The Psychological Anthropology of Wayne Edward Oates

The Psychological Anthropology of Wayne Edward Oates

A Downgrade from the Theological to the Therapeutic

SAMUEL E. STEPHENS

WIPF & STOCK · Eugene, Oregon

THE PSYCHOLOGICAL ANTHROPOLOGY OF WAYNE EDWARD OATES
A Downgrade from the Theological to the Therapeutic

Copyright © 2020 Samuel E. Stephens. All rights reserved. Except for brief quotations in critical publications or reviews, no part of this book may be reproduced in any manner without prior written permission from the publisher. Write: Permissions, Wipf and Stock Publishers, 199 W. 8th Ave., Suite 3, Eugene, OR 97401.

Unless otherwise indicated, all Scripture quotations taken from the New American Standard Bible® (NASB), Copyright © 1960, 1962, 1963, 1968, 1971, 1972, 1973, 1975, 1977, 1995 by The Lockman Foundation. Used by permission. www.Lockman.org.

Wipf & Stock
An Imprint of Wipf and Stock Publishers
199 W. 8th Ave., Suite 3
Eugene, OR 97401

www.wipfandstock.com

PAPERBACK ISBN: 978-1-7252-6839-5
HARDCOVER ISBN: 978-1-7252-6840-1
EBOOK ISBN: 978-1-7252-6841-8

To Hannah, my helper and friend.
She walks in a manner worthy of the Lord,
pleasing Him in all respects,
bearing much fruit (Col 1:9–12).

To Audrey Anne and Alice Ruth,
my heritage and reward from the Lord (Ps 127:3).

Contents

Acknowledgments		ix
Introduction		xi
1	Pastoral Counseling in the Age of Psychology	1
2	Shepherding Without a Staff *Profiling a Pastoral Psychologist*	18
3	Pastoral Counseling *A Clinical and Therapeutic Affair*	43
4	Pilgrimage of Personality *Understanding People in Process*	66
5	Disordered Personality *Identifying Threats to Healthy Selfhood*	97
6	Reorganized Personality *Utilizing Tools to Achieve Self-Acceptance*	111
7	Looking Back to Look Ahead	127
Bibliography		133

Acknowledgments

THE COMPLETION OF THIS book has come about through the influence of three men who have taught me much about the personal ministry of the Bible and have demonstrated to me in different ways what a genuine love for God's people looks like. Frank Catanzaro was the first man to teach me about biblical counseling. He taught me not to take myself too seriously, not to be intimidated by the high-sounding philosophies of the world, and most importantly not to view my ministry in the context of measurable successes but rather through the lens of my genuine and heart-felt surrender and worship of God. John Babler was the first man to give me an opportunity to provide biblical counsel to a hurting and wayward soul in a formal setting. In many ways this experience showed me the urgency and great importance of the faithful ministering of Scripture. Dale Johnson has had more to do with the subject of this book than anyone else. He is a man of incredible integrity, humility, courage, intelligence, and knowledge. However, most importantly, he is a committed shepherd of souls. It is my privileged to count him as my mentor, friend, coworker, and brother in the faith.

This book could also not have been written without the help of several skilled archivists who gave their time and expertise to help me track down manuscripts, newspaper clippings, and countless file folders. Among these servants is Mrs. Megan Mulder, who is the Special Collections Librarian at the Z. Smith Reynolds Library at Wake Forest University, where Wayne Oates bequeathed all of his personal notes, correspondences, and other firsthand documents. Mrs. Mulder and her staff were invaluable in their assistance to me during my residence. I am also thankful for the thoughtful assistance of Dr. Adam Winters, who serves in the Archives and Special

Collections at the James P. Boyce Centennial Library on the campus of The Southern Baptist Theological Seminary.

Above all I am especially grateful to my beautiful wife and the mother of my children, who has been my biggest support in this entire process. From the beginning, she has consistently offered me the much-needed encouraging word, but more than anything else she has faithfully prayed for me. I am blessed to have a godly and gracious wife as my helper in this life.

Introduction

IN THE YEARS LEADING up to my time as a seminary student, I had considered counseling as a professional and specialized career that was only peripherally related to the church, if at all. Counselors were people who had years of education, utilized psychological theories and methods to help people with their problems, and had a clinical practice similar to any other mental health professional. Besides taking an introduction to psychology class at some point in college, I could not tell you the difference between Freud and Skinner much less the philosophies behind their theories. Regarding any personal exposure to counseling, I did not have a frame of reference for that either. In instances where I did have a friend seeking counsel from their pastor on a particular issue (and even that was rare) that counsel was often shallow and brief. Eventually counseling would be *deferred* and my friend would be *referred* to some other counselor outside of the church.

While attending seminary, I found that a majority of my classes related to preaching, discipleship, evangelism, and worship, assumed the Bible as the sole and sufficient source of truth guiding principles and practice, but counseling was often treated as a unique and distinct discipline which treated the Bible merely as a helpful and supplementary resource. The truth is, I did not think much about counseling while at seminary because I was not convinced it had anything to do with me. I was going to be a pastor, denominational leader, or professor (I have always been ambitious), and as far as I could tell, counseling was not going to be something I was expected to do. All of this changed when I took a biblical counseling class my third year in seminary. It was in this class that I was first exposed to a whole facet of church life that I had never considered. For the first time, I was challenged to consider what the biblical goal of preaching, discipleship, evangelism, and worship ought to be. All of these aspects of ministry are about, in one way or another, conforming and transforming wayward souls into the priceless image of Jesus Christ. Counseling was no different. My indifference and ignorance concerning modern psychological theories, for the first time, was laid before me as I was made aware of their godless principles, foundations, assumptions, allegiances, and biases. From that day forward, my life has not been the same. I have fully entered and engaged in a fight that only a few years ago I was rather oblivious to and remains largely invisible today. This is the fight for biblical sufficiency in soul care.

The impetus of this book comes from all that I have learned, and continue to learn, about the history of counseling within American Protestantism. When I began to study more about the modern biblical counseling movement and was directed to the Scriptures to consider practical implications for church practice, pastoral care, and one-another ministry, I was struck with the fact that biblical counseling is a fundamental result of the church being and doing what God designed it to be and do. It did not take long for the cognitive dissonance to set in. *Why am I just now finding out about this? Why has my previous view of counseling as a profession outside of the church been the norm? Why is biblical counseling treated as a novel idea to so many?* These questions eventually led me to study the history of how pastoral counseling was taught in seminaries in the decades leading up to today. That is when I was introduced to the life and work of Wayne Edward Oates.

By no means a household name, Oates played a silent yet significant role in shaping how pastors and church members across the world's largest Protestant denomination viewed counseling. Through an extensive academic and writing career which spanned four decades, he influenced generations of pastors to engage with counseling by utilizing psychology. Interestingly, many of his former students have praised him for his biblical approach to pastoral counseling, but I seek to demonstrate that his anthropology, which served as the root of his pastoral counseling theory, was shaped by concepts, values, and principles derived from modern psychology and which contrasted starkly with a view of man as presented in Scripture.

It is my intention through this study to accomplish several things at once. I desire to show how broadly secular psychology has been utilized to impact pastoral counseling in the church. In this, I want to highlight the important role that anthropology plays in any counseling system. We should be deeply concerned with the object and source of truth (epistemology), the ethical values born from that truth applied in practice (axiology), and the nature of reality in which all counseling is firmly placed (metaphysics), but we cannot miss the fact that counseling is a task that intimately involves people. What we believe about who we are, the struggles that we face, and where we can go for help and healing matters. A theologically oriented anthropology sets each of these points within the proper context. This has been the dominant approach to understanding human nature throughout antiquity up until the modern era. Unfortunately, with the Enlightenment and later the birth of modern psychology, a therapeutically oriented anthropology rooted in self-centeredness, self-sufficiency, and self-worship, has become the dominant perspective of the day. Ultimately, my hope is that I can spark interest in these matters for the sole purpose of seeing the church of Jesus Christ once again reengage with the God-glorifying, Christ-honoring, and Spirit-empowering ministry of counseling.

The chapters of this book are divided into two main parts. In part 1, I seek to provide the historical context that Oates found himself in, as well as explore the many influences in his own life that directly contributed to his shift away from a theologically oriented counseling approach. Chapter 1 is designed to establish the unique contributions of this book by presenting the problems addressed by my central thesis. This chapter includes other introductory material which should help the reader better understand and grasp the background and context for this topic. Chapter 2 introduces the reader to Wayne Oates's formative influences and early life and explore motifs which characterized him as a pastoral psychologist. While Oates was coming of age in the early twentieth century, his life was shaped by mentors and teachers who introduced him to liberal theology and contemporary psychology, both of which often contradicted a clear reading of the Scriptures. Through an exploration of his conversion and call to ministry, important overarching themes which later characterized his life and ministry will be explored. Chapter 3 addresses key aspects that comprised Oates's approach, theory, and practice of pastoral counseling. The chapter will begin by addressing his theory of collaboration and how this understanding provided a gateway to Oates's prolific use of secular psychology. Related to Oates's understanding of the pastoral counselor as a collaborator with those within the mental health field, is the theory of correlation which further moved Oates to adopt psychological terms and concepts by relating them to biblical doctrine. I will then seek to explore how Oates's particular approach to pastoral counseling relates to the field of the psychology of religion and what part phenomenological philosophy and method play.

In part 2, I present Oates's anthropology as one that has embraced a psychological and therapeutic orientation despite the general use of theological language and constructs. In chapter 4 the question of human nature will be addressed from the anthropological view gathered from Oates's writings. I will begin this chapter by identifying Oates's idea of selfhood and personality and further develop the context for Oates's thinking about human nature from a clinical perspective. Various theological, philosophical, and psychological influences will be uncovered in Oates's thinking about man's nature, including elements of process and existential philosophy, along with developmental and personality psychology. In chapter 5, I will explore Oates's thinking on the purposes, problems, and uses of religion in the life of man. The majority of this chapter includes concepts found throughout his writings used to demonstrate what he identified as various "threats" to man achieving an organized selfhood. The ultimate problem of man, according to Oates, will be shown to be primarily man-centered instead of God-centered in the preservation of personality as it faces self-destruction and disorder. In chapter 6, the solution to man's problems will be explored and will not only include Oates's general approach to counseling by highlighting its humanistic undertones, but it will also present concepts used by him that contextualize man's solution in therapeutic terms. This will ultimately expose themes in Oates's anthropology associated with liberal theology, including a redefinition of faith, trust, conversion, redemption, etc., and secular psychology, including a focus on man's felt needs, actualization, personality organization, and self-clarification. This book will conclude with remarks on the work as a whole by summarizing the contributions of the research to contemporary discussions related to the state of Christian soul care and pastoral counseling. I will also attempt to provide suggestions for further research in the future and implications of the research on the topic explored herein.

1

Pastoral Counseling in the Age of Psychology

IN THE YEARS FOLLOWING the World War II, America had experienced an explosive interest in the therapeutic use of psychology as returning soldiers and civilians alike faced a host of growing and seemingly insurmountable mental health problems.[1] Clinical psychologists and psychiatrists sought to associate their work more with the traditional and trusted health sciences in an effort to create a niche market to meet unique postwar demands. While the burgeoning mental health industry was being realigned with traditional health sciences through the influence of scientism that emphasized specialization, industrial efficiency, and professionalization, there was also a shift in the perception of the role of Protestant pastors. Edward Thornton, widely regarded as the chronicler of the clinical pastoral education (CPE) movement, noted that in an effort to maintain credibility and relevancy in a new age that placed great value on scientific acumen and professional credentials, "pastors plunged into the traffic flowing across the health sciences bridge."[2]

---

1. Muravchik, *American Protestantism*, 13. For an overview of the CPE movement at its height (ca. 1917 through 1956), see Johnson, "Fifty Years of Clinical Pastoral Education," 223. For another differing perspective, see Shorter, *History of Psychiatry*.

2. Borchert and Lester, *Spiritual Dimensions of Pastoral Care*, 12. See also Cabot and Dicks, *Art of Ministering to the Sick*, 4.

While ministers engaged with the growing psychotherapeutic culture and the mental health industry in an attempt to "enhance their pastoral care," theological seminaries and Christian colleges "began offering, and eventually requiring, psychology coursework and hospital chaplaincy internships."[3] Before the 1930s, virtually no theological institution included a field experience component within its curriculum; however, with the rising influence of experience-based learning, seminarians were now spending part of their total degree "in some work in churches and other institutions which provide practical experience through which ideally the student's academic preparation is sharpened in its relevance to human needs, and in which his maturity is furthered through his bearing responsibility for religious ministry."[4]

The CPE movement, which was initially conceived and developed outside of the theological seminary and the local church, ultimately became embraced by both. This clinical approach to ministerial education involved a trained, experienced, and skilled supervisor who helped students deal with issues and problems faced on the front lines of ministry. The end goal was the "fusion of scientific understanding with Christian wisdom and concern."[5] The clinical model was perpetuated through the formation of professorships in the "pastoral field which would be filled by men who had been nurtured in the clinical training movement."[6] The most notable thinkers related to this new approach to pastoral training, namely Anton Boisen and Seward Hiltner, viewed classical pastoral care as antiquated and outmoded. They saw seminaries and churches as having failed to utilize the advances in the new behavioral sciences to educate or train ministers for meeting social and individual needs of a modern age. Clinical supervisors often challenged the "dogmatic beliefs" of their students, most of whom were seminarians preparing for ministerial work, in order to "ensure they did not conflict with the psychological understandings that clinical training fostered."[7]

Boisen argued that "theological schools needed a thorough overhauling, mainly because they failed to use scientific methods in the study of

---

3. Muravchik, *American Protestantism*, 3.

4. Niebuhr et al., *Advancement of Theological Education*, 112–13. See also Farley, *Theologia*, 175–203.

5. Niebuhr et al., *Advancement of Theological Education*, 123.

6. Oglesby, *New Shape of Pastoral Theology*, 37. See also Bruder, "Clinical Pastoral Training," 25–27.

7. Murvachik, *American Protestantism*, 30. See also Holifield, *History of Pastoral Care*, 231.

religious experience."[8] Largely in agreement with his predecessor, Hiltner's conception of pastoral theology necessitated that ministers of the gospel approach anthropological, cosmological, soteriological, and hamartiological concerns through the lens of modern psychology for an *enlightened* perspective. Any conclusion that communicated a less-than-flattering view of human nature or offered a direct challenge to concepts of self-esteem was to be questioned or rejected altogether.[9] Both Boisen and Hiltner were important figureheads within a coordinated effort to establish a new theory and practice of pastoral counseling firmly grounded in the principles of modern clinical psychology replacing a classical approach to soul care which was birthed from conservative biblical theology.[10] Though not as easily recognized, there was another important player whose contributions helped to transition the counseling work of the pastor from the realm of the biblical and theological to the realm of the psychological and therapeutic.

Born in Greenville, South Carolina, the early years of Wayne Edward Oates (b. 1917; d. 1999) were marked by poverty, hard labor, and low self-esteem. Through a turn of events which included serving as a page to a sitting senator, Oates was eventually able to attend Mars Hill Junior College, where he answered the call to full-time ministry under the tutelage of his friend and mentor, Olin T. Binkley. During his years at Mars Hill, and later at Wake Forest College in North Carolina, Oates was introduced to the writings of various theologians and secular psychologists which would provide a foundation for his own later theological and philosophical convictions.[11] After graduating from Wake Forest, Oates briefly attended Duke University before transferring to The Southern Baptist Theological Seminary (SBTS) in Louisville, Kentucky where he graduated with a Doctor of Theology in 1947. As early as the mid-1940s, Oates had joined the faculty of Southern Seminary as an instructor in the psychology of religion. As a professor who

---

8. Holifield, *History of Pastoral Care*, 244–45. According to Kemp, "The chief purpose of this clinical training was to supplement the academic training of the seminary, to provide the students with understanding and techniques to prepare him more adequately for the work of the pastorate" (Kemp, *Physicians of the Soul*, 254).

9. Muravchik, *American Protestantism*, 47–48. Hiltner received a liberal theological education at the University of Chicago in the early 1930s. In his graduate work, he studied the social-historical method of theology under Shailer Mathews and John T. McNeil. He once noted about his professors, "These liberals had been emancipated, most of them from extreme conservatism of some kind. . . . As I now see it, they were in process" (Adams and Hiltner, *Pastoral Care*, 226).

10. Aden and Ellens, *Turning Points in Pastoral Care*, 175.

11. Oates, *Struggle to Be Free*, 52. Collins noted that Oates's pastoral care was influenced by contemporary psychology, and therefore a departure from the classical perspective (Collins, "Pastoral Concern," 1). See also Bush, "Human Suffering," 253.

readily utilized advances in current psychological sciences, Oates promoted and popularized clinical education within the Southern Baptist Convention and across the Southern United States.[12] He would serve on the faculty at Southern Seminary for nearly three decades, eventually leading a department dedicated to the psychology of religion and pastoral care.[13] While some have hailed Oates as the father of pastoral counseling within the Southern Baptist Convention, others have identified him among the most influential figures within the field of pastoral care and counseling in the twentieth century.[14] Several scholars and practitioners also agree that any comprehensive study of the *new* pastoral theology, along with its application in counseling, should include the teaching and writing efforts of Wayne Oates which served as a monumental contribution to a modern approach to the care of souls.[15]

THE QUESTION AT HAND

With a thorough reading and study of primary sources, it can be said that a majority of Oates's writings were concerned with the nature and purpose of humankind. This should not come as much of a surprise. The interests of counseling are naturally and necessarily concerned with anthropological questions. With this in mind, the author was led to ask about the significance of modern psychological principles and presuppositions as they sought to inform or shape how Oates viewed his fellow man. Were these *significant* influences or were they merely supplemental? Did Oates attempt

---

12. Thornton, *Professional Education for Ministry*, 153.

13. Oates, *Struggle to Be Free*, 257. This information was summarized from a transcribed personal interview conducted with Oates in 1988. Mays specifically mentioned that Oates was introduced to developmental psychology and process philosophy at Wake Forest College (Mays, "Contemporary Theology," 49).

14. Thornton, *Professional Education for Ministry*, 276. See also Clinebell, *Basic Types of Pastoral Counseling*, 17; Oglesby, *New Shape of Pastoral Theology*, 37. Johnson identified Gaines S. Dobbins as the one responsible for laying the foundations of professionalization within pastoral counseling and for being the "father of *modern* pastoral care" in the Southern Baptist Convention (Johnson, "Professionalization," 184–94). While I agree with Johnson's conclusion, this work seeks to highlight the fact that Oates, having built upon the foundations previously established by his predecessors, is an important figure in his own right for contributing to and standardizing a therapeutic anthropology through his extensive teaching and writing career.

15. Aden and Ellens, *Turning Points in Pastoral Care*, 19–20. See also Thornton, *Professional Education for Ministry*, 155, and Borchert and Lester, *Spiritual Dimensions*, 12–13. This latter work is a *festschrift* dedicated to the life and ministry of Wayne Oates. Many of the contributors of this volume were students of Oates or active leaders within the field of pastoral counseling.

to correlate or synthesize two disparate conclusions about human nature, or was he indeed, as many have suggested or claimed, a prime example and standard of a biblically oriented pastoral counselor? While understated by many, there should be little doubt that Oates had a significant influence on generations of pastors and how they consider the task of counseling within the church, but what *exactly* is the nature and result of this impact?

In order to get answers to such questions, I recognized that it was imperative to unpack the very heart of Oates's pastoral counseling philosophy, his anthropology. How Oates understood human nature, the problems people face, and the answers to these problems needed to be freshly examined and comprehensively constructed not from what his students and contemporaries said *about* his views, but what Oates said and wrote concerning his *own* views. A study of the life, ministry, and writings of Wayne Edward Oates reveals that his anthropological views were therapeutically oriented, being shaped by concepts and principles derived from secular psychological influences, and which stood opposed to a theologically oriented anthropology associated with the classical biblical model. The purpose of this book is to identify and expound upon the various influences which aided in the development of Oates's psychological approach to counseling and to bring to bear the implications behind such conclusions.

It is not lost on me the ambitious nature of constructing an anthropology from a lifetime of writing, speaking, preaching, and teaching. Therefore, in this attempt, I will provide a truncated biblical anthropology which will seek to provide an alternative to Oates's understanding of man. Also, by necessity, various theological influences will be explored as they directly relate to Oates's adoption of secular concepts in the formation of his psychological anthropology. It is not the purpose of this volume to categorize any of these exhaustively; however, I will attempt to achieve two allied purposes. First, this book is a response to the vast majority of academic literature which contends that Oates's anthropology is wholly biblical. Second, I seek to contribute to the growing literature which outlines and demonstrates the influences of modern psychology in Southern Baptist history as seen within the field of pastoral counseling, care, and theology.

IMPORTANT TERMS

Anthropology

Since the nineteenth century, the theological pursuit of the biblical understanding of human nature has shifted as many began formulating a doctrine of humanity by integrating the "data of the social sciences within a framework based on divine revelation."[16] For the purposes of this work, *anthropology* will be used to refer to the biblical and theological questions, implications, and contexts concerning the spiritual nature, ailments, and cures of men and women as unique creations of God.[17]

Modern Psychology

Modern psychology developed during the Enlightenment and continued to crystallize as a distinct discipline by the late nineteenth and early twentieth centuries. During this time "modern science was successfully challenging religious authority and tradition as the dominant worldview and source of truth."[18] Compared to new scientific and professional advances of the age, religious institutions were not respected or highly esteemed as they once had been.[19] In his book *Psychotherapy and a Christian View of Man*, David E. Roberts urged Christians to forgo what he saw as "ecclesiastical shackles" which tended to alienate the broader culture and the offerings of modernity. If not cast off, these shackles "would have prevented man from carrying through important forms of progress, enlightenment, and self-understanding."[20]

David Benner identified the founding of modern psychology with the establishment of Wilhelm Wundt's psychological laboratory at Leipzig, Germany, in 1879. He noted that Wundt's psychology was empirical in nature and that "the method of psychology had to involve the observation of experience."[21] Throughout this book, *psychology* will refer to general secular and scientific attempts to understand man's personhood, problems, and solutions vis-à-vis wide-ranging psychotherapeutic and psychiatric approaches.

---

16. Davis, *Theology Primer*, 18.

17. Packer et al., *New Dictionary of Theology*, 28–29. See also Akin, *Theology for the Church*, 340–478. Other words and phrases will be used synonymously throughout this book. These terms include, but are not limited to, the doctrine of man, doctrine of humanity, understanding of man, and the like. The term *man* will be understood to refer to both men and women, and humanity in general.

18. Bergin and Richards, *Spiritual Strategy*, 23. See also Benner and Hill, *Baker Encyclopedia of Psychology & Counseling*, 952–57.

19. Bergin and Richards, *Spiritual Strategy*, 24.

20. Roberts, *Psychotherapy*, 92.

21. Benner and Hill, *Baker Encyclopedia of Psychology and Counseling*, 952–57.

Theological Liberalism

Evangelical and theological liberalism highlights "current naturalistic and anthropocentric viewpoints" and also depicts the Bible as a "fallible human record of religious thought and experience rather than divine revelation of truth and reality."[22] Theological liberalism allows for the complete integration and application of extrabiblical information as normative and elevates secular sources of knowledge to the status of theological revelation.[23] Evangelical and theological liberalism uniquely marked the new pastoral theology not only in its attempt to orient pastoral care and counseling toward a man-centered perspective, but it also emphasized the "value of religious experience" and the liberal spirit of inquiry was open to new scientific findings and tolerant of seemingly combative philosophies.[24]

Psychology of Religion

This term will be used to refer to an academic and clinical field of study which represented the efforts of social scientists in studying the "motivations, expressions, dynamics, developments and effects of religion" through empirical means in order to discover how to make the Bible's message "clear and relevant to the needs of humankind."[25] This once-popular and thriving movement, which hit its zenith in the mid-twentieth century, can be traced as far back as the late nineteenth century with the work of psychologists including Wilhelm Wundt, William James, E. D. Starbuck, E. S. Ames, and James Leuba. While this broad and multilayered field has undergone three general phases of emphasis throughout its history, the unifying theme of the utilitarian nature and intrinsic value of religion for the sake of an individual's growth and personal development has remained consistent.[26]

Therapeutic

Howard Clinebell pointed out that the etymology of the word *therapy* comes from the Greek θεραπευτές (*therapeutes*), meaning "attendant or servant"—i.e., the help by a servant in illness. Its root meaning is essentially

---

22. Packer et al., *New Dictionary of Theology*, 385.
23. Henry, *Revelation and the Bible*, 14. See Demarest, *General Revelation*, 76.
24. Scruggs, *Baptist Preachers with Social Consciousness*, 18.
25. Elwell, *Evangelical Dictionary of Theology*, 968.
26. Elwell, *Evangelical Dictionary of Theology*, 970.

interpersonal—the beneficial effects of one person on another."[27] Hiltner's view of the value of therapy was the "restoration of functional wholeness that has been impaired as to direction or timing. The aim of shepherding is to help the person to move as far in the direction of healing as circumstance permits."[28] This term will be used to characterize human-centered counseling approaches which highlight the importance of establishing empathetic relationships, refraining from judgmental language in order to preserve self-esteem, and helping counselees find answers "according to their own values, preferably ones that did not contradict a liberal Christian view of the world."[29] The problem with therapeutically oriented counseling is that it focuses on the fortification and building up of an individual's personality and self-esteem and stands diametrically opposed to a biblical view of the world which finds God, not man, as the only focus of true worship.[30]

REVIEW OF RELATED LITERATURE

Historical Significance of the Subject

With the publication of his work *The Triumph of the Therapeutic: Uses of Faith after Freud*, sociologist and cultural commentator Philip Rieff launched a groundbreaking social critique on modern America's obsession with psychology which sought to expose the "un-therapeutic and even, in some respects antihuman" irony of the various human potentiality movements.[31] While Rieff pointed to the moral bankruptcy resulting from the widespread acceptance and application of popular psychology, Stephanie Muravchik, in her book *American Protestantism in the Age of Psychology*, presented a very different assessment. While demonstrating that American faith, virtue, and social warfare had not been corrupted by psychological influences since World War II, Murvachik argued that these elements have instead been reinforced by the convergence and general acceptance of

---

27. Clinebell, *Basic Types of Pastoral Counseling*, 59.

28. Hiltner, *Christian Shepherd*, 19–20. It is important to note that Boisen, Hiltner, and Oates utilized this term within a psychological, sociological, and existential context and not in its original meaning which was limited to medical treatment for a disease.

29. Murvachik, *American Protestantism*, 44.

30. See Clebsch, "American Religion," 249–64. Philip Rieff used this term to describe a type of person who had been liberated from the burden of caring for others in order to care only for his self-perceived needs and desires (Rieff, *Triumph of the Therapeutic*, 50).

31. Rieff, *Triumph of the Therapeutic*, xi. Another major work indebted to Rieff includes Lasch, *Culture of Narcissism*.

psychology by not only the general public but by the Protestant clergy.[32] A landmark historical treatise by church historian E. Brooks Holifield, entitled *A History of Pastoral Care in America: From Salvation to Self-Realization*, offered a more nuanced perspective by contextualizing the influence that modern psychology has made within the field of pastoral counseling. In his tracing of the developments within the field, Holifield emphasized the key role that the clinical pastoral education movement played in reshaping pastoral care and counseling within professional, psychological, and therapeutic frameworks.[33]

A major source that was relied upon by Holifield in contextualizing the new pastoral counseling approach was Edward Thornton's *Professional Education for Ministry: A History of Clinical Pastoral Education*. As a product of the teaching ministry of Wayne Oates, Thornton offered an eyewitness perspective of Oates's pastoral counseling. This resource not only outlined the progression of the clinical pastoral movement, but also articulated a modern, psychologically oriented pastoral approach in which an individual's felt needs became the center of care.[34] In an edited volume entitled *Turning Points in Pastoral Care*, editors LeRoy Aden and J. H. Ellens, along with a host of contributors who were one-time pupils of Anton Boisen and Seward Hiltner, agreed with Thornton's positive assessment of the field of pastoral counseling as a vehicle for integrating psychology and pragmatic philosophies with theology and Christian tradition to create a more informed, efficient, and therapeutically aware minister.[35] Thomas Oden, an influential theologian who wrote on subjects concerning the intersection of psychotherapy and theology, maintained reservations about the philosophic presuppositions of many of the fathers of the new pastoral theology. He criticized figures such as Seward Hiltner, Edward Thornton, Carroll Wise, and Wayne Oates as relying too heavily on secular counseling practitioners rather than demonstrating reliance on Scripture.[36] In an article

---

32. Murvachik, *American Protestantism*, 2–3.

33. Holifield, *History of Pastoral Care*, 231ff.

34. Thornton, *Professional Education for Ministry*, 235. While not expounded upon in the dissertation, an understanding of the clinical pastoral education (CPE) movement is vital to an accurate understanding of Oates and his approach to pastoral counseling. The researcher investigated the following books written by the founders of CPE, many of whom were mentors of Oates: Johnson, "Fifty Years of Clinical Pastoral Education," 223; Boisen, *Out of the Depths*; Cabot and Dicks, *Art of Ministering to the Sick*.

35. Aden and Ellens, *Turning Points in Pastoral Care*, 70. See these seminal works: Boisen, *Exploration of the Inner World*, and Hiltner, *Preface to Pastoral Theology*.

36. Oden, *Contemporary Theology and Psychotherapy*, 88. Oden seems to connect the anthropology of Oates with that of Carl Rogers regarding the "psychological paradigm of the fall" (89–93). This is referenced in Edgar, "Pastoral Identity," 1.

published in the *Journal of Pastoral Care*, Oden suggested that "pastoral counseling had lost its pastoral identity by neglecting the classical models of Christian pastoral care."[37] This article brought reactions in favor of Oates's approach as biblical and derivative of church history and scholarship.[38]

Major Themes in Oates's Writings

Throughout his long career, Wayne Oates published numerous books and articles. One theme found throughout Oates's writings is the exploration of the relationship between religion and the behavioral sciences. In 1955, Oates published *Religious Factors in Mental Illness*, in which he explored the value of religion from the perspective of the mentally ill patient in order to "interpret his religious experience as it goes on within him and between him and his spiritual community."[39] This book, written during a sabbatical leave while teaching at Union Theological Seminary, demonstrated the direct influence of Seward Hiltner, Anton Boisen, and Paul Tillich on his thinking.[40] Topics related to counseling specialization, referrals, clinical training, and psychiatric diagnosis were all explored in the context of pastoral counseling. Three years later, with the publication of the booklet *What Psychology Says about Religion*, Oates's affirmation of the application and contribution of psychology to the discussion and interest in religion became more explicit. Not only was the audience widened to include lay people, but his reliance upon secular psychological authority became more evident.[41] Psychology

---

37. Oden, "Recovering Lost Identity," 4–20.

38. Stein, "Reactions to Dr. Oden's 'Recovering Lost Identity,'" 21. A large majority of resources relating to pastoral counseling that mention Oates do so from a noncritical perspective. Many of these will be dealt with later, but one in particular is demonstrative of the tone of the whole (Borchert and Lester, *Spiritual Dimensions*, 119–41; Edgar, "Pastoral Identity," 7).

39. Oates, *Religious Factors in Mental Illness*, vii. See Tillich, "Communicating the Gospel," 3. In this article Tillich promoted a recontextualization of the Gospel on the basis of the life stage, or life circumstance, of the individual for whom it is intended. Over twenty years later, Oates would publish *The Religious Care of the Psychiatric Patient*, which echoed many of his earlier conclusions, but would go a step further in emphasizing a stronger bond between ministers and physicians, a heavier reliance upon psychiatry, use of developmental psychology as a framework for the human life, and focus on humanistic needs of clients. While some developments in thought can be demonstrated, a consistency in thinking (Oates, *Religious Care*, 16).

40. The influences of these men will be highlighted throughout the following chapters.

41. Oates, *What Psychology Says about Religion*, 11. Oates characterizes Carl Rogers as "one of the truly great psychologists of our time" in regard to him revolutionizing the relationship between counselors and clients. See Rogers, "Personal Formation," 342.

was praised as an objective scientific pursuit while religion was redefined in anthropocentric terms. The influence of his mentor, Olin T. Binkley, was in view as he stated in his book *The Churches and the Social Conscience* that religion acquired social currency and value in terms of expediting social change and good will.[42]

Another theme that is revealed in Oates's writing is his interest and focus on human personality. As early as 1957, Oates made his first attempt at articulating his own perspective on the psychology of religion. For him, a theory of personality provided the best framework by which a psychology of religion could be understood.

> The concept of personality provides a comprehensive, organizing principle for a systematic psychology of religion. . . . In a very real way psychology of personality is a rallying point at one and the same time for a secularization of the doctrine of man and an awakened religious concern among contemporary psychologists of personality.[43]

Oates seemed to recognize that a psychology of personality, as expressed by secularists, missed the mark of a full biblical understanding of man; nonetheless, he affirmed its utilization as a positive contribution to a Christian doctrine of man. This affirmation was demonstrated in his reliance upon secular psychologists of personality, including Gregory Zilboorg, Gardner Murphy, William James, Harry Stack Sullivan, and Gordon Allport, among others.[44] Oates not only referenced psychologists to support his argument, but he also referenced several theologians who had constructed their own theology of personality. These theologians included a mix between classic liberal and neoorthodox and included names such as Friedrich Schleiermacher, Martin Buber, Karl Barth, Emil Brunner, Reinhold Niebuhr, and Paul Tillich.[45]

---

42. Binkley, *Churches and the Social Conscience*, 4.

43. Oates, *Religious Dimensions of Personality*, 16. Oates warned, "Without a specific, conscious, and ordered study of personality *in both its theological and scientific dimensions*, the theologian and preacher cannot avoid interpreting the basic nature of the Christian faith in what may be essentially non-Christian terms" (Oates, *Religious Dimensions*, 48–49, emphasis added).

44. Oates, along with many of his colleagues and students, claimed not to follow one particular school of psychology; however, a close look at the backgrounds of many of his common psychological references demonstrates an influence from both depth and humanistic psychology.

45. While theological liberalism will not be exhaustively explored in this book, it is important to note its impact on Oates's conception of anthropology. According to Halverson and Cohen, theological liberals "have always asserted the claims of reason against a petrified orthodoxy and have sought freedom for diversity of belief in the

In 1973, Oates published another significant volume entitled *The Psychology of Religion*. This volume was unique not only due to the fact that nearly half of its chapters were copied from corresponding chapters in *The Religious Dimensions of Personality*, but that a majority of the content of the book, excluding some updated terminology and resources, remained virtually unchanged from nearly twenty years prior.[46] Probably the seminal book written by Oates related to his understanding of man was *Christ and Selfhood*.[47] Representing the apex of his academic career at Southern Seminary, this volume revealed Oates's philosophical commitments in his choice of terminologies, citations, and approach to inquiry. He demonstrated that his own theological lens was focused through a psychological filter thus exposing an anthropology that was stridently unbiblical. In one instance he stated, "The ways in which fluctuating psychological modes of life both have been shaped by and have exerted shaping influence upon the interpretation of the Person of Jesus Christ throw vivid light upon our knowledge of ourselves."[48]

Yet another category by which Oates's writings can be understood is his work concerning the nature, role, and duties of the Christian minister. Perhaps his most well-known book, *The Christian Pastor*, has been republished in three editions. The title is borrowed from an earlier work written by Washington Gladden, originally published in the late 1890s. However, Oates admitted that his purpose was to reinterpret this subject matter (pastoral ministry) for a new generation taking into mind his own generation's "needs and resources" which for him had more to do with societal and cultural relevancy than with personal holiness.[49] While it served as a practical guide, his conception of pastoral ministry was marked by the

---

Church" (Halverson and Cohen, *Handbook of Christian Theology*, 207). Other liberal theologians who were read widely by Oates include William Adams Brown, William Newton Clarke, Shailer Mathews, and Robert Lowry Calhoun.

46. A close examination of the endnotes to corresponding chapters in *The Religious Dimensions of Personality* demonstrated a consistency in Oates conception of psychology of religion and anthropology. He quotes the same sources and relies upon the same psychologists and theologians that he utilized in his earlier work.

47. Oates, *Christ and Selfhood* (1961) and *Behind the Masks* (1987). This later work is yet another example of Oates's interest in anthropology. In this volume, he expresses many of the same sentiments and comes to many of the same conclusions as in his older writings, outside of his inclusion of psychiatric terminology and literature.

48. Oates, *Christ and Selfhood*, 22. This book received both positive and critical examinations. For more, see St. Amant, review of *Christ and Selfhood*, 215; and Jansma, "Review of *Christ and Selfhood*," 43.

49. Oates, *Christian Pastor*, 8. The second edition of this book was published in 1964 and the revised and expanded edition was published in 1982.

same influences found within his other writings. He relied upon the familiar work of Gaines S. Dobbins, Anton Boisen, Seward Hiltner, Russell Dicks, Daniel Day Williams, and other leaders within the clinical pastoral education movement and the new pastoral theology.[50] His other volumes dealing with the work of the pastor continued to emphasize the therapeutic process based on building empathetic relationships, the importance of utilizing relevant psychological techniques, and forming a referral-based relationship with members of the mental health team.[51]

The final category explored by the author further outlines the topic of pastoral counseling. While it could be argued that all of Oates's books dealt with this topic, these works explicitly presented his approach, theory, methodology, and conception of counseling. Oates wrote many books on specific topics which counseling often addressed in the lives of hurting people.[52] These were addressed often to an audience of laypeople. However, he did write with the professional pastoral counselor in mind. In his *New Dimensions of Pastoral Care*, Oates urged pastors to view themselves as independent "pioneers" who would be prepared to discover fresh new ways to incorporate and take advantage of the behavioral sciences in the care of souls.[53] This book presented statements that exposed his unbiblical commitments regarding anthropology. He noted, "Psychology helped pastors to understand that a human person lives life in stages and if we are to care for him properly, we must understand him that way . . . and we must know the relevant information about prior stages to know the present accurately."[54]

In his book *Psychotherapy and a Christian View of Man*, David Roberts presented a model upon which Oates built his therapeutically oriented anthropology. Other elements of his thinking including the concepts of health and salvation are directly shaped by Paul Tillich in the third volume of his *Systematic Theology*. Oates considered the golden age of pastoral care education and teaching to be demonstrated at Union Theological Seminary during the decade of the 1950s. However, not everyone agreed with Oates affirmative view of the field. In his article in the *Journal of Pastoral Care*, Joachim Scharfenberg argued that the field was at risk of being dominated

---

50. Dobbins, *Building Better Churches*; Boisen, *Religion in Crisis and Custom*; and Williams, *Minister and the Care of Souls*.

51. Oates, *Minister's Own Mental Health*; Oates and Neely, *Where to Go for Help*; and Oates, *Pastor's Handbook*, vol. 1.

52. Oates, *Anxiety in Christian Experience*; Oates, *Revelation of God*; Oates and Oates, *People in Pain*; and Oates, *Managing Your Stress*.

53. Oates, *New Dimensions in Pastoral Care*, 2.

54. Oates, *New Dimensions in Pastoral Care*, 7–8.

by secularism and that any distinguishing characteristics that set pastoral counseling apart as a ministry of the Word of God could be lost.[55]

Academic Dissertations Focusing on Oates

In order to quantify the unique contribution of this volume and also to gauge the level of critical analysis of Oates by scholars in the field, I investigated a trail of related dissertations and graduate theses which had been published over a period of twenty years concerning the theory and practice of Oates's pastoral counseling. The earliest academic thesis researched, published in 1968 by William Mays, is entitled "Contemporary Theology and Pastoral Care: A Study of the Writings of Wayne E. Oates."[56] Influenced by both Edward Thornton and Samuel Southard, both former colleagues of Oates, Mays argued that the "evidence forces the conclusion that Oates's theology does permeate his pastoral care. He has been highly successful in penetrating and refining pastoral care and counseling methods with his own theological presuppositions."[57] Mays claimed that Oates provided a clear Christian view of man, yet this dissertation did not take into account or explain how a biblical anthropology resulted from Oates's thought as he relied upon modern psychology as a "basis of relevancy" used to define man.[58] Published a few years later, "The Pastoral Concern for Man in the Thought of Wayne Edward Oates" further expounded Mays's work.

J. C. Collins was in agreement with Mays's conclusions; however, he seemed to go one step further in stating that "Oates' basic theological insight stem from a Christocentric understanding of man and a Trinitarian view of God."[59] Similarly to Mays, Collins's background and training in clinical pastoral education seemed to contribute to an uncritical approach to Oates's pastoral counseling. Throughout this work Collins did not support

---

55. Scharfenberg, "Babylonian Captivity of Pastoral Theology," 133. See also Oates, *Protestant Pastoral Counseling*, 15–21. Oates did share some of these concerns. He believed that a spirit of self-criticism should not be forsaken by those within the field and an anthropocentric point-of-view should be guarded against. However, when taken as a whole, the influence of secular psychology, humanistic philosophy, and liberal theology is made evident to support his conclusions.

56. Mays, "Contemporary Theology and Pastoral Care." This work is cited in many dissertations as an unpublished work; however, since that time it has been physically printed and bound. The researcher was able to access it through the library at Southern Seminary in Louisville, Kentucky.

57. Mays, "Contemporary Theology and Pastoral Care," 101.

58. Mays, "Contemporary Theology and Pastoral Care," 72–74.

59. Collins, "Pastoral Concern for Man," 47.

statements affirming the theological and christocentric foundations of Oates counseling approach, instead he used a large portion of his dissertation to argue for the validity of Oates's method of integrating psychology with theology.[60]

Oliver Curtis's dissertation contrasted the anthropologies of an atheist, Erich Fromm, and a Christian, Wayne Oates. Curtis asserted that Oates seemed to contextualize his "Christian selfhood" in psychological language which closely parallel's Fromm's conception of man's problem and solution.[61] His defense of Oates, however, was weakened by the fact that Curtis continued to favorably connect Oates with either non-Christian psychologists including Hall, Lindzey, Freud, Maslow, and Rogers or with theologians, such as Tillich, who de-emphasized the authority and sufficiency of Scripture in order to embrace liberal principles devoted to an existential, person-centered faith.[62]

Martin Keller Jeane analyzed Oates's method and approach to pastoral counseling as coming from a phenomenological perspective. This perspective, suggested by Jeane and affirmed by Collins, served as the groundwork for Oates's therapeutic approach to counseling and revealed that anthropology was Oates's starting point for building a system of care.[63] Jeane claimed that Oates could be distinguished from others due to his influence on a responsible biblical and theological support for pastoral work.[64] In "Pastoral Identity in the Thought of Wayne E. Oates," John Henry Edgar defended Oates against critics who claimed that his method of correlation was an excuse to utilize psychological terms by simply translating them from biblical concepts. In this way, Oates could make use of the relevant research, data,

---

60. Collins, "Pastoral Concern for Man," 65. This can best be summarized as Collins stated, "Oates's method [of correlation] is bifocal in that he takes the best from biblical insights and theological tradition and attempts a meaningful relation to the best in behavioral insights and current understandings of man."

61. Curtis, "Role of Religion," iii.

62. Curtis, "Role of Religion," 96. See also Oates, *Religious Dimensions of Personality*, 301; Maslow, "Theory of Human Motivation," 341.

63. Jeane, "Analysis of Wayne Edward Oates' Phenomenological Method." Jeane identified Edmund Husserl (1859–1938) as the influence on Oates's phenomenological approach. See Husserl and Gibson, *Ideas*, and also, Oates, *Protestant Pastoral Counseling*, 184.

64. Jeane, "Analysis of Wayne Edward Oates' Phenomenological Method," 4. Jeane later went as far as to state, "An informed person does not question Oates' intense relationship with the Bible" (49). Jeane attempted to raise the question as to whether Oates's phenomenological approach affected his reliance upon Scripture; however, his conclusion is that it does not.

and concepts of the behavioral sciences without sacrificing any theological commitments.[65]

The most recent attempt at capitalizing on the influence and impact of Oates on pastoral counseling was published in 1988. In his dissertation, Rodrick Durst claimed that Oates's anthropology was thoroughly and unapologetically Christian in its foundation, formation, and conception.[66] Durst's dissertation could be considered the closest to the topic and subject matter approached in this volume. However, while Durst noted that Oates's view of man was informed, and in some sense redefined, by secular psychotherapy and liberal theology, he did not expound upon specific ways these influences manifested in an outlined anthropology. Durst also provided only one chapter that addressed anthropology. He also continued to argue for Oates's Christian anthropology in the face of evidence that Oates's agenda for pastoral psychology has "been to render the verifiable results of clinical psychology into a terminologically useful form for pastoral ministry."[67]

The Legacy of Wayne Oates

Agreeing with Boisen's attribution of the achievements and contributions of the depth psychologies, Oates noted that the purpose of therapy was the "bringing of the unconscious into the conscious which provides meaning for one's senseless behavior."[68] He maintained throughout his career that

---

65. Jeane, "Analysis of Wayne Edward Oates' Phenomenological Method," 211. Edgar admitted that Oates's use of liberal theological principles was related to his own theological presuppositions; however, he noted that his use of liberal theology and behavioral science was for the goal of making the "church more relevant to the needs of modern society" (Edgar, "Pastoral Identity," 70). Bush and Collins both covered Oates's method of correlation as well.

66. Durst, "Theological Dimensions of Human Existence," 3.

67. Durst, "Theological Dimensions of Human Existence," 124. See also Oates, *Religious Dimensions of Personality*, 219–41. The term "pastoral psychology" will be used to refer to the subdiscipline within the psychology of religion that was popular in the mid-twentieth century. Pastoral psychology sought to incorporate secular principles, theories, and methods into the practice of pastoral ministry. This approach became so popular that several academic and ministry-focused journals (e.g., *Pastoral Psychology, Journal of Psychology and Christianity*, and *Journal of Psychology and Theology*) were founded which touted the application of psychology for the general improvement and support of the Christian minister's work. See Hofmann, *Ministry and Mental Health*, and Boisen, *Exploration of the Inner World*, 239.

68. Oates, *Pastoral Counseling*, 63. Oates credited David Roberts for leading the way for the "assimilation of insight therapy" into theology. See Roberts, *Psychotherapy*. This influential textbook was used in pastoral counseling courses in many seminaries and theological institutions through the 1970s.

responsible and well-educated pastors should be versed in the fundamental literature in the secular field of counseling and psychotherapy.[69] Oates stated, "Scientific techniques of psychological and therapeutic counseling have exerted a vital influence upon the minister's interpretation of his own role in such a way that he is today likely to sense counseling needs quickly."[70] As a result of these philosophical and methodological commitments, Oates's anthropology was birthed and developed outside of the scope, authority, and influence of the Bible.

The therapeutic process was aimed at developing the personality, assuaging guilt, and providing comfort in the face of dis-ease, unhappiness, and disappointment. The minister as therapist followed the mandate of an old French proverb regarding the counseling task which had for its goal, "to heal sometimes, to remedy often, to comfort always."[71] Rogerian non-directive counseling informed Oates's conception of the therapeutic minister in that clinical training would sensitize the counselor to the self-centered needs of the client and that he would allow the client to come to his own solutions for his own problems.[72] As part of therapeutically informed pastoral care, any judgments made by the shepherd were not to demean or place demands upon wayward sheep. The implication behind this was that the sheep would lose their sense of individuality and become dependent upon the shepherd. Instead, the minister as shepherd is one of equal cooperation "in the growth of human personalities" so that people may fully exercise "his own free power of decision" in order to become a complete person.[73] Ultimately, according to Oates, the shepherd's role as therapist was to focus upon the needs, desires, and interests of the sheep.[74] Unfortunately, as will be seen in the following chapters, many of his key anthropological conclusions stand in stark relief from a biblical understanding of man.

---

69. Oates, *Christian Pastor*, 114. Oates specifically referred to Rogers, *Counseling and Psychotherapy*, and Dicks, *Pastoral Work and Personal Counseling*.

70. Oates, *Where to Go for Help*, 18. See also Hiltner, *Preface to Pastoral Theology*, 101.

71. Oates, *Pastoral Counseling*, 9.

72. Oates, *Where to Go for Help*, 19.

73. Oates, *Christian Pastor*, 30. See also Hiltner, *Pastoral Counseling*, 32. A troubled person is referred to as a "divided personality" instead of a divided soul (cf. Jas 1:8).

74. Oates, *Christian Pastor*, 108. This distinctive of the pastor represented a client-centered and man-centered approach to the pastor's work. The question that must be asked is, does the pastor represent man's interests or God's interests? See also Hiltner, *Christian Shepherd*, 28.

2

Shepherding Without a Staff

Profiling a Pastoral Psychologist

WHILE OATES PREFERRED TO think of himself as a simple country minister, the designation of pastoral psychologist has been applied to him by those who sought to depict his approach to counseling as biblical. Among these sources, Collins approved of Oates's contributions to pastoral theology and counseling by noting that his "theological and psychological insights concerning man and their personal application hold rich, varied resources for both pastor and laymen."[1] Durst likewise claimed that Oates had "developed his pastoral psychology as a dramatization of the continuing encounter of psychology and theology in regard to the redefinition of human personality."[2]

---

1. Collins, "Pastoral Concern for Man," iii. As far as many of his contemporaries were concerned, Oates maintained theological and biblical integrity regarding his counseling (Collins, "Pastoral Concern," 16). Jeane agrees with Collins's conclusion that Oates's work is distinguished in his biblical and theological work in pastoral care even to the point where he suggests that only uninformed people would seek to question Oates's commitment to the Bible. (Jeane, "Analysis," 4, 18, 49). However, the fact that "Oates begins with theological truth holding the Bible in one hand and human experience in the other" seems to differ greatly than an anthropology and counseling methodology driven by Scripture (Oates, *Bible in Pastoral Care*, 75).

2. Durst, "Theological Dimensions of Human Existence," 116. John Edgar noted that the conception of human nature for most Protestant ministers, during the years in which Oates began engaging in pastoral counseling, leaned heavily upon the latest advances in the behavioral and psychological sciences instead of upon Scripture as a

Within these assessments, both Collins and Durst acknowledged a direct link between Oates's role as a pastoral psychologist and his understanding of man.³ Seeing many of the problems facing people as stemming from the social crises of his day, Oates sought to offer an ongoing dialogue between the fields of theology, psychology, and psychiatry in an effort to broaden the possibilities of interdisciplinary collaboration toward finding solutions.⁴ His approach to pastoral psychology, one that combined modern pastoral theology with a psychological framework for Christian ministry, attempted to translate the "dialects of the secularized value systems of the behavioral sciences into the wisdom, words, and power of the good news of God in Jesus Christ."⁵

In order to articulate a doctrine of man derived from the writings of Wayne Oates as it relates to his counseling, it is necessary to explore salient aspects of Oates's life, including themes and motifs present throughout his early years, self-descriptions of his conversion experience as a young man, and the lasting legacy of his multifaceted career in academia. The following biographical sketch is intended to provide pertinent information relating to Oates's overall conception of pastoral counseling, ultimately pointing to how psychological foundations became the cornerstone of his understanding of man.⁶ Following this section, the author will briefly outline a biblical anthropology which will serve as the standard of comparison by which to adequately assess Oates's anthropology and its unsettling implications.

EARLY LIFE AND STRUGGLES (1917–1932)

Early in life, Wayne Oates became familiar with hardship, tragedy, and poverty. His mother, Lula, was a sharecropper turned textile mill worker, and

---

definitive guide. Interestingly, Edgar, like Durst, concluded that Oates, while indebted to elements of theological liberalism and secular psychology, maintained a biblical view of man (Edgar, "Pastoral Identity," 77).

3. In his book *Protestant Pastoral Counseling*, Oates noted that anthropology served as the heart for his entire conception of pastoral counseling. In many ways, Oates's doctrine of man (i.e., anthropology) informed all other aspects of his pastoral counseling approach. (Oates, *Protestant Pastoral Counseling*, 184, and Jeane, "Analysis," 4).

4. Bush, "Human Suffering," 3–5.

5. Borchert and Lester, *Spiritual Dimensions*, 58. While rejecting secularization and the behavioral sciences which tend to remove God "from our sense of responsibility for our actions," Oates affirmed that pastoral counselors need "humanistic assessments of human behavior which, when put into relationship to God, become translatable into Judeo-Christian concepts of sin" (Borchert and Lester, *Spiritual Dimensions*, 62–63).

6. For the purposes of this book, I will focus upon relevant aspects of Oates's biography from his early years to the time of his departure from Southern Seminary in 1974.

his father, whom Oates would only meet twice, had committed adultery and abandoned the family weeks after Oates's birth.[7] The remainder of the family included two brothers and one sister, all of whom were much older than Oates. His maternal grandmother was remembered by the young Oates as his primary religious influence in the home.[8]

As suggested in his 1983 autobiography, a dominant motif which characterized Oates's early life and later shaped his thinking was the ever-present conflict between struggle and freedom. A strong desire to be free from poverty was one of his earliest drives. In the years leading up to the Great Depression, Oates had become consumed by the seemingly insurmountable financial restraints, destitution, and lack of opportunity that the mill towns afforded.[9]

The only deliverance that a young Oates could find from the harsh reality of his life was through public education. He noted, "I had found in school the avenue of my freedom from the grinding poverty, ugliness, filth and brutality I saw happening around me. I sensed that learning words would give me power for the struggle to be free."[10] As a student, Oates was known to be a keen observer of himself and others. During the first years of public education, his interest in human nature was piqued through the influence of his teachers as they exposed him to new and different ideas. As early as the second grade, Oates remembered first understanding that he had a "mind within my mind that was *more* than my mind" and that he was set apart from others as a unique individual.[11] While he claimed that this introduction to the internalized "me" was the first step in his escape from poverty, Collins suggested that Oates's view of himself had more to do with "his struggle for selfhood" than anything else.[12]

---

7. Oates, *Struggle to Be Free*, 14.

8. Oates, *Struggle to Be Free*, 17. By the time of his birth, Oates's two older brothers had already moved out of the home, leaving him to be reared by his mother, grandmother, and for a shorter time, his sister. According to one of his close friends, Dotson M. Nelson Jr., Oates characterized his adolescent years as being in "bondage to poverty." See Nelson, "Life and Works of Wayne Oates," 5, Wayne E. Oates Papers, box 16: folder 5.

9. Dillon, "Wayne E. Oates," 1, Wayne E. Oates Papers, box 37: folder 51.

10. Oates, *Struggle to Be Free*, 24.

11. Oates, *Struggle to Be Free*, 22. Oates's later reading of Immanuel Kant's *The Science of the Right*, further confirmed this first "revelation" of self-perception. Kant's philosophy encouraged him to pursue freedom and personal rights without apology for this was the right of every man. Existential philosophy became a hallmark of Oates's thinking through mentors in his life including Olin Binkley, Gaines Dobbins, and Anton Boisen (Jeane, "Analysis," 26).

12. Collins, "Pastoral Concern for Man," 10. Oates distinguishes between identity

A gifted student, Oates was encouraged by his teachers to take confidence in and foster his natural intellectual capabilities and interests. He wrote, "By the time I reached the sixth grade I was writing on my own. I wrote and illustrated a 'book' entitled 'Man and Nature,' in which I pointed out that inventions such as the camera and the airplane were man's copies of nature—the human eye and the bird that could fly."[13] Once again, an attention to anthropological concerns seemed evident.

Public school provided a physical and intellectual escape from the abject poverty of the mills; yet while he excelled academically, Oates still struggled with feelings of inferiority.

> My earliest feeling of inferiority came just when Erik Erikson said it would—in the first years of school. For me it was a struggle to see whether high achievement as a student would win out over the fact that often my lunch was a cold biscuit with fatback in it while other children paid for lunch in the school lunchroom.[14]

As the end of his eighth grade year approached, the nearly fourteen-year-old was faced with the grim, yet seemingly inevitable, reality that his future was in the cotton mills of his youth.[15] However, as providence would have it, in November of 1930, Oates was informed by his teachers that he had been selected to serve as a page to a sitting United States senator. Serving alongside other young boys his age, Oates moved into a boardinghouse in Washington, DC, where he would live for the next three years.[16]

During his first year in Washington, DC, Oates was aware of the disparity that existed between himself and his peers. While the other pages were well-educated and wealthy, he was socially awkward, shy, and his speech could be characterized as rustic. He noted that during this time he was "tormented, hazed, ridiculed, and beat up on by these people."[17] While his

---

and selfhood. According to Collins's readings of *Christ and Selfhood*, he stated, "Identity is man's ability to transcend himself and to be aware that he is a person. When that identity finds a governing and organizing center, the identity becomes a selfhood" (Oates, *Christ and Selfhood*, 24). This will be covered more in chapter 4.

13. Oates, *Struggle to Be Free*, 22.

14. Oates, *Struggle to Be Free*, 29. This motif of low self-esteem began in his first days of public school and followed him into his young adulthood. (See Nelson, "Life and Works," 5.)

15. See Nelson, "Life and Works of Wayne Oates," 5.

16. Oates, *Struggle to Be Free*, 24. This senator was Ellison D. "Cotton Ed" Smith of South Carolina (D) who served in office from 1909–1944 (Collins, "Pastoral Concern for Man," 8).

17. Oates, *Struggle to Be Free*, 31.

self-esteem hit an all-time low, Oates decided to cut the ties that continued to bind him to his identity as the son of an impoverished cotton mill worker.

He sought help from his supervisor, Mr. Leslie Biffle, who mentored him in everything from social manners to personal hygiene and tutored him in his knowledge of the English language. He also took night classes throughout his tenure as page in an effort to continue in his education.[18] By the time of his second year as a page, Oates established his new identity. He recollected, "This newfound increase in confidence, self-worth, and personal dignity created a wide gap between my home environment and me. . . . I crossed a Rubicon of self-worth. There was never to be again a turning back—no matter what happened. I could hold my head high and not be ashamed."[19]

By the spring of 1933, due to his age, Oates became ineligible to continue serving in the Senate and moved back to Greenville, where he graduated from Parker Hill High School the following spring.[20] After graduation he worked several odd jobs and eventually spent two years working in the very textile mills he had struggled to escape a few years earlier. While learning the family trade as a weaver, Oates never stopped desiring to continue his formal education. One of the three purposes that Oates identified as motivations for him going to college was his search for an adequate philosophy of life, something at this point he knew that he had not yet fully developed. Noting the important role a college education could have in developing such a philosophy Oates stated:

> Life as the college student, experiences it, [sic] is an adventure in intellectual and spiritual conquest, and in social and ethical adjustment. A college student, in other words must advance in wisdom and stature and in favor of God and man. In short, he must grow up and he must live with people. How, then, may we arrive at an adequate philosophy of life.[21]

---

18. Dillon, "Wayne E. Oates," 2.

19. Oates, *Struggle to Be Free*, 33. While Oates confessed that poor decisions accompanied his change of personality (e.g., he was involved in several physical alterations with any pages who confronted him), he writes with a sense of achievement and pride in the fact that he was indeed able to take advantage of his former adversaries and drive a further wedge between who he wanted to be and who he was when he arrived in Washington, DC (Nelson, "Life and Works," 6).

20. Oates, *Struggle to Be Free*, 39.

21. Oates, "Why I Decided to Go to College," 8, unpublished personal essay, Wayne E. Oates Papers, box 3: folder 20. Among the other motivating factors that Oates listed was overcoming his undesirable "familial and environmental heritage" and leaving a lasting legacy to generations to follow.

Encouraged by a friend to pursue a college education, Oates visited Mars Hill Junior College, near Asheville, North Carolina. After meeting the president of the institution, R. L. Moore, and being approved for a work grant, he made plans to matriculate in the fall of 1936.[22]

CONVERSION AND CALL TO CARE (1932–1943)

Through a study of the personal correspondence and published writings, the author discovered either inconsistencies in the narrative surrounding Oates's conversion or no mention of it as a major life event.[23] In an interview given when he was sixty-seven years old, Oates recalled that it was through his personal experiences during the early years of his public education that his understanding of Christianity first took shape.[24] While Oates remembered having a consciousness of God from his early years, the narrative and details surrounding his conversion to Christianity do not begin until the summer of 1932 when Oates was home from Washington, DC.

Conflicting Conversion Narratives

In an effort to distance himself from his background in poverty, his feelings of inferiority, and to impress a young girl, Oates began attending church. Soon he was approached by the pastor's wife and was asked if he would like to become a Christian. He answered in the affirmative. That same evening he made a public profession of Christ and was soon baptized. In recalling this experience Oates noted:

---

22. Oates, *Struggle to Be Free*, 40–41.

23. Oates's conversion, something that should be considered as a major event in any biography, was either not mentioned at all or it was mentioned in contradicting terms among the several resources surveyed. Even his autobiographical references to this event lacked clarity. When mentioned, there seemed to be a disparity behind when his authentic conversion occurred, what his age was, and what circumstances surrounded the event.

24. Bush, "Human Suffering," 251. As mentioned earlier, Oates credited his grandmother for his earliest recollections about teaching on Christianity. However, as he noted in his autobiography, Oates formed his own conception about God's relation to him through two life experiences. A streetcar operator in Greenville showed kindness to the young Oates. He noted, "In the concrete operations of my mind, I decided that God had to be like this streetcar motorman. He was a strong God. He guided and controlled the world the way this man did the streetcar. . . . He *laughs!* He likes *me.* We're friends. No religious teachers taught me this. I decided it for myself" (Oates, *Struggle to Be Free*, 23).

> To me this meant that I had as much right as anybody else to pray. It meant that I felt responsible to God from then on for my behavior and my sense of purpose in my work. Yet, it was a remarkably *contentless* experience. I did not get any specific instructions as to who Jesus Christ is, as to what I had agreed to be and become, beyond simply being a "good person," a thing I had been striving for all along. . . . He [the pastor] gave me no instructions about what redemption in Christ was all about. This is what I mean by *contentlessness*. I had faith, but not according to knowledge.[25]

In his autobiography, Oates seemed to place doubt on the authenticity of his conversion during this episode in his life. However, regarding this same narrative, he later recalled that he had *indeed* become a Christian when he turned sixteen years old. He noted that when asked by the pastor's wife if he had believed in the Lord Jesus Christ, he replied, "I always have."[26] Bonny Dillon, in an essay relating to Oates's pioneering work in pastoral counseling, agreed that Oates was authentically converted at sixteen in a small Baptist church in Greenville.[27]

However, another conversion narrative was discovered in the existing literature that apparently contradicts these previous accounts. During the time Oates was attending Mars Hill Junior College, his pastor, William L. Lynch of Mars Hill Baptist Church, first introduced Oates to the writings of Harry Emerson Fosdick, Leslie Weatherhead, and psychologist and philosopher William James. Particularly through reading James's definition of conversion, Oates identified his "real conversion."[28] This definition was found in *Varieties of Religious Experience*.

---

25. Oates, *Struggle to Be Free*, 37–38. The authenticity of Oates's conversion to Christianity at this point in his life is muddled by the language he employed. In his autobiography, he is emphatic in his statements regarding the lack of content and faith surrounding this initial decision to become a Christian. However, he seemingly ignores these concerns by stating that he became assured that his prayers now "got higher than the ceiling."

26. Oates, *Struggle to Be Free*, 252. Oates's autobiography was published in 1983, three years after Oates told Theodore Bush in a personal interview that his conversion at sixteen was authentic.

27. Dillon, "Wayne E. Oates," 1, Dillon referenced Oates, *Pastoral Counseling in Social Problems*, 64. Nelson does not go into any detail regarding the time that Oates became a Christian. Oates's Christian faith, which Nelson noted was "planted . . . almost by accident" came about while he still serving as a page in Washington, DC (Nelson, "Life and Works," 6).

28. Oates, *Struggle to Be Free*, 43. Nelson, "Life and Works of Wayne Oates," 7.

> To be converted, to be regenerated, to receive grace, to experience religion, to gain an assurance, are so many phrases which denote the process, gradual or sudden, by which a self hitherto divided, and consciously wrong inferior and unhappy, becomes unified and consciously right superior and happy, in consequence of its former hold upon religious realities. This at least is what conversion signifies in general terms, whether or not we believe that a direct divine operation is needed to bring such moral change about.[29]

With the introduction of William James's pragmatism, Oates came to emphasize the utilitarian value and empirical nature of conversion. James conceived of the concept of conversion in terms of a personal and self-willed experience that resulted in the shift of one's habits, affections, and life goals from one center to another.[30] Conversion was not to be considered merely a static, supernatural transaction between God and man, but a dynamic growth process within a context of the natural sphere in which a person could come to better understand his or her needs.[31] Oates related his conversion experience with feelings of being freed from his past as a poor mill worker and the ability to now rise above his situation and conquer any obstacle in his field of view.[32] This "religious experience" was understood by him in terms of liberation and individualism.[33] Instead of his conversion

---

29. James, *Varieties of Religious Experience*, 157. James is recognized as the founding father of American psychology and has been identified as one of the most significant educational psychologists in American history. See Sprinthall et al., *Educational Psychology*, 11. Oates utilized James's concept, and in some instances the very definition, in a number of his books. (Oates, *Struggle to Be Free*, 43; Oates, *Christian Pastor*, 17; Oates, *Psychology of Religion*, 73, 93–94; Oates, *Religious Factors in Mental Illness*, 189.)

30. James, *Varieties of Religious Experience*, 157. See also Oates, *Religious Factors in Mental Illness*, 34; Durst, "Theological Dimensions of Human Existence," 32, and Boisen, *Out of the Depths*, 212.

31. Oates, *Psychology of Religion*, 95. Oates would later come to the conclusion that James's understanding of conversion, one that was rooted in a developmental framework and centered on meetings psychosocial needs, should be considered normative within the field of psychology of religion. See also Starbuck, *Psychology of Religion*, 403; Murphy, *Personality*, 490–91; Roberts, *Psychotherapy*, 118.

32. Oates, *Struggle to Be Free*, 43. For Oates, Jesus offered "redemption from feelings of inferiority."

33. Collins, "Pastoral Concern for Man," 30–31; Oates, *Pastoral Counseling in Social Problems*, 64. Interestingly, Oates noted that among the religious experiences he had in his life, his profession of faith was "significant but not profound." It should be noted that Collins identified Oates as being seventeen and the year being 1935 when his "profession of faith" took place, two facts that run in contradiction with other accounts.

being the cornerstone on which his life story hinged, he instead positioned it in self-serving terms.

Call to Pastoral Care

By the summer of 1937, under the continued guidance of his pastor and teachers at Mars Hill Junior College, Oates abandoned his plans to become a lawyer and politician in favor of the ministry. Regarding his call to ministry, Oates stated, "I came to a steadfast certainty both that I wanted to be a minister and that God was inviting me to be a minister. No visions, ecstasies, or loud voices accompanied the certainty. The intelligence of the eternal God worked through his creation of my own mind to bring closure to a decision to be a minister."[34] In the fall of 1938, Oates transferred to Wake Forest College, at that time an all-male institution, to further his ministerial training and preparation for the pastorate.

Olin T. Binkley and Religious Psychology

At Wake Forest, Oates was not only able to continue pursuing interests he had picked up after his call to ministry, including his penchant for classical and New Testament Greek, but it was here where he met the professor, mentor, and friend who would greatly influence him regarding the application of psychology for the pastoral ministry.[35] Only nine years older than Oates, Olin Trivette Binkley had graduated with his doctorate of philosophy from Yale University and was pastoring a church in Connecticut by the time he was twenty-four years old. When Oates started taking classes at Wake Forest College in 1938, Binkley had also just started his first year as professor of religion.[36] During that year, Oates enrolled in a course taught by Binkley per-

---

34. Oates, *Struggle to Be Free*, 48–49. Oates found early on that his emphasis in ministry would be a focus on people. Oates rejected the revivalist approaches because what he labeled as "sales-pitch evangelism" did not go far enough to provide a more "prescriptive, individualized, and growth-oriented approach to the proclamation of the good news of Jesus Christ" (49). See also Nelson, "Life and Works of Wayne E. Oates," 7–8.

35. Oates, *Struggle to Be Free*, 50. Binkley's influence in Oates's life and thinking cannot be overemphasized. Toward the end of Oates's career and life, he continued to name Binkley as being one of his closest confidants and major influences on his thinking concerning pastoral counseling. See Oates, "Appreciation Response by Oates," April 3, 1984, Wayne E. Oates Papers, box 1: folder 20; Nelson, "Life and Works of Wayne E. Oates," 9. Various correspondences between Oates and Binkley, Olin T. Binkley Papers, box 11: folders 6–7.

36. "Dr. Olin Trivette Binkley, 91," *Wake Weekly*, September 2, 1999, Olin T. Binkley

taining to marriage and family that would have a lasting impact on his life and career.[37] It was through Binkley's teaching where Oates sought how to apply psychology and counseling to the pastoral ministry. Through course lectures and assigned readings, Oates utilized a psychological approach to pastoral care.[38] In other courses, Binkley introduced his student to the work of various clinical psychologists who were key figures in the psychology of religion. These psychologists, including men such as Karl Stolz and E. D. Starbuck, held wide and varying interests which included the origins and development of personality, the inner religious life of man, and the study of human experience through empirical observation.[39] Binkley's knowledge of psychology and its usefulness in the study of religion dated back to his studies at Yale in 1930. It was here where Binkley came to understand psychology as "the science of the mind" and that the psychology of religion, as a subspecialty of general psychology, attempted to "apply the general method of psychology to those particular experiments we call religion."[40] In Binkley's courses, the interests of the human mind and the science of psychology were introduced and nurtured in Oates's thinking. Oates's academic

---

Papers, box 17: folder 13. It is important to note that as the chair of the department of religion at Wake Forest College, Binkley was instrumental in teaching Oates the value of the historical-critical study of the Bible. This nontraditional approach to the study of the Bible captivated Oates and remained the prominent view of Scripture for him throughout his career. See Wills, *Southern Baptist Theological Seminary, 1859–2009*, 355; Binkley, "Education of Ministers in Contemporary Society," 265.

37. Oates, "Long Friendship," 38–39. This course was the earliest in marriage and family ever taught at the collegiate level in the United States. Binkley, a student of Ernest Groves, who was a pioneer in marriage and family therapy, taught courses related to marriage counseling, Christian ethics, sociology and psychology throughout his career well into the 1960s. See also Oates, *Struggle to Be Free*, 99; and Bush, "Human Suffering," 253.

38. Bush, "Human Suffering," 254.

39. Binkley, "Psychology of Religion Notes," Olin T. Binkley Papers, box 28: folder 6. Karl Stolz approached religion as a "fact" available to be studied in order to explain why people put their trust in God, how they first came to believe in him, and how religion impacts personality adjustment. See Stolz, *Psychology of Religious Living*, 7, 21. Binkley also required as a course text a seminal volume in the field of psychology of religion, E. D. Starbuck's, *Psychology of Religion*, which was first published in 1901. In this key text, Starbuck argued that psychology usefully serves religion by bringing it out of the "domain of feeling" and into the realm of the scientific and intellectual understanding (Starbuck, *Psychology of Religion*, 17).

40. Binkley, "Psychology of Religion, Personal Notes, Yale 1930," Olin T. Binkley Papers, box 118: folder 1. Binkley, among three other men, including Gaines Dobbins, Ralph Bonacker, and Anton Boisen, influenced Oates in his doctoral research regarding the significance and positive contribution of psychoanalysis, specifically Sigmund Freud, for the advancement and clarification of the Christian faith.

acumen would eventually culminate in Binkley's suggestion that Oates one day consider a professorship in psychology and philosophy.

When Oates graduated from Wake Forest in the spring of 1940, he transitioned from being Binkley's student to becoming his colleague as he took on the role of instructor of psychology and philosophy.[41] While this was Oates's first move in a long career in academia, it was hardly financially substantive. Looking to grow his ministerial experience, while supplementing his meager salary, Oates took on two pastorates in small churches near the college. While he had never had a course on preaching or pastoral care, Oates leaned heavily on his mentor's knowledge and experience as Binkley provided Oates with clinical supervision throughout the two years he served as pastor.[42] As an ethicist and sociologist, Binkley viewed religion in terms of expediting social change and social good will.[43] Consequently, the combination of Oates's particular background in poverty and Binkley's teaching and supervision led Oates to be wary of joining the "party-line thought of Southern Baptists" concerning the view of the pastor as primarily an evangelist and church grower.[44] Instead, Oates decided to embark on a tireless visitation campaign in order to meet the needs of his congregation and those in the surrounding community.

For the first time, Oates was faced with the ills of humanity in varying forms ranging from families struggling with mentally unstable children to those who had succumbed to addictions, adultery, and suicide. While these crisis scenarios provided opportunities for Oates to utilize psychological and theological principles he had learned from Binkley, there was

---

41. Speaking of Binkley's influence on the direction of his unique career, Oates noted, "From my identification with him as a teacher, I resolved to express my ministry through the classroom and the clinic as well as the pulpit." Oates, *Struggle to Be Free*, 51.

42. Oates, *Struggle to Be Free*, 54; Nelson, "Life and Works of Wayne E. Oates," 9. It is interesting to note that in his pulpit ministry, Oates was taught by J. B. Weatherspoon to utilize psychological concepts and to carefully include the "essence of human psychology in his sermons" without revealing the processes involved in finding the essence. I argue that this example of subtle speech is evident in Oates's counseling ministry as it is in his pulpit ministry (Bonny Dillon, "Wayne E. Oates: Pioneering in Pastoral Counseling," 2, in Wayne E. Oates Papers, box 37: folder 51). Olin Binkley, Harold Tribble, and J. B. Weatherspoon, all influences on Oates at Wake Forest and later at Southern Seminary, learned from their progressive theological neighbors that only gradual and "calm pedagogy," not open conflict, would eventually see the broader Southern Baptist denomination become open to progressive and liberal theological ideals (Wills, *Southern Baptist Theological Seminary*, 377).

43 Oates, *What Psychology Says about Religion*, 41. See also Binkley, *Churches and the Social Conscience*, 4, 25.

44. Oates, *Struggle to Be Free*, 55; Nelson, "Life and Works of Wayne E. Oates," 9.

one instance that left an indelible mark.[45] Oates was approached by a local physician, Dr. Cheeves, who had diagnosed a woman at Oates's church with stomach and intestinal problems. This woman also had a husband who was known to be an alcoholic. The physician recommended that Oates visit the woman with the hope that he could address her illness, fears associated with her husband, and the causes behind his abuse of alcohol. After an initial meeting with the woman, Oates remembered:

> I conferred with the doctor and he said she was genuinely sick with stomach, intestinal, and blood pressure problems. These were aggravated by her fear of her husband, who was a heavy drinker. He encouraged me to continue to see her, to get acquainted with each of her children, and to try to understand what caused the husband to need so much booze. He urged me to listen, convey, and pray with them. These things I did, and I was amazed to see that her health improved, her husband's sadness lifted and his drinking decreased, and her children began laughing and playing again. . . . Not long after this, Dr. Cheeves was called into the military. He, upon leaving, urged me to give myself to studying and teaching about the relation of the ministry and medicine. He said, "It's the wave of the future."[46]

It was during this season of ministry that Oates's conception and practice of pastoral care as a clinical endeavor, which utilized psychological knowledge for the purpose of promoting mental health, became solidified.[47]

CAREER IN COUNSELING (1943–1974)

Another mark of influence left on Oates while he was at Wake Forest included a rejection of "pack thinking" in favor of drawing his own conclusions on the basis of evidence instead of succumbing to the status quo.[48] Individual thinking and a pioneering spirit of inquiry were qualities which were

---

45. Olin T. Binkley, "WFC Lecture Notes: Psychology of Religion (1938–1944)," Olin T. Binkley Papers, box 28: folder 4. Examples of psychological influences relied upon by Binkley, besides those already mentioned, also included E. D. Thorndike, G. S. Hall, William James, Edward Scribner Ames, and George Albert Coe. Examples of theological influences include the following: Walter Rauschenbusch, William Adams Brown, William Newton Clarke, Reinhold Niebuhr, and Shailer Mathews.

46. Oates, *Struggle to Be Free*, 57–58. This particular experience served as a precursor to Oates extensive work in CPE and foreshadows his close relationship to Dr. Spafford Ackerly and his work at the Norton Psychiatric Clinic in Louisville, Kentucky.

47. Oates, *Christian Pastor*, 14–15.

48. Oates, *Struggle to Be Free*, 52; Nelson, "Life and Works of Wayne E. Oates," 9.

embraced by Oates as he saw them reflected in Binkley and other likeminded students.[49] From Oates's perspective, the years he had spent as a rural pastor only served to cement in his identity the idea of the pastor as a pioneer. He took advantage of opportunities to learn new methods from his mentors and often utilized innovations in the behavioral sciences in order to tend to the needs of those whom he was serving. Many years into his career, Oates would reflect on himself as a pioneer by stating, "Pioneers always relish the lure of the yet-untried. They have deft hands that sift out the grain of true promise from the chaff of false illusion and a patient but sharp surgical skill in cutting through the red tape that stifles action."[50]

Oates eventually decided to pursue formal theological education, which led him, along with his wife, Pauline, to move to Duke Divinity School located in Durham, North Carolina. In 1943 the couple made a fateful decision, with the encouragement and recommendation of Binkley, to transfer to Southern Seminary in order for Oates to complete his theological education.[51] Binkley, who started his academic career in Louisville in 1944, had been invited to join the faculty the previous year but initially denied the invitation because he understood that his approach to theology, as evidenced by his historical-critical study of the Bible and his utilization of social science, would be stifled at Southern Seminary than they had been at the more liberal-leaning Wake Forest College.[52] Despite some of his misgivings, Binkley urged Oates to come to Southern to study under other professors who shared similar convictions as Binkley.[53]

---

49. Dillon, "Wayne E. Oates," 4.

50. Oates, *New Dimensions in Pastoral Care*, 2, and Oates, *Struggle to Be Free*, 69.

51. Letter from Hugh Peterson to Olin Binkley, April 1, 1943, Wayne E. Oates Papers, box 11: folder 3. In his response dated April 20, 1943, to Peterson, the registrar and dean of students at Southern Seminary, Binkley referred to Oates as a "superior student" with "excellent intellectual ability, unusual capacity for hard work" and demonstrating "promise of great usefulness to the Christian ministry." See also *SBTS Catalog of Students*, 1943–1944 academic year, 110.

52. Wills, *Southern Baptist Theological Seminary, 1859–2009*, 338.

53. Dr. Ellis A. Fuller, who served as the sixth president of SBTS, was instrumental in bringing Binkley on the faculty as a professor of Christian ethics and sociology. Under Fuller's administration, the seminary's curriculum diversified to include the emerging social sciences, and instructional methodology reflected the influences of progressive educational approaches of the modern era. The perceived need for professionally trained religious education experts, according to the seminary leadership at the time, would lead to a separate school of religious education being formed in 1953. See Oates, "Ellis A. Fuller: Man of Transition and New Beginnings," 3–4, Wayne E. Oates Papers, box 25: folder 22; Wills, *Southern Baptist Theological Seminary, 1859–2009*, 327; Shands, "Ellis Adams Fuller, Man of God."

Harold W. Tribble and Modern Theology

In a letter written to Binkley during his first term at Southern, Oates praised his new theology professor, Harold Tribble, for his efforts in introducing the need for incorporating the findings of scientific research in the study of the Bible and Christian doctrine. Oates wrote,

> He [Tribble] is trying to give the boys the facts that scientific research of the past fifteen years has uncovered concerning the Scriptures. He has to blast away old conceptions before he can start. In doing so, he has to try to undo in the second and third years of a student's life here what has become firmly implanted there in the first year by the Old and New Testament departments and the Biblical Introduction classes. These classes are being taught as though scientific research had discovered nothing in the past forty years. The hypocrisy of it all is that they parade themselves under a pseudo-scholarship that chloroforms the boys into thinking they are omniscient when they have come through these treadmills, erroneously called classes. Dr. Tribble is doing a wonderful work here, but I think he is trying to sweep the ocean back with a broom.[54]

As the figurehead of the contingency of liberal faculty members at Southern, Tribble saw it as his duty to raise the intelligence of Southern Baptists through progressive scholarship, which entailed historical-critical methods of Bible study and necessitated scientific investigation.[55] Tribble was well aware that Fuller's policy of keeping Southern Seminary a confessional institution, one in which the churches of the Southern Baptist Convention determined the direction and content of the curriculum, would halt it from ever becoming faculty-driven in academic pursuits and policy formation. However, he did place his hope in his students, including Oates, that when they would become professors they would fight for the freedom to pursue scholarship without constraints.[56] Tribble's efforts at educational reform,

---

54. Personal correspondence from Wayne Oates (September 26, 1943), Olin T. Binkley Papers, box 11: folder 3.

55. Wills, *Southern Baptist Theological Seminary, 1859–2009*, 314. This perception of professorial responsibility would come to challenge the toned-down and "realist" approach of the SBTS administration under the leadership of Duke McCall culminating in the demand for resignations of more than a dozen professors after Tribble had already left as faculty at Southern. This conflict, according to McCall, centered on the fact that the dissenting professors "advanced ecumenism, liberal theology, and historical criticism of the Bible" and they did not "represent grassroots Baptists" (Wills, *Southern Baptist Theological Seminary*, 380).

56. Wills, *Southern Baptist Theological Seminary, 1859–2009*, 332. In the years of

along with this commitment to academic freedom in the use of extrabiblical scientific advancements, endeared Oates to him to the point that Tribble's perspective would be adopted by Oates as he would seek to bring reform to the curriculum at Southern Seminary as a faculty member.[57]

In 1925, after receiving his doctor of theology, the young Harold W. Tribble joined the faculty of Southern Seminary as the assistant to then president and head of the theology department, E. Y. Mullins. Tribble would serve in this role until he advanced to chair the department as professor of theology in 1929 shortly following Mullins's death.[58] Before joining the faculty at Southern Seminary, Tribble studied at the German universities in Tübingen and Bonn, where he came to appreciate and study the work of various neoorthodox theologians, most notably Karl Barth, Rudolph Bultmann, and Emil Brunner.[59]

While a broad movement, neoorthodoxy generally emphasized some views held closely by the conservative constituents of the Southern Baptist Convention; however, it was still in many ways far removed from traditional theological views which affirmed the inerrancy and infallibility of Scripture and the superiority of special revelation over general revelation.[60] While

---

Fuller's and McCall's presidencies, many of the Southern Seminary faculty desired to model the seminary after the divinity schools of the Northern Baptists all of which served as examples of progressive scholarship and touted academic freedom for faculty in the pursuits of their interests (Wills, *Southern Baptist Theological Seminary*, 327). See also Oates, *Struggle to Be Free*, 102–03.

57. Wills, *Southern Baptist Theological Seminary, 1859–2009*, 335. Building off of the work of Gaines Dobbins, Oates would become a visible figurehead at Southern Seminary in the effort to incorporate psychology of religion, clinical pastoral education training, and practical studies into the department of theology. See personal correspondence from Oates to Binkley (December 19, 1953), Olin T. Binkley Papers, box 11: folder 6.

58. While it is outside the scope of this work, it is important to note that Mullins was greatly influenced by the psychological work of William James. For an in-depth treatment of this influence as it relates to the curricular shift of pastoral ministry instruction and focus on scriptural content toward "pragmatic and psychological considerations" at Southern Seminary, see Crouch, "Influence of William James."

59. McDonald, "Man of the Month: Harold W. Tribble," *The Tie*, November 1946, 6; Harold Tribble Papers, box 1: folder 1. Tribble was well-educated, having earned an additional master's degree from the University of Louisville, a PhD in philosophy from the University of Edinburgh, and having completed additional studies at universities in Bonn, Germany, and Basel, Switzerland. See untitled obituary draft, Harold Tribble Papers, box 1: folder 1; Wills, *Southern Baptist Theological Seminary, 1859–2009*, 312, 340.

60. In its earliest years, this movement of theologians making efforts to reclaim traditional Christian doctrine from classical liberalism was strong in its assertion of the discontinuity of Christianity in all its aspects from the dominant thought-forms of the West. Unfortunately, many of these same theologians agreed with liberal theologians that the "whole area of spatio-temporal fact and event is the valid object of scientific

Tribble's mentor, E. Y. Mullins, incorporated elements of neoorthodox theology, Tribble's application differed markedly from Mullins. For example, Tribble seemed to favor Brunner's open view of general revelation which provided Tribble and other liberal-leaning faculty members at Southern Seminary an opportunity to "retain much of their experientially oriented liberalism and at the same time advocated such neoorthodox emphases as the gravity of human sinfulness and the centrality of the Bible."[61]

Besides the influence of neoorthodoxy, Tribble also studied the work of William Newton Clarke and Friedrich Schleiermacher and freely promoted their perspectives in his courses at Southern.[62] By the late nineteenth century, William Newton Clark (1840-1912) presented the first mature systematization of the "new theology" in his *Outline of Christian Theology*, a textbook that was used by Tribble and many other professors throughout the twentieth century and that served as a catalyst in the liberalization of Protestant thought in American seminaries.[63] Instead of the traditional approach to theology, one in which Scripture was held as authoritative for faith and practice and was primarily christocentric in its message, Clarke's theology was born out of progressive perspectives which syncretized man's growth and development with the larger structures of organic macroevolution.[64]

Before Clarke's birth, the German theologian Friedrich Schleiermacher (1768-1834), known as the "father of liberal theology," argued that

---

inquiry" in the sense that the "hypotheses of science in the area of natural and historical fact are regarded as authoritative" (Halverson and Cohen, *Handbook of Christian Theology*, 258).

61. Wills, *Southern Baptist Theological Seminary, 1859-2009*, 313-14. For Tribble and like-minded faculty members, including Dobbins, Weatherspoon, and Binkley, liberal and historical-critical scholarship would lead to truth and "this truth was essential to the advance of a relevant gospel in the modern world" (Wills, *Southern Baptist Theological Seminary*, 332).

62. Tribble, "Book List for Systematic Theology 1941, First Term," Harold Tribble Papers, box 17: folder 12. Among the theologians referenced for this course were Clarke (*Outline of Christian Theology*), Schleiermacher (*Christian Faith*), and Shailer Mathews (*Faith of Modernism*).

63. See Smith, *Changing Conceptions of Original Sin*, 194. Clarke was the teacher of William Adams Brown, a long-time professor at Union Theological Seminary, and influenced Brown's theological treatise *Christian Theology in Outline* (ca. 1906). Both Clarke's and Brown's texts were used in theological education for years. Concerning the new theology espoused by Clarke and himself, Brown noted, "By the new theology we mean the type of theology whose method is determined by the modern scientific movement and which is hospitable to its results." Oates was beholden to many professors at Union Theological Seminary who held views consistent with Brown including Reinhold Niebuhr, Roberts, and Tillich (Davis, *Theology Primer*, 48-49).

64. Smith, *Changing Conceptions of Original Sin*, 189-90, and Clarke, *Outline of Christian Doctrine*, 129.

the essential nature of Christianity should be found in personal experience instead of objective special revelation. Schleiermacher refuted the "universal sinfulness" of man due to a faulty belief in a historical account of Adam and Eve's sin in the garden. Instead he relegated sin to a "mere disturbance" of the human condition.[65] The Bible's authority became subservient to advances in scientific research, historical critique, and modern psychological inquiry, all the while traditional biblical doctrines, including the sinfulness of humanity, became open to reinterpretation. Under Tribble's direction, Oates was exposed to an anthropology that was inconsistent with traditional biblical teachings and instead characterized humanity as possessing both a good and evil nature in which mankind could naturally progress on their own.[66]

Gaines S. Dobbins and Practical Training

By the time that Oates had arrived in Louisville in 1944, Tribble was nearing the end of his tenure at Southern before moving on to serve as president of two prominent institutions, Andover-Newton Theological School, near Boston, and later Oates's alma mater, Wake Forest College, where he would oversee its move to Winston-Salem.[67] While Tribble's impact upon the formation of Oates's larger theological framework seemed to be substantial, the long-term mentorship, friendship, and guidance of Gaines Stanley Dobbins did even more to shape Oates into the image of a pastoral psychologist for the twentieth century.

In 1920, E. Y. Mullins, then president of Southern Seminary, hired Dobbins to join the small faculty as a professor of church efficiency and Sunday school pedagogy in an effort to introduce practical studies into the wider seminary curriculum. For the next thirty-six years, Dobbins filled a variety of roles, including not only leading a new department which would

---

65. Schleiermacher, *Christian Faith*, 292.

66. Clarke, *Outline of Christian Doctrine*, 242. Clarke noted, "Humanity possess upward tendencies, and has proved itself a slowly rising race. Man does advance as ages pass." Gross forms of evil are outgrown. See also Tribble, "Book List for Systematic Theology 1941, Second Term" (The Nature of Sin—Lecture 20), Harold Tribble Papers, box 17: folder 12.

67. It is interesting to note that Binkley's and Tribble's careers intersected in several points. Not only did Tribble end his career as president of the institution where Binkley started his career, but Binkley became the first president of Southeastern Baptist Theological Seminary, whose campus originally housed Wake Forest College. See also personal correspondence from Binkley (October 7, 1947), Harold Tribble Papers, box 1: folder 29; personal correspondence from Binkley (June 21, 1950), Harold Tribble Papers, box 1: folder 29.

focus on practical application over theoretical content but eventually serving as dean of a newly formed school of religious education and even interim president of the seminary.[68] Dobbins, who had studied under both George Albert Coe and John Dewey, was a firm believer that psychology was the most important resource for the theologian and church leader next to the Bible.[69] Oates's first interaction with Dobbins was in the classroom. During his first year of graduate work at Southern Seminary, Oates learned from Dobbins the essential elements of pastoral ministry and leadership. Recalling his time as a student in this particular course, Oates noted that Dobbins "probed deeply our motivations for learning and enabled us to realize our own genuine selfhood in the process."[70] Dobbins's practical, experimental, and hands-on approach to ministerial training was fresh and exciting and offered Oates the opportunity to grow in his understanding of human personality. Edgar pointed to Oates's interest in anthropology by noting that Oates decided to attend Southern Seminary to "further his theological education of the human personality." In Dobbins's use of psychology and emphasis on church efficiency as lenses into the study of human personality, behavior, and motivation, Oates found the type of professor and mentor he had been looking for.[71] As a student of Dobbins, Oates did not restrict himself to traditional, assembly-line-like forms of education; instead he was encouraged to freely interact and stay in contact with the real "issues of life." At one point he wrote to Binkley that Dobbins was "awake to what is going on in the world of today and does not restrict us [students] to a lot of canned putrefaction."[72] Oates's disdain for what he called "factory education," which stifled freedom of academic expression was made evident.

68. Johnson, "Professionalization of Pastoral Care," 62–63. See also Crouch, "Influence of William James," 88–90; Hull, *Seminary in Crisis*, 12; answered correspondence (1950–1951), Olin T. Binkley Papers, box 13. This focus on the "practical" curriculum over the traditional educational approach which emphasized the quality of content naturally led to the interest in a clinical approach to training pastors for the work of the ministry.

69. Holifield, *History of Pastoral Care*, 160.

70. Oates, "Gaines S. Dobbins," original manuscript, 1–2, Wayne E. Oates Papers, box 7: folder 9; Bush, *Human Suffering in the Theology of Wayne Oates*, 225. Oates mentioned George Albert Coe's influence on Dobbins's teaching method which positioned the teacher in a facilitator role as co-experimenter with the student in the education process. He stated, "Dr. Dobbins did not focus the classes' attention upon himself. He did not perceive himself as the center of the learning process. He saw himself as the catalyst of learning but not the fountain of knowledge" (Oates, "Gaines S. Dobbins," 9).

71. Edgar, "Pastoral Identity," 29.

72. Oates, personal correspondence to Binkley (September 26, 1943), Olin T. Binkley Papers, box 11: folder 3. Oates also made a general reference to "Dobbinology" in this letter, although he does not call it by this name here. See also Oates, *Struggle to Be*

Dobbins's Ministry of Introduction

Dobbins was one of the greatest influences in Oates's early career and life. Not only was he instrumental in bringing Oates on as a member of the faculty at Southern and worked alongside him in the formation of the department of psychology of religion and pastoral care, but more importantly, Dobbins's unique "ministry of introduction" exposed his young protégé to various theologians, psychologists, psychiatrists, and pastoral counselors who would come to directly impact Oates's anthropology.[73]

It was a psychology of religion course where Dobbins first introduced Oates to Spafford Ackerly, a medical doctor who served as a professor of psychiatry at the University of Louisville. Ackerly and Dobbins were likeminded in their belief that only through clinical experience of working with patients could seminary students be most prepared for the work of the ministry.[74] As the director of the psychiatric ward of the Norton Memorial Infirmary, a clinic associated with the department of psychiatry at the University of Louisville, Ackerly provided field supervision to Dobbins's students as they engaged in clinical pastoral training.[75] The combination of Dobbins's experimental educational tutelage in psychology of religion and Ackerly's knowledge of clinical psychiatry, contributed to a fascination of psychological studies applied to pastoral ministry that would mark Oates's career and writings.[76] This eventually led Oates to not only strongly advo-

---

Free, ch. 5; Nelson, "Life and Works of Wayne E. Oates," 10–11.

73. Collins, "Pastoral Concern for Man," 25. Collins identified, along with Thornton, that Oates was a pioneer in the "new understanding of pastoral care." The researcher suggests that this "new understanding" was solidified, in part, through the teaching and mentorship of Dobbins (Collins, "Pastoral Concern for Man," 5).

74. Oates, *Anxiety in Christian Experience*, 120. It is important to note how psychiatry informed Ackerly's view of religion. According to Oates, Ackerly once remarked that the "purpose of religion is the creation of new life, the development of feeling tone, and the regeneration of psychic energy" (Oates, *Bible in Pastoral Counseling*, 92).

75. Oates, *Religious Factors in Mental Illness*, 15. The Norton Memorial Infirmary served as the setting for early experiments in clinical pastoral education at Southern. Oates described it as "voluntary, nonprofit hospital where the emphasis is upon early treatment and intensive ward care. The clinic administration aims at the development of a therapeutic community in which every person who is in contact with the patients shall be the award of the therapeutic implications of his own relationship to them" (Oates, *Religious Factors in Mental Illness*, 47).

76. Oates, *Religious Factors in Mental Illness*, xi. The Norton Memorial Infirmary not only served as the training ground where Oates "cut his teeth" on clinical pastoral training as a student, but later as a faculty member, Oates would send his students to the clinic to work with Ackerly and other colleagues. The clinic would ultimately become his place of work toward the end of his career when he transitioned to the employment of the University of Louisville School of Medicine as a professor of psychiatry. (Oates,

cate for the inclusion of clinical pastoral training with the curriculum at Southern Seminary as a student and later a faculty member, but his clinical experience at the infirmary aided in the systematization and conceptualization of what would become Oates's approach to pastoral counseling and his psychologically informed anthropology standing in stark contradiction to a historical and biblical anthropology.

Dobbins had an interest in a clinical approach to training pastors several years before Oates came to Southern as a student in 1943. In addition to Mullins bringing Dobbins to Southern in the 1920s with the explicit purpose of incorporating practical studies within the curriculum, Dobbins invited Seward Hiltner, regarded by many historians to be the father of the new pastoral theology, to visit the seminary in 1937 as a consultant and guest lecturer. Even though Hiltner's visit predated Oates's time as a student at Southern, there is little doubt that Dobbins's familiarity with Hiltner and his vigorous support of his work in the advancement of the new pastoral theology was greatly impressed upon Oates so much so that Hiltner's psychological perspective would not only become a familiar undercurrent in his writings, but Hiltner and Oates would later become colleagues and close friends.

While Southern had not yet formally implemented any practical training component within the curriculum, Dobbins had been working on plans to establish a clinical training program in partnership with Louisville General Hospital as soon as the Council for Clinical Training (CCT), an accrediting organization within the broader clinical pastoral education movement, could provide a supervisor to oversee the seminary students; however, no suitable supervisor was available at that time.[77] Interestingly, even before Hiltner's consultation in 1937, Anton Boisen, considered the father and the seminal figurehead of the clinical pastoral training movement, was invited by Dobbins to lecture in his courses related to pastoral counseling and ministry.[78] In fact, Dobbins and Ackerly, both personal friends to Boisen, were instrumental in persuading him to visit Louisville in order to speak jointly

---

When Religion Gets Sick, 11.)

77. Thornton, *Professional Education for Ministry*, 153. See also Johnson, "Fifty Years of Clinical Pastoral Education," 223–31; Collins, "Pastoral Concern for Man," 5–6. The CPE movement was at its apex by the 1950s, but had a history in theological education as far back as the early 1900s.

78 Johnson, "Professionalization of Pastoral Care," 12. Both Hiltner and Boisen were not only major shapers of the professionalization of pastoral ministry and counseling, but also directly impacted Oates's conception of pastoral counseling. See also Hiltner, *Pastoral Care in the Liberal Churches*, 236.

to medical students in psychiatric residency at the University of Louisville and seminary students at nearby Southern Seminary.[79]

Accompanying the breakout of World War II, it seemed that every aspect of American society began to evidence the influence of modern psychology. This included everything from the therapeutic and strategic application of psychology for American military interests to the development of business efficiency models, which were based in psychological understandings of human motivation, to boost economic growth. The pastorate was no exception to this rule, with an increased pressure for pastors to become "mental health professionals" themselves.[80] It was in this cultural milieu that Southern Seminary was called to provide support for the local hospitals due to staffing shortages. Dobbins was contacted by various hospitals in the area to help provide theological students who could work on a part-time basis in the service of the patients. It was during this time that Dobbins introduced Oates to another individual, Ralph Bonacker, who would serve as another key figure in the formation of Oates as a full-fledged pastoral psychologist. Even before Oates was his student, Dobbins had worked closely with Bonacker, who worked at the Norton Memorial Infirmary alongside Ackerly, in his efforts to widely integrate the study of the social sciences and incorporate a clinical-practical educational model into the curriculum at Southern which would provide opportunities for students to experience modern approaches to ministerial training.[81] During the 1943–1944 academic year under Dobbins's direction and leadership, Bonacker began offering evening courses at the infirmary for seminary students interested in clinical pastoral education. With Dobbins's encouragement, Oates registered for this course, with Bonacker serving as his field supervisor, and formally began his lifelong involvement and advocacy of psychologically oriented clinical training.[82]

---

79. Bush, "Human Suffering in the Theology of Wayne Oates," 256; Jeane, "Analysis of Wayne Edward Oates' Phenomenological Method," 32. Described by Oates as an "intrepid explorer of the inner world," Boisen's clinical training of pastors emphasized the study of individuals as sources of authority, self-discovery as a process of growth and healing and detecting "destructive forces" in the context of personal experience (Oates, *Struggle to Be Free*, 91).

80. Edgar, "Pastoral Identity," 76–77.

81. Edgar, "Pastoral Identity," 90; Chow, "Wayne E. Oates' Contribution," 2, Wayne E. Oates Papers, box 15: folder 2.

82. Thornton, *Professional Education for Ministry*, 154; Oates, *Struggle to Be Free*, 95. This experimental course involved a thirty-six-week internship at the hospital where students would get personal interaction with medical staff and patients. While Bonacker facilitated daily oversight within the institution hosting the training, in order to receive seminary credit, students would need to meet weekly with Dobbins for

In 1944, Freudian psychoanalysis was growing in popularity and practice across the country. In fact, the wide-ranging CPE movement was later considered by Oates as having a "hand-in-glove relationship . . . with psychiatry and [Freudian] psychotherapy."[83] As an Episcopalian chaplain certified by the CCT, Bonacker was not only educated in theology, but was trained in and utilized Freudian psychoanalysis as well.[84] As organizations affiliated with the clinical pastoral education movement, groups like the CCT and the Institute for Pastoral Care (ICP) reflected the common convictions held by leaders within the movement that the pastoral ministry was in need of a systematic renovation due to its weakness, unhelpfulness, and general incompetence in not only meeting needs, but also in its engagement with the burgeoning psychologies of the modern era.[85]

CONSIDERING A BIBLICAL ANTHROPOLOGY

After identifying the psychological influences that shaped Oates's anthropology from a historical perspective, the author will consider a biblical anthropological perspective in order to provide clearer distinctions regarding Oates's commitments. The purpose of this section is to outline a concise and brief biblically and theologically informed anthropology in order to provide the reader with a starting point by which to evaluate the psychological anthropology of Wayne Edward Oates.[86] J. Patout Burns defined *theological anthropology* as necessarily involving an investigation of "the resources, the limitations, and the destiny of the human person" with the understanding that "humanity's present condition does not correspond to God's ultimate purpose and original intention in its creation."[87] As it relates to this work, the following anthropological considerations involve understanding the

---

debriefing and supplementary instruction. Oates saw much value in courses like this which, he earnestly believed, would put an end to "factory education."

83. Oates, *Struggle to Be Free*, 59.

84. Oates, *Struggle to Be Free*, 95; Edgar, "Pastoral Identity," 91–92. Oates recognized that Freud's thinking was associated with anti-Christian doctrine and was aggressive in its secularizing impact. Nonetheless, he largely affirmed psychoanalysis as an appropriate lens by which to study theology and anthropology. He believed that Freud's Jewish heritage and clinical anthropology were "very compatible with Christian thinking" (Oates, "Significance of the Work of Sigmund Freud," 183–93).

85. Holifield, *Pastoral Care in America*, 231, and Thornton, *Professional Education for Ministry*, 152.

86. Due to the focus of this book, I am not making an attempt to discuss several subtopics of anthropology (e.g., the monism-dualism debate, constitutional aspects of man, etc.).

87. Burns, *Theological Anthropology*, 1.

identity and ontological nature of man, the intrinsic problems faced by man in his current position, and the solution to his spiritual problems. In each of these considerations, it should also be noted that the Trinitarian God plays a central and vital role in the proper definition of man.[88] While the following section is purposed to provide a critical context for the remainder of the book, in subsequent chapters, the author will provide a more detailed biblical critique of Oates's conclusions regarding his understanding of man.

Man's Identity

The first consideration to be noted regards the very identity of man. There is a vitally important distinction made concerning man in the opening chapters of the Old Testament book of Genesis that must be noted on the outset. Humans, unlike God, are created beings (Gen 1:26–27; 5:1–2). It is only through God as Creator that man has the ability to remain preserved in life and "have our being" (Neh 9:6; Acts 17:25–28). It is important to note that man is not only a creature, but he is a created *person*. The Bible speaks to man as a person in that he is created in the *imago Dei*, the very image of God. Genesis 9:6 states, "Whoever sheds man's blood, By man his blood shall be shed, For in the image of God He made man."[89] The Hebrew phrase בְּצֶלֶם אֱלֹהִים in this verse refers to the likeness of God being represented by only one of his creations, humankind. As this verse suggests, it is considered sacred to reflect the likeness of God, so much so that the murder of man was taken as a direct assault against a holy and righteous God.[90] In addition to this, it is important to note that a right understanding of man can only be reached through a right understanding of God.[91] Humans are completely dependent upon God for his creation as for the sustaining of his life. They are his handiwork and therefore owe the entirety of their being to him (Gen 2:7; Col 1:16–17; Ps 139:14; 1 Cor 6:19; Heb 11:3). Modern psychological theories attempt to come to a comprehensive and functional anthropology without considering God. The danger in this approach is that if metaphysical descriptions are based on atheistic presuppositions, then

---

88. Hoekema, *Created in God's Image*, 4.

89. All Scripture references are from the New American Standard Bible unless otherwise noted.

90. Grudem, *Systematic Theology*, 449–50.

91. Garrett, *Systematic Theology*, 213. See also Delitzsch, *System of Biblical Psychology*, 55.

not only are all subsequent anthropological observations tainted, but the prescriptions for man are likewise skewed.[92]

Man's Position

The second consideration involves the spiritual position that man finds himself in naturally. It must first be noted that God created man for a specific purpose. While he was designed to fulfill this purpose in many ways, in general, it was to bring glory and praise to God with his very existence (Eccl 12:13; 1 Cor 10:31; Isa 43:7; Eph 1:11–12).[93] However, with the fall of man into sin, his new nature was marked by disobedience, a rebellious heart, and spiritual death (Eph 2:3; Jas 3:2; 1 John 1:8; Rom 3:23; Jer 17:9–10).[94] The presence of sin that marked the human heart was treated seriously enough by God that fellowship was broken and the original purpose of man to glorify God became tainted and twisted to promote self-gratification and self-worship (Gen 3:6–7; Rom 1:21–25).[95] Concerning this unfortunate state, Paul noted that in his fallen state, man was resigned to a reality of "having no hope and [being] without God in the world" (Eph 2:12). The impact of sin, while not totally destroying the image of God in man, marred it to the point where human spirituality, physicality, and mentality were transformed by sin's degenerative effects. From the noetic (mind) to the ontic (being), man in sin is a compromised creation in every way imaginable.[96]

Man's Solution

The final consideration broaches the subject of the solution to the sin problem addressed in the previous section. As was stated earlier, man was created by God for a particular work, however, due to the introduction of sin into the world, man could no longer in and of himself fulfill the purpose for which he was created. The gospel changes the narrative in that while man was still in his sin, the atoning death of Jesus provided a way for man to be restored and washed clean (Titus 3:5; John 3:3–7, 16–17; Rom 10:9–10; 2 Cor 5:17; 1 Pet 1:22–25). In spite of the emphasis within modern psychology on man's ability to navigate and manage his own life, a biblical anthropology promotes

---

92. Bulkley, *Why Christians Can't Trust Psychology*, 194.
93. Grudem, *Systematic Theology*, 442.
94. Hoekema, *Created in God's Image*, 139.
95. Grudem, *Systematic Theology*, 492.
96. Berkouwer, *General Revelation*, 31. See also Moroney, *Noetic Effects of Sin*.

an understanding that man is totally unable to cleanse himself. It is only through the Son of God and the power of his Holy Spirit that man can be made righteous and once again become useful to God's original purpose and plan (Lam 3:58; Ps 69:18, 107:2; 1 Cor 1:30, 7:23; Gal 3:13–14, Heb 9:11–12).

CONCLUSION

In this chapter, I sought to provide historical background in order to gain a better understanding of the influences and experiences that shaped Wayne Oates's counseling and anthropological views. His early years were marked by poverty and struggles which contributed to a strong drive to improve his financial and intellectual status. For Oates, a formal education provided salvation from poverty and low self-esteem and afforded to him his first introduction to psychology and counseling through several key figures including his lifelong mentors Olin Binkley, Harold Tribble, and Gaines Dobbins. In addition to this biographical sketch, I provided a biblical anthropology brief, in order to provide a framework and backdrop for the remainder of the dissertation necessary to measure and contrast Oates's anthropological commitments from a theological context.

3

Pastoral Counseling

A Clinical and Therapeutic Affair

WILLIAM HULME NOTED THAT psychologically oriented pastoral counseling was an invention of modernity. This counseling approach was a departure from the German idea of *seelsorge* (soul care) which dated back to the Protestant Reformation. Hulme noted, "In former days the pastor's counseling was oriented in pastoral theology; today it centers on pastoral psychology. The impetus for the new movement has come more form the laboratories of the psychological sciences than from the scholarship of theologians. It is a psychologically oriented *seelsorge*."[1]

As early as the mid-1940s, the CPE movement initiated by Anton Boisen and the new pastoral theology articulated by Seward Hiltner had found expression in a culturally relevant and pragmatic pastoral counseling curriculum within the seminaries of the Southern Baptist Convention.[2]

---

1. Hulme, *Counseling and Theology*, 1–2. It is important to note that the Christian church has had a longer history related to the cure of souls which was informed by a biblical anthropology that was not man-centered; however, modern psychology's promise of salvation without the need of repentance, forgiveness, or a savior offered a "rival doctrine of man" which eventually took root in many Protestant churches in America. See North, *Foundations of Christian Scholarship*, 42.

2. Oates, *Introduction to Pastoral Counseling*, v. See also Thornton, *Professional Education for Ministry*, 153. Oates noted that his objectives for a clinical pastoral education curriculum was motivated and aligned with Boisen's views (Oates, *Introduction to Pastoral Counseling*, 98).

In addition to these important figures, Wayne Oates played a key role in the development of a new department at The Southern Baptist Theological Seminary that combined the study of modern psychology, religion, and pastoral care and counseling. His eclectic career spanned many years and included an "extensive private practice of counseling, as well as his teaching of graduate theological students in pastoral care and medical students in psychotherapy."[3] Oates admitted that pastoral care throughout the twentieth century was marked by secular psychological theory and method.[4] Pastoral counseling during Oates's career was approached from an integrative perspective in which secular psychological theories, and the behavioral sciences, were not only referenced but actively pursued and applied as a guide for how pastors cared and counseled their flock.[5] In this perspective, the Scriptures were not generally viewed as sufficient or authoritative for the counseling task.[6]

As has been mentioned, Oates was guided by a diverse group of counselors, ministers, and academic theologians who made use of the findings of modern psychology. These various influences contributed to Oates's pastoral counseling and how he viewed and approached it through a psychological lens and framework.[7] For Oates, contemporary psychology and the behavioral sciences were analytical and practical tools in the hands of pastors as they brought greater clarity and nuanced insight into anthropology. As ministers understood the complexities of man in their development, personality, and moral constitution, the thinking was that they would be more equipped to minister in times of crisis.[8] This, of course, necessitated a view of Scripture in which extrabiblical sources were viewed as equally valid as the truth revealed in Scripture, if not superior.

Among those who influenced Oates, one thinker in particular stands out as providing the psychological grounding upon which Oates built his

---

3. Borchert and Lester, *Spiritual Dimensions*, 122. The establishment of this new department would not have been probable without the guidance and groundwork laid by Gaines Dobbins and current president of Southern Seminary, Ellis A. Fuller.

4. Oates, "Pastoral Care (Contemporary Methods, Perspectives, and Issues)," in *Dictionary of Pastoral Care and Counseling*, unpublished manuscript, Wayne E. Oates Papers, box 2: folder 10.

5. Hester et al., "Pastoral Care among Southern Baptists," in *Encyclopedia of Southern Baptists*, unpublished manuscript, Wayne E. Oates Papers, box 2: folder 19.

6. Oates, *Bible in Pastoral Care*, 18.

7. In a course taught by Oates entitled "Religion and Psychotherapy: Philosophy, Current Needs, and Prospect," Oates references works by David Roberts, Albert Outler, Paul Tillich, Karl Menninger, and Carl Rogers, all of whom were either directly or indirectly involved in clinical psychology.

8. Oates, "New Morality," 286, and Oates, *Christian Pastor* (1982), 23.

own counseling approach.⁹ Paul Tillich, considered to be one of the most "influential liberal Protestant theologians of the twentieth century," contributed greatly to the advancement of psychological theory and method within the field of pastoral counseling, a field which would later be known as pastoral psychology.¹⁰ As a member of the editorial advisory board of the influential *Pastoral Psychology* journal, of which Oates would regularly contribute, Tillich stressed the integration of modern psychology and psychiatry with a religious understanding of human personality. In his utilization of the insights of psychology in dealing with anthropological concerns, Tillich's approach and convictions were apparent. This was made even more explicit when he noted that "the theology which underlies pastoral counseling should be one which itself has been influenced by the insights of psychotherapy, not only in the questions it asks, but also in the formulation of the answers in correlation with the questions."¹¹ After leaving Germany before the onset of World War II, Tillich taught at Union Theological Seminary, a bastion of progressive and liberal theology, until his retirement in 1955, where he was appointed as a professor at Harvard University.¹² Tillich's theological method has been compared to that of Washington Gladden, William Newton Clarke, and William Adams Brown, all of whom influenced Oates's thinking.¹³ Oates saw in Tillich the penultimate "bridge" that would span the chasm between the biblical picture of man and the image set

9. Bush, "Human Suffering in the Theology Wayne E. Oates," 9–10, 72.

10. Spiceland, "Tillich, Paul (1886–1965)," in Elwell, *Evangelical Dictionary of Theology*, 1200.

11. Hofmann, *Ministry and Mental Health*, 13. See also Mays, "Contemporary Theology and Pastoral Care," 5; and Tillich and Rogers, "Paul Tillich and Carl Rogers," 55.

12. Oates, *New Dimensions in Pastoral Care*, 19. The golden age for pastoral care teaching and education, according to Oates, was demonstrated at Union Theological Seminary during the 1950s. He mentions the work of David Roberts (psychotherapy and biblical anthropology), Paul Tillich (health and salvation), John T. McNeill (history of soul care), and Lewis Sherrill (religious education and psychotherapy). Oates studied under Tillich and worked alongside him as a colleague on multiple occasions while Oates taught at Union during his sabbatical leave from Southern Seminary. The two formed a close friendship and Oates valued Tillich's opinion on several matters related to the topic at hand.

13. Smith, *Changing Conceptions of Original Sin*, 219–21. Tillich saw it as his responsibility to reinterpret classical understandings of theological doctrines in such a way as to have them grasped by "every new generation" (Smith, *Changing Conceptions*, 219). Durst made a strong comparison between Tillich and Oates regarding their efforts of bridging the gap between contemporary psychology and theology. He noted that the first volume of Tillich's *Systematic Theology* was published in 1951, the same year as the first edition of Oates's book *Christian Pastor*. After this, Oates made it his goal to continue "lively, responsible dialogue in print with contemporary theological, Christological, and anthropological thought." See Durst, "Theological Dimensions," 11.

forth by contemporary psychology. In an article written for an issue of *Pastoral Psychology* dedicated to Tillich, Oates wrote, "Thus he [Tillich] opened the door once again for the use of the psychological method in theology. Implicit within these discoveries of psychologists are clues to the ultimate concern of men. Implicit within religious doctrines are the very human materials of the meaningful symbols of man."[14]

For Tillich, anthropology lay at the very core of psychological and pastoral pursuits. In characterizing the nature of this discipline as both an art and a science, Oates stated that the "psychologist becomes an interpreter of human life as well as one who describes what he sees."[15] In his own study of the intersection of psychology and religious experience, Oates noticed four distinct stages by which psychology progressively dialogued with and influenced religion. In the earlier stages of development, Oates depicted the field of psychology as being either silent as to the nature of religion (e.g., Ivan Pavlov) or noisy in its overt rejection of religion (e.g., John B. Watson, Sigmund Freud). In the contemporary context, the one in which Oates found himself, psychology was still very critical of religion, but it also was starting to move toward a position of cautious affection and interaction (e.g., Gordon Allport, Erich Fromm, Karl Menninger, Rollo May, Henry Stack Sullivan). It was this later group of contemporary psychologists that had contributed to clarifying religious motivations and perspectives and whose work was most useful to Christian pastors.[16] Noting Oates's perspective, there are four key components, each of which was shaped from modern psychological principles, presuppositions, and theories, that make up his pastoral counseling. Before expounding upon the particular ways secular psychology framed Oates's understanding of humanity, which we will see stood as an antithesis to a biblical understanding of man, it is necessary to offer a conceptual overview of the nature and practice of his pastoral counseling by examining these foundational pillars.

---

14. Oates, "Contribution of Paul Tillich," 12. Oates clearly demonstrates not only the central role anthropology plays in his pastoral counseling, but his indebtedness to Tillich. He noted, "Psychology helped pastors to understand that a human person lives his life in stages and if we are to care for him properly, we must understand him that way . . . we must know the relevant information about prior stages to know the present accurately." See Oates, *New Dimensions in Pastoral Care*, 7–8.

15. Oates, *What Psychology Says about Religion*, 17. Tillich's influence reached into Oates life, and the general culture, in more than one way. While he was primarily thought of as a theologian, he also directly impacted the field of psychology.

16. Bush, "Human Suffering," 94–95.

COLLABORATIVE EFFORT

Oates wrote prolifically concerning the role and work of the Christian minister. His first major work, *The Christian Pastor* (1951), was published with the distinct purpose of reinterpreting pastoral work for a new generation while considering his current generation's "needs and resources."[17] CPE, according to Oates, best prepared the minister in taking advantage of innovative psychological resources, while also attempting to meet the needs his parishioners. In many ways, the work of the pastor could be summarized in the work of a crisis ministry. In order to help people in an advanced and psychologically informed society, the Christian pastor needed to assume, in addition to knowledge of the Bible, the psychological significance of the crisis in a person's life.[18] Regarding pastoral care, the Christian minister was to bring a God-consciousness to bear within the counseling relationship and to resolve any conflict, whether internal or external, with the goal of helping the counselee resolve his or her own life purposes.[19] In the tradition of Boisen and Hiltner, Oates viewed pastoral care and counseling through a clinically efficient and psychologically relevant lens.

With the publication of his groundbreaking book in 1950 entitled *The Individual and His Religion*, Gordon Allport ushered in a time of collaboration and cooperation between psychologists and theologians by "exploring areas of mutual concern" between two groups that had, for the most part, been at odds.[20] Another influential book within the field of pastoral psychology that was published in the same year also argued that collaborative efforts between the fields of contemporary psychology and theology were

---

17. Oates, *Christian Pastor*, 8.

18. Oates, *Christian Pastor*, 13–14. The crisis ministry called for the "reorganization of the total personality of an individual and his family, and the result may easily be disorganization" (Oates, *Christian Pastor*, 13). The language used by Oates regarding the reorganization of the inner life and special attention made to personality can be seen throughout Boisen's and Hiltner's works. See the following for examples: Boisen, *Exploration of the Inner World*, viii, 204, 248, and Hiltner, *Pastoral Counseling*, 32, 66.

19. Oates, *Pastoral Counseling*, 12. When asked by a psychiatrist concerning the difference between his work as a pastoral counselor and the work of a psychiatrist, Oates is recorded as having said, "You have a choice as to whether you bring God into the focus of the patient's attention. I [Oates] am different in that if I am introduced as a minister, I have no choice but that God tacitly or overtly becomes the focus of the relationship.' The psychiatrist then asked, 'Whose God becomes the focus of the relationship?' I replied, 'The patient's God, not mine'" (Oates, *Pastoral Counseling*, 12). Boisen wrote about the importance of projecting an "idea of God" onto his clients. See Boisen, *Exploration of the Inner World*, 196.

20. Butman, "Psychology of Religion," in Elwell, *Evangelical Dictionary of Theology*, 969.

needed and would benefit both sides. Only through partnering together could hopelessness and hostility in the world be adequately addressed.[21] From the early days of his academic career, Oates had been in favor of Christian pastors seeking to collaborate with psychologists and psychiatrists in the mental health field. In his dissertation, which was written on the contributions of Sigmund Freud's theories to Christian faith and practice, Oates noted that Freud's therapies dealt with the same subject matter inherent and related to Christian theology and ministry.[22] Accordingly, the depth psychologies (e.g., Freudian Psychoanalysis, Gestalt Therapy, Adlerian Therapy) served a useful purpose for Christian pastors in their helpfulness in probing the deep mysteries of the personality.[23] Oates noted that the responsible pastoral counselor who takes the call of God seriously should not ignore "all known means of understanding the human person in sickness and in health."[24] Thus, for Oates, the work, mission, and call of the Christian pastor was linked to the work, mission, and call of mental health professionals.

Ministry and Mental Health

During the 1950s and the 1960s, professional pastoral counselors were highly valued and sought after. Professionalism was characterized by objectivity and scientific methodology. By the late 1960s, the idea of the professional clergyman was further nuanced to refer to one who was "precisely competent to help all people become responsible participants in society."[25]

21. Roberts, *Psychotherapy and the Christian View*, 6. In this book, Roberts purposed to reach the theologian and the mental health professional by attempting to provide an argument for the successful synthesis of these fields in answering anthropological concerns (xiii).

22. Oates, "Significance of the Work of Sigmund Freud," i–ii. Oates admitted in the first page of his preface that the topic of his dissertation was "usually associated with the antithesis of the Christian faith" (i). However, the central task of this thesis was to remove any terminological or conceptual differences between Freudian psychology and Christian theology and highlight what the two had in common (Oates, "Significance of the Work of Sigmund Freud," 72). Knowing this, it is interesting to note that speaking to Freud's anthropology, Oates stated, "In its origins he sees personality as a bundle of animal impulses; he sees solidified adult character, burdened with the sense of guilt, and torn by conflicting desires. Here is the source of all pathology in the spirit of man: the clash between his sense of the demands of society, his sense of his own ideals, and his sense of need for instinctual satisfaction" (Oates, "Significance of the Work of Sigmund Freud," 55).

23. Oates, *Christian Pastor* (1951), 93.

24. Oates, *Religious Care*, 3.

25. Oglesby, *New Shape of Pastoral Theology*, 228–29. Oates noted, "The pastoral

Pioneers in CPE understood the focus of the professional minister to be not so much concerned with biblical soul care, but rather with individual and social mental health. The task of shepherding was now concerned with "adopting an approach that prioritized the individual emotional needs" of patients.[26]

Oates, like his predecessors, viewed the pastoral counselor as a type of consultant within the realm of the helping professions.[27] Pastors were to be viewed as service-providers who were able to utilize "scientific knowledge of human relationships" with theology in an integrated and clinical methodology.[28] Professional ministers were aware of their particular time restraints and jurisdictional boundaries of expertise and should be prepared to defer and refer to others when needed. Without highly specialized training, like that of "full-time counselors and psychotherapists," ministers "need to be able to recognize those problems which are beyond his particular level of skill, so that he can make a wise referral."[29] While distinct from state-sponsored specialists, Oates claimed that the minister should be and was a professional in his own right. He should be confident in his specialized training and clinical experience.[30]

Through collaborative efforts, pastors could gain experience with mental health professionals in clinical settings. These firsthand experiences

---

counseling movement in America has rightly concentrated much attention and energy upon the development of professionally valid forms of clinical pastoral education for the minister. The processes of accreditation, qualification, and authorization of the pastor as a counselor are of great importance to Protestant theological educators" (Oates, *Pastoral Counseling*, 87). See also Cabot and Dicks, *Art of Ministering to the Sick*, 9.

26. Muravchik, *American Protestantism*, 30.

27. Oates, *Pastoral Counseling*, 18. See Clebsch and Jaekle, *Pastoral Care*, 63. Clebsch and Jaekle regarded pastoral care as the exclusive care of "troubled people" to the point where there were times when soul care should be halted in order to meet social needs and responsibilities (5). See also Cabot and Dicks, *Art of Ministering to the Sick*, 4.

28. Oates, *New Dimensions in Pastoral Care*, 5. See also Oates, *Minister's Own Mental Health*, 11. See Boisen, *Exploration of the Inner World*, 183–84.

29. Clinebell, *Basic Types of Pastoral Counseling*, 52–53. During this era, the pastor was viewed more as a general practitioner and member of other helping professions, including psychiatrists, social workers, and psychotherapists (Clinebell, *Basic Types*, 176). See also Oates, *Protestant Pastoral Counseling*, 112–13; Oates, *Where to Go for Help*, 20, and Hiltner, *Ferment in the Ministry*, 101.

30. Oates, *Minister's Own Mental Health*, 13. Oates tended away from specialization not because he didn't see value in professionalization, but because it provided barriers to further collaboration with other members of the healing team. According to James Glasse, who is a reference for Oates on this topic, professionalism has more to do with the pastor's knowledge and level of self-respect among his client and peers. See Glasse, *Profession*, as quoted in Oates, *New Dimensions*, 48. See also Oates, "Clinical Pastoral Training's Contribution to Theology," 6, Wayne E. Oates Papers, box 6: folder 24.

were seen as necessary for pastors in building a psychiatric profile of their clients. Competent pastoral counselors understood that engaging in empirical research about the complexities of human personality paired with the application clinical techniques and methodology in their counseling would lead to the most comprehensive care for their client.[31] The behavioral sciences have contributed to the faith and practice of pastoral counselors through the provision of quantifiable descriptions of human motivations. Oates remarked, "We have elaborate data on depressed, hostile, suspicious, manipulative, withdrawn, dependent, apathetic, and compulsive persons."[32] The root of this conviction, for Oates at least, was not in the fact that pastoral counselors were merely ignorant, but that they would be faced with issues that were out of their range of training and knowledge. Speaking to situations like this, Oates said that these pastors should feel "no embarrassment about searching out a qualified and ethically serious physician who can render whatever therapy is needed," and in fact, doing this would safeguard the pastor's overall mental health and help him avoid "personality handicaps" inherent in his own life.[33]

Therapeutic Impact

While Oates affirmed that the Scriptures were to be treated as the "royal road" leading to the ultimate hope for people seeking counsel, he likewise held that other religious traditions *outside* of the Christian faith could "be used similarly by people who have been educated and reared in the culture where those symbols are alive."[34] Interestingly, Oates held to this counterproductive and unorthodox stance in his approach to pastoral counseling.

---

31. Oates, *Christian Pastor* (1951), 89; Oates, *Pastoral Counseling*, 16. During this era, integration was considered the popular approach of inquiry into religious concern for others. According to Oates, these observations must be a mix of the "existential as well as scientific." For more on this topic, see Oates, *Psychology of Religion*, 61.

32 Oates, *New Dimensions in Pastoral Care*, 55. Oates's commitment to CPE throughout his career demonstrates his conviction that clinical and laboratory contexts provide the best setting to receive the empirical value of this type of study of man. Both of Oates's mentors, Boisen and Hiltner, agreed that the more pastors are knowledgeable about the affairs of mental health professionals, the more efficiently they can help their patients. See Hiltner, *Pastoral Counseling*, 98, and Hiltner, *Fervent in the Ministry*, 101.

33. Oates, *Christian Pastor* (1951), 114. Competency and personal mental health were not all that was at stake, but if the pastor did not take advantage of the behavioral sciences, albeit in conjunction with Christian tradition, the pastor's credibility and therapeutic integrity could also be put into question (Oates, *Christian Pastor*, 10).

34. Oates, *Religious Care*, 96. See also Oates, "Gospel and Modern Psychology," 181, and Oates, "New Emphases in Psychiatry and Religion," 141.

What pastoral psychologists sought in the application of psychological theory in their counseling approach was the creation of a therapeutic context in which the end goal for every client was ultimately the meeting of their self-centered felt needs.[35] Hiltner wrote that the historical and classic image of the pastor as a shepherd carrying a wounded sheep on his shoulders needed to be reanalyzed and reimagined for a contemporary age. The sheep should no longer be depicted as stupid, incapable, or weak, and the shepherd should no longer be seen as a knowledge-centered authority who has the answers. Instead, the shepherd is to be a service-oriented facilitator who refuses to "moralize the sheep about having run off course."[36] In similar fashion, Oates agreed that the minister's job is one of cooperation with other members of the helping and healing team "in the growth of human personalities" so that people may fully exercise their power to choose to become complete.[37] In a therapeutically centered approach to pastoral counseling, members of the healing team should be wary of using theological terminology because of the symbolism that it internally holds. Instead the therapeutic minister should explore the inner world of the patient or client in order to better understand his problems.[38] Whether intentional or not, and with influence from a wide range of psychologists, including Erik Erikson, Gordon Allport, and Carl Rogers, the result of collaboration between secular psychologists and Christian theology resulted in a therapeutic emphasis in Oates's conception of counseling for pastors which tended to focus more on reaching individualized wholeness instead of personal holiness.[39]

CORRELATIVE THEORY

According to John Jefferson Davis, correlation is a theory and process rooted in existential thought in which questions from a naturalistic context are

---

35. Oates, *Pastoral Counseling*, 9. Published the year he left Southern Seminary, Oates stated that the goal of counseling was to resolve conflict and to meet the need of the client, in short, to help them clarify their own life purposes.

36. Hiltner, *Ferment in the Ministry*, 104–6. In order to demonstrate his competency, expertise, and status as a member of the helping team, Hiltner added that the pastor "should have a Bible, or a reversed collar, or a Communion kit to demonstrate what he represents and to differentiate his service from that of physicians and other hospital helpers" (Hiltner, *Ferment in the Ministry*, 109).

37. Oates, *Christian Pastor* (1951), 30.

38. Oates, *Religious Care*, 95. See also Oates, "Inner World," 16. More about this will be expounded upon in the following section on correlation and in chapter 4.

39. Oates, *Christian Pastor* (1982), 25, 31. More on this will be explored in the following section concerning phenomenology.

translated and corresponded to answers drawn from theology, namely from special divine revelation.[40] Once again, Paul Tillich's dual impact in both the fields of psychology and theology, including Oates's pastoral counseling, was felt regarding this particular theory and method. Writing on the contribution of Tillich's correlative method, Oates wrote:

> He has provided the pastoral psychologist with theological method for translating the power of the gospel into idiom of twentieth century thought, namely a psychological way of thinking, a psychological idiom. Through the method of correlation, Tillich seeks to unite message and situation. . . . The method of correlation is an effort to adapt the Christian message to the modern mind without at the same time destroying or losing the essential character of the Christian message.[41]

In the same issue of *Pastoral Psychology*, Donald Browning, long time professor of pastoral theology at the University of Chicago, wrote on three leading methods of pastoral theology that were prevalent in the mid-twentieth century. Of these methods, Browning noted that Tillich's correlational approach was grounded in the use of psychology, sociology, and relied upon what they have to say about the human condition. Therefore, psychotherapy, instead of Scripture, ended up influencing his views of man, sin, salvation, and justification.[42]

Terry Cooper, a noted historian whose background and expertise is related to pastoral theology, counseling, and psychology, noted that

---

40. Davis, *Theology Primer*, 21. Davis goes on to define existentialism as a philosophical worldview in which "neither traditional metaphysics nor the natural sciences are adequate for understanding the deepest issues of human life" (26). While existentialism is broad, the common core is an emphasis on personal experience as the capstone of truth, authority, and reality.

41. Oates, "Contribution of Paul Tillich," 12–13. While Oates mentioned that Tillich correlative theory maintains the integrity of the Christian message, he later noted that correlation actually started with an anthropocentric foundation instead of a God-centered foundation. Oates's admiration of Tillich can be described in almost salvific terms. He wrote, "Paul Tillich was like a flash streaking of brilliance and lightning on the dark horizons of post-World War II theology and pastoral psychology. We who sat in darkness saw a great light and were renewed by it" (Oates, "Contribution of Paul Tillich," 16). See Tillich, *Courage to Be*, 41.

42. Browning, "Analogy, Symbol, and Pastoral Theology," 42–43. Knowing of Tillich's influence on pastoral counseling and on Oates, many of Browning's conclusions are disconcerting. In this same article, he made mention of not only Tillich's close ties to existential psychology and philosophy, which mandated a man-centered ontology, anthropology and metaphysic, but his outright rejection of the concept of the monotheistic God of the Scriptures as the Supreme Being. See also Tillich, "Impact of Pastoral Psychology," 18; Tillich, *Courage to Be*, 184–85, Tillich, *Systematic Theology*, 255.

throughout his career Tillich urged theologians to remain in constant dialogue with influential theorists in the therapeutic community in order to better understand, utilize, and take advantage of the latest psychological terminologies and concepts in their own work. In the belief that theologians had much to learn from psychologists, Tillich often made use of contemporary psychological terms in an effort to reinterpret theological concepts for consumption in the twentieth century.[43] Tillich's correlative method was depicted in his many points of agreement with Carl Rogers, who along with Tillich was one of the most widely read and influential theorists in the field of pastoral theology in the twentieth century.[44] For instance, even though Rogers and Tillich both used the same term *estrangement* to describe a key problem for humans in need of community, Rogers understood this as a cognitive and developmental incongruence while Tillich understood it as an internal dissonance which impacted one's relationship with self, others, and the "ground of being."[45] In his final public appearance in March of 1965, Tillich appeared on a television program in which he dialogued with Carl Rogers regarding how their philosophical perspectives differed from and related to one-another. Throughout the presentation Tillich and Rogers were in agreement in many areas, prompting Rogers to point out the apparent inconsistency in Tillich's widespread agreement with secular psychology and his continued use of theological/religious framework and tone. Rogers stated:

> I realize very well that I and many other therapists are interested in the kind of issues that involve the religious worker and the theologian and yet, for myself, I prefer to put my thinking on those issues in humanistic terms, or to attack those issues through the channels of scientific investigation. . . . I would be interested in knowing why you tend to put your thinking—which certainly is very congenial to that of a number of psychologists these days—why you tend to put your thinking in religious terminology and theological language.[46]

43. Cooper, *Paul Tillich and Psychology*, 1–2. Cooper, a student of Browning, noted that Tillich was intimately tied to several secular psychologists, including Erich Fromm, whom he met earlier in pre-Nazi Germany, Rollo May, a close friend and biographer of Tillich, Ruth Benedict, and Carl Rogers. These psychologists, among pastoral counselors, including Seward Hiltner and David Roberts, were members of the New York Psychology Group which met regularly throughout the 1940s in order to discuss a wide range of topics involving the relationship between faith and social science. Many of these members were influenced by Sigmund Freud and Karl Marx (Stokes, 25).

44. Wise, "Client-Centered Counseling," 127.

45. Cooper, *Paul Tillich and Psychology*, 16–17.

46. Tillich and Rogers, "Paul Tillich and Carl Rogers," 60. It should be noted that

In response to Roger's inquiry, Tillich answered his conviction that the language of science is adequate in expressing the vertical dimensions and relationships of man to the infinite. In this, Tillich's self-inflicted "heavy yoke" and purpose was to radically reinterpret theological terms and concepts, along with their classically held meanings, into a language that would be more palatable to a new generation who was skeptical toward religion in general.[47]

Of the dissertations which explore various facets of Oates's counseling and theology, there is general agreement with the fact that Oates adopted the method of correlation and applied it to his conception of pastoral counseling. While noting that Oates did not typically describe how he arrives at a particular point of correlation between theological concepts and psychological ones, Collins added that for Oates these concepts "converge" on one another at level of belief to the point where there is inconsequential difference between the seeking after redemption of sin and discovering "integration and self-consistency."[48] Durst pointed out that the basic concepts of psychotherapy as put forth by David Roberts also influenced Oates's correlative principle which had its starting point in a uniquely human perspective which moved toward Christian doctrine to elucidate the human problem. Like Tillich and Roberts, Oates's correlative methodology claimed to help contextualize, legitimize, and reinterpret the gospel in light of twentieth-century needs. Oates equated several aspects of Christian anthropology with contemporary personality theory.[49] In a lengthy piece written for Crozer Theological Seminary on the presuppositions behind his pastoral counseling, Oates argued that the counselor "must actually hear clinically the questions that people are asking in their own market-place speed. Then he must bring the materials of the Christian faith alongside these with an attempt at correlation."[50] In this article, Mays rightly pointed out that Oates's

---

Tillich used "religious terminology and theological language" as noted by Rogers; however, these terms, including such words as salvation, sin, healing, and forgiveness, bore little resemblance to a biblical meaning. When using such language, Tillich was clear about his use of them for symbolic and metaphoric purposes. See also Tillich, *Courage to Be*, xi.

47. Tillich and Rogers, "Paul Tillich and Carl Rogers," 60.

48. Collins, "Pastoral Concern for Man," 61; Douglas, "Psychology in Theological Education," 87; Oates, *Christ and Selfhood*, 283–87; Oates, *Revelation of God*, 11.

49. Durst, "Theological Dimensions of Human Existence," 38, 67, and 124. See also Oates, "Contribution of Paul Tillich," 11–15; Roberts, *Christian View of Man*, 93, 153; Oates, *Religious Dimensions*, 219–41; Oates, *New Dimensions*, 283.

50. Oates, "Pastoral Counseling," 3. While admitting that presuppositions differed greatly in many respects, Oates later stated, "I have a great respect for the work of Dr. Carl Rogers. I think his book on counseling, *Client-Centered Therapy*, is one of the truly

theological method centered on studying people first, and only after mastering the subject of study could he seek to apply religion to their lives through the utilization of more palatable language.[51]

PSYCHOLOGIZING RELIGION

While the social sciences were coming into prominence and extensive use in all quarters of American society at the turn of the twentieth century, the traditional Judeo-Christian ethic was still a palpable characteristic of the broader cultural landscape. From the inception of modern psychology as a stand-alone discipline in the late 1800s, theorists, scientists, and philosophers have been intrigued by the nature, value, and impact of religious ideation related to the individual, whether mentally sick or well. Questions as to the motivations, expressions, and effects of religion have been a part of scholarship in the field in its earliest days as an academic discipline.[52] In 1890, E. D. Starbuck presented a paper which proposed that religion should be exposed to scientific inquiry and study and that this particular study would benefit both the scientific and religious community in the end. In the introduction of *Psychology of Religion: An Empirical Study of the Growth of Religious Consciousness*, Starbuck made a statement regarding religion that would turn out to be prophetic:

> Science has conquered one field after another, until now it is entering the most complex, the most inaccessible, and, of all, the most sacred domain—that of religion. The Psychology of Religion has for its work to carry the well-established methods of science into the analysis and organisation [sic] of the facts of the religious consciousness, and to ascertain the laws which determine its growth and character.[53]

---

significant contributions to the understanding of the counseling relationship" (Oates, "Pastoral Counseling," 6). See also Oates, *What Psychology Says about Religion*, 11; Rogers, "Personal Formation," 342.

51. Mays, "Contemporary Theology and Pastoral Care," 11; Oates, *Religious Dimensions of Personality*, 29; Oates, *Religious Factors in Mental Illness*, vii.

52. Butman, "Psychology of Religion," 969. See Douglas, "Psychology in Theological Education," 85.

53. Starbuck, *Psychology of Religion*, 1. Starbuck's philosophic framework (including anthropological convictions) was deeply mechanistic and naturalistic and influenced by his field supervisor at Clark University, G. Stanley Hall, whose work in developmental psychology has impacted the way many view human physical and psychological growth and his professor at Harvard, William James (Starbuck, *Psychology of Religion*, 382). Hall was the one who urged Starbuck to publish his findings in the study of the psychology of conversion (Starbuck, *Psychology of Religion*, xi).

American philosopher William James, who was mentioned earlier as an influence in the thinking of Oates, was indebted to Starbuck's work which led him to conclude in *Varieties of Religious Experience* that religion had pragmatic and utilitarian value due to its relation to the mental, or unseen, constitution of man. This being of general interest to psychologists, James led the way to strip religion of its supernatural and theological ties in order to study it as more of a cultural phenomenon.[54]

By the mid-1920s, the psychology of religion had been engaged by philosophers, psychologists, and theologians alike. In theological contexts, in particular, this discipline was being offered in seminaries most often within religious education departments.[55] In the late 1930s through the 1940s, Oates was a student in psychology of religion courses at Wake Forest College taught by Olin Binkley. In his lectures, Binkley made frequent references to the work of pioneers in American psychology, including E. S. Ames, James Leuba, George Albert Coe, Edward Thorndike, and Karl Stolz.[56] In his personal notes Binkley defined the "psychological study of the religious mind" as dealing with "religious consciousness, religious beliefs, and religious behavior" as well as the "study of the birth and growth of religion in the race and the development of religion in the individual."[57] In similar fashion, other influencers on Oates conception of pastoral counseling, namely Boisen and Hiltner, were convinced that the scientific method should and could be adequately applied to the study of religious phenomena and that there should be no restriction of methods or resources in the study of religion in individual and social contexts.[58] Gordon Allport, who came to be known as one of the world's foremost theorists dealing with the concepts of personality and social psychology and who also popularized the psychology of religion in non-theological contexts, influenced the field of pastoral psychology.[59] In one of his books, *The Individual and His Religion*, Allport sought to reclaim the understanding of man and his problems from a religious and philosophical context to a psychological and naturalistic

---

54. James, *Varieties of Religious Experience*, 2–3. It should be noted that the work of James Leuba actually predated that of Starbuck. Leuba, who had a direct impact on James, subordinated and reduced theological aspects of religion to its moral value (James, *Varieties of Religious Experience*, 201).

55. Kelly, *Theological Education in America*, 143–44.

56. Stolz, *Psychology of Religious Living*, 125.

57. Binkley, "Psychology of Religion Lecture Notes (1938–1944)," 4, Olin T. Binkley Papers, box 28: folder 4.

58. Boisen, *Exploration of the Inner World*, 58; Boisen, *Religion in Crisis and Custom*, ix; Hiltner, *Clinical Pastoral Training*; Hiltner et al., "Credentials," 45.

59. Hiltner, "Gordon W. Allport," 65–67.

perspective. He undertook the task of "discovering the place of religion in the life-economy of the individual" and utilizing a psychological understanding of religion in order to bring about a correct perspective.[60]

The role that psychology of religion played in Oates's counseling was not only demonstrated by his frequent referencing of the psychologists listed above, but also served as the subject matter of some of his most academic and lengthy works. One such work, *The Psychology of Religion*, was considered by Oates to be one of his most important and comprehensive texts on the subject.[61] According to Oates, the study of the psychology of religion served as the conceptual basis for pastoral counseling for the producing of healthy characteristics related to religious or spiritual ideations in persons, and it also provided tools to offset anything that would hinder the development of healthy religion in a person.[62] In line with his stances on collaborating with those in the mental health field and seeking to correlate psychological terminology with theological concepts, Oates's view and relationship with psychology was generally congenial because he saw it as offering the pastor the ability to empirically quantify and grasp religious sentiment, convictions, and other seemingly intangible qualities. For Oates, this becomes an important aspect reaching a successful conclusion in the counseling task.[63] By placing the individual and his experiences at the core of the counseling task, those who promoted the psychology of religion sought to appreciate innate holiness in humanity, while simultaneously grounding religious experience in the empirical realm. Ultimately, the whole point of this field was to bring the "definitions of human life into dialogue with each other and to speak to God in both a sacred and secular manner."[64]

---

60. Allport, *Individual and His Religion*, xi. Allport's influence can be seen on Oates in the numerous times he is quoted or referenced in the following works: *Bible and Pastoral Care*, *Psychology of Religion*, *Christian Pastor*, and *Religious Care*. Allport's influence will be explored in later chapters.

61. This book, published in 1973, was a revised edition of a much earlier work entitled *The Religious Dimensions of Personality* (1957). Other works dealing primarily with this topic include the following: *Religious Factors in Mental Illness* (1955); *What Psychology Says about Religion* (1958); *Minister's Own Mental Health* (1961); *Protestant Pastoral Counseling* (1962); *When Religion Gets Sick* (1970); and *Religious Care* (1978).

62. Oates, *Psychology of Religion*, 43. See also Oates, *Anxiety in Christian Experience*. In this volume, Oates quotes one of his mentors, Spafford Ackerly, as having stated that the "purpose of religion is the creation of new life, the development of feeling tone, and the regeneration of psychic energy" (Oates, *Psychology of Religion*, 120). Oates echoes a similar sentiment in *The Bible in Pastoral Care*.

63. Oates, *When Religion Gets Sick*, 26.

64. Oates, *Psychology of Religion*, 15.

PHENOMENOLOGICAL PERSPECTIVE

In the early twentieth century, German-born philosopher Edmund Husserl (1859–1938) founded a new philosophical movement known as phenomenology, which in its most basic form is the attempt to objectively study topics traditionally understood as subjective or abstract.[65] Husserl, who influenced later metaphysical philosophers, including Martin Heidegger and Jean-Paul Sartre, envisioned phenomenology as the science of essential being which was dedicated to establishing knowledge of pure essence without the influence of outside prejudice or personal bias.[66] Husserl suggested that true understanding could only come through a "disciplined naiveté" in which the scientist-philosopher would "bracket" his own presuppositions, essentially setting them aside temporarily, in order to participate objectively in the study at hand.[67] In this, personal experience vis-à-vis sense perceptions became the mediator between the scientist and the object of study.[68] Jeane pointed to Husserl's phenomenology as the framework for Oates's counseling approach. In his dissertation which detailed this influence, Jeane noted, "For Husserl to deal phenomenologically was to analyze intentionally an aspect of experience in order to discover the essence of that experience.... He believed this was a presuppositionless approach."[69]

Phenomenology is rooted in existential thought. Initially articulated by Danish philosopher Søren Kierkegaard, existential philosophy has gone

---

65. Menon et al. *Interdisciplinary Perspectives*, 172. Husserl was influenced by American philosopher and psychologist William James. In particular his notion that one's judgment concerning the physical realm must be suspended in order to properly view the object within the immediate context. See Wilshire, *William James and Phenomenology*, 7; Oates, *Religious Dimensions of Personality*, 108.

66. Husserl and Gibson, *Ideas*, 44. First published as *Ideen zu einer reinen Phänomenologie und phänomenologischen Philosophie* in 1913.

67. Oates, "Existential Psychotherapy," personal notes, 5, Wayne E. Oates Papers, box 30: folder 19. Oates's existential psychotherapy was influenced by Søren Kierkegaard (*Sickness unto Death*), Martin Heidegger (*Being and Time*), and Paul Tillich (*Courage to Be*). Tillich in particular owed much of his thinking to Husserl.

68. Husserl and Gibson, *Ideas*, 101. Husserl came from a long line of philosophers, psychologists, and theologians who maintained existential ideas, including Barth, Bultmann, Brunner, Tillich, Kierkegaard, Sartre, and Heidegger. Existentialism, while a broad philosophical umbrella, does share a common premise that existence precedes essence.

69. Jeane, "Analysis of Wayne Edward Oates' Phenomenological Method," 2. This can be seen in particular in the 1982 edition of *The Christian Pastor* as Oates seeks to do away with prejudiced listening. In order to better improve the therapeutic relationship with the client, Oates attempted to suspend belief as he listened (Oates, *Christian Pastor*, 169).

through several forms.⁷⁰ While broadly applied to philosophers of various backgrounds, theories, and presuppositions, existentialism is generally distinguished from other philosophical approaches. As noted, existence is stressed over essence. Rationalists tended to equate everything with essence or with the objectivity of the thing known, while existentialists viewed the world as dynamic and changing.⁷¹ Also, existence, as the ultimate basis for reality, was equated with an individual's self-perception, thus, the context of his immediate situation becomes the interpreter of reality, purpose, and destiny.⁷² Accordingly, existentialists held that neither a traditional metaphysic nor scientific advancement could be adequate to replace the laboratory of individual experience for comprehending the nature of man.⁷³

Writing on topics intersecting and related to existential philosophy, psychology, and religion, existentialists, including Niebuhr and Tillich, believed that man's existential and essential natures should be separated. This belief was manifested in their insistence that man's essential nature was not distorted based on their view of the Judeo-Christian tradition of the goodness of creation. For Tillich in particular, existential thought promoted and offered a pathological approach to human nature. It pointed first to the universal struggles of the "human psyche" and agrees that one cannot begin to explore what it means to be human without first exploring the realities of man's problems.⁷⁴

Another well-known psychologist, Abraham Maslow (1908–1970), believed that existentialism offered a lot to the psychological study of man. As the founder of the Association of Humanistic Psychology, Maslow saw an existential metaphysic as placing an individual's own concept of self as the cornerstone of human nature and being. Instead of relying upon *a priori*

---

70. Halverson and Cohen, *Handbook of Christian Theology*, 120. Kierkegaard wrote much dealing with religion and his approach to God. This shaped modern Protestant theology and was later expressed by the work of Karl Barth (1886–1968), Reinhold Niebuhr (1892–1971), Paul Tillich (1886–1965), and Martin Buber (1878–1965).

71. As this book proceeds, the author will connect this aspect of existential thought to the process philosophy of A. N. Whitehead and show how both left a mark on Oates's view of man. See Oates, *Christ and Selfhood*, 193; Whitehead, *Religion in the Making*, 16; Williams, *Minister and the Care of Souls*, 12; Jeane, "Analysis of Wayne Edward Oates' Phenomenological Method," 41.

72. Halverson and Cohen, *Handbook of Christian Theology*, 122–24.

73. Davis, *Theology Primer*, 26.

74. Cooper, *Paul Tillich*, 67; Oates, "Organizational Development," 352–53; Tillich, *Systematic Theology*. In Tillich's theological method, experience is the "medium through which sources [of truth] speak" (Cooper, *Paul Tillich*, 40). It is the theologian's responsibility to engage with "creative interpretation of existence" in order for theology to be accepted, understood, and grasped by the modern mind (Cooper, *Paul Tillich*, 5–7).

reasoning, personal experience and knowledge of self became the "locus of value."[75] Carl Rogers's client-centered therapy also reveals an existential, and thus phenomenological, foundation. In his approach to psychotherapy, it was necessary for the counselor to fully understand his client and avoid being too quick to evaluate or make judgments.[76] Ideally, this type of understanding would lead to "unconditioned positive regard" in which the counselor is oriented around the client's sense of self. Rogers's goal was for the client to feel secure to explore himself without threat within the counseling relationship. In order to make this happen, a non-judgmental environment must be created and sustained.[77]

The theological and psychological approaches from the men above are evident in Oates's thought and reveal a phenomenological method to counseling. Like Rogers, Oates urged pastoral counselors that they "must first be a student of the person [client] in the privacy of the person's own mind before you can be a teacher of the person in the interpretation of the person's difficulties."[78] This approach necessitated an anthropological method that demonstrated pastoral empathy. The client, according to Oates, must be made to feel heard and understood by the counselor. Through Husserl's bracketing, or "suspending your judgment," this could be accomplished.[79] Oates admitted that since the 1950s, there had been much discussion within the field as to whether pastoral counselors should attempt to be passive or ethically neutral. While avoiding answering this concern directly, the

---

75. Maslow, *Motivation and Personality*, 9. Maslow believed that existentialism, as a brand of philosophy, rested on phenomenology because of its utilization of personal, subjective knowledge as the "foundation upon which abstract knowledge is built." See also Gough, "Maslow, Abraham Harold," 449.

76. Rogers, *On Becoming a Person*, 18–20. See also Oates, *Pastoral Counseling*, 12–15. Client-centered therapy impacted how Oates counseled by his admission that he was ultimately bound by the client's perception of God as he or she understood him to be. In a section of his book *Pastoral Counseling*, Oates apologizes to his readers lest they perceive him as a "God-talk" proponent. He is clear that "religious jargon" is not necessary in order for him to be pastoral during counseling.

77. Rogers, *On Becoming a Person*, 76.

78. Oates, *Christian Pastor* (1982), 80. This was the common approach of other pastoral counselors during this era. Collins noted that this phenomenological approach "seeks to enter into the other person's frame of reference" in order for the client to ultimately decide his or her own course (Oates, *Christian Pastor* [1982], 121). Other pastoral counseling resources utilizing this approach include: Clinebell, *Basic Types of Pastoral Counseling*, 29–33; Browning, "New Trends in Pastoral Care," 849–51; Southard, "Phenomenological Approach," 1277–78.

79. Oates, *Christian Pastor* (1982), 169. See also Oates, *Pastoral Counseling*, 59; Thurneysen, *Theology of Pastoral Care*, 132; Oates, *New Dimensions of Pastoral Care*, 10; Oates, *Psychology of Religion*, 33–34.

implication behind his answer is an approval of the phenomenological approach of the pastor emptying himself of all his prerogatives, even including his representation as ambassador of God in order to take on the "form of the person to whom he is called" as "part of the good news of the Lord Jesus Christ, whether it is called by that name or not."[80] It is evident that Oates held to a phenomenological perspective in his counseling approach throughout much of his life and career. In *The Presence of God in Pastoral Counseling*, Oates capitalized on his ability to turn aside from his "fixed and well-acquainted ways of doing things, understanding people, and stereotypical thinking" by setting aside his presuppositions.[81]

BIBLICALLY INCONSISTENT ANTHROPOLOGY

While the remainder of this book will present a detailed account of Oates's anthropology and how it differs from a biblical anthropology, it is important to note how anthropology serves as the hinge upon which his overall conception and practice of pastoral counseling rested. Each of the previous elements of his pastoral counseling listed (e.g., collaboration, correlation, psychology of religion, and phenomenology) were articulated from a particular anthropological stance. Anthropology served as the fundamental aspect of Oates's theology, and thus his conception of pastoral counseling. As a major theme with which he interacted, Oates attempted to demonstrate both the diversity and unity of psychology and theology as he presented man as a figure caught in an internal struggle for identity.[82] In this,

---

80. Oates, *New Dimensions in Pastoral Care*, 11. See Hiltner and Colston, *Context of Pastoral Counseling*, 45–46.

81. Oates, *Presence of God in Pastoral Counseling*, 61. Oates does make a caveat that by setting aside (e.g., bracketing) one's presuppositions and worldviews, one does not have to abandon his or her convictions, but just set them aside in order to take an open-minded position toward counselees in order that the counselor may be truly empathetic. See also Oates, *Psychology of Religion*, 275; Oates, *When Religion Gets Sick*, 103, 114; May, *Existence*, 64–65.

82. Bush, "Human Suffering," 10, 56–57. Oates went on to state in *The Bible in Pastoral Care* that the Bible, as the "record of revelation of God and men" serves as the "instrument of the revelation of the personality of both the minister and the person with whom he counsels" (Bush, "Human Suffering," 22). In using Jas 1:22–24 to support this conclusion, Oates interpreted the passage to imply that the Bible primarily serves as a mirror on which a person may project his own self-concept. However, this interpretation suggests a man-centered reading as opposed to traditional readings which highlight man's wickedness (i.e., inability to see clearly) juxtaposed with the perfect law of God to which nothing can be added by man. See Henry, *Acts–Revelation*, 974–75, and Martin, *James*, 54–55. See also Oates, *Religious Dimensions of Personality*, 213–14; Oates, "Legalism and the Use of the Bible," 29; Oates, "Diagnostic Use of the Bible," 43.

the understanding of human nature directly impacts and determines the therapeutic process.[83] While Oates's emphasis on anthropology is present throughout his published writings, there are general points of inconsistency regarding a biblical perspective.

Oates maintained that theologians could benefit from secular psychology especially regarding the acquisition of a clearer understanding of mankind. In fact, according to Oates, one of the greatest contributions of modern psychology is that of understanding religious man in terms of the personality development.[84] For those theorists dealing within the field of personality theory, Oates urged his fellow theologians and counselors to heed what they have to say and remain open-minded regarding their scientific knowledge of man.[85] In *Christ and Selfhood*, which dealt particularly with the contributions of psychology, theology, and philosophy on concepts of personality and identity, Oates demonstrated how his own theological lens had been informed by secular psychology. He stated, "The ways in which fluctuating psychological modes of life both have been shaped by and have exerted shaping influence upon the interpretation of the Person of Jesus Christ throw vivid light upon our knowledge of ourselves."[86]

While Oates often touted the benefits of utilizing psychological science and research in understanding man, he also made mention that such sources of knowledge could involve danger. He cautioned, "Contemporary psychotherapy and psychologies of personality are in a subtle way preparing the Western mind for an easier acceptance of humanistic, mystical religions of the East as over against the redemptive religious faith of Christianity."[87] In the same work he criticized how often Christian theologians unconsciously, or at times even carelessly, adopted secular definitions of man. In many theologians' use of secular psychology, biblical doctrines may become compromised and fall short of the Hebrew-Christian view of man. Oates further warned, "Without a specific, conscious, and ordered study of personality in

---

83. Oates, *Minister's Own Mental Health*, 13.

84. Oates, *What Psychology Says about Religion*, 51. See also Allport, *Becoming*, 94–95.

85. Oates, *Religious Dimensions of Personality*, 25. Oates made reference to Gregory Zilboorg and Mary Thelen as providing empirical evidence through psychology for a seemingly secular theory of man's fall (Oates, *Religious Dimensions of Personality*, 49). See also Thelen, *Man as Sinner*, 32.

86. Oates, *Christ and Selfhood*, 22. Oates later mentioned that ancient and contemporary psychologies are relevant in understanding man. Bush later supported this claim by noting, "Oates suggests that Christians would find it beneficial to study 'modern psychotherapy' which, he observes, has serious 'inferences as to the psychology of religious experience'" (Bush, "Human Suffering," 103).

87. Oates, *Religious Dimensions of Personality*, 25–26.

both its theological and scientific dimensions, the theologian and preacher cannot avoid interpreting the basic nature of the Christian faith in what may be essentially non-Christian terms."[88] Anthropologies derived from secular theorists carry a pseudo-soteriology which exposes an anthropocentric worldview highlighting man's self-enlightenment and self-sufficiency.[89] Interestingly, Oates's stern warnings to the well-meaning theologian were contradicted by noting that secular psychologists and theologians share an overlapping concern for people in need, thus functionally minimizing any distinctions in definitions of terms such as *religion* and *personality* to the point that congruency is formed between two "quite different philosophical and theological presuppositions."[90]

Another point of inconsistency in Oates's anthropology compared to clear biblical teaching can be seen in Curtis's work. In his dissertation which explored, in part, Oates's anthropology, Curtis claimed that Oates's view of man was wrapped up in the sovereignty of God. Quoting Oates, he mentioned that a Christian view of man "does not begin with the nature of man. Rather it begins with the truth about God. The sovereign Lordship of Christ as a trenchant truth about God poignantly accentuates the basic character of man."[91] Curtis is consistent with this assertion in an earlier statement that the sovereignty of God laid the groundwork for Oates's idea of man's transcendent worth; however, he also stated unequivocally that through correlating revelational Christianity with human science in a phenomenological context, the conclusion could be made that the "reality of God must be centered in the nature of man and structures of man's existence."[92] While Curtis's work was designed to distinguish and defended Oates's understanding of man as God-centered; in actuality, it highlights inconsistencies in Oates's anthropological structure. The previous quote from *Protestant Pastoral Counseling* was used by Curtis to clear Oates of any accusation that he held to an anthropology that was open to humanistic or man-centered tendencies. Curtis pointed to the fact that there have been many systems of

---

88. Oates, *Religious Dimensions of Personality*, 48–49, emphasis added.

89. Bush, "Human Suffering," 68.

90. Oates, *Religious Dimensions of Personality*, 49.

91. Curtis, "Role of Religion," 172. See also Oates, *Protestant Pastoral Counseling*, 26. In this work, Oates admitted that the field of pastoral counseling faced a great challenge in its disposition to emphasize the sovereignty of man in such a way as to challenge orthodox theology that centered all reality, personhood, and truth on the sovereignty of God (Oates, *Protestant Pastoral Counseling*, 21).

92. Curtis, "Role of Religion," vii. While Fromm was openly atheistic and antagonistic toward the concept of God, Oates seemed to contextualize his "Christian selfhood in psychological language which closely parallels Fromm's conception of man's problems and solutions" (Curtis, "Role of Religion," v).

thought within the field of pastoral counseling that have threatened to upend a Christian anthropology. In the midst of this threat, Oates was viewed by his students as the champion who sought to uphold Christ-centered and biblical principles related to understanding man.

Curtis noted that one such system that was particularly antagonistic toward a Christian anthropology was the psychological theory of Sigmund Freud.[93] The particular mention of Freud causes damage toward Curtis's defense of Oates due to the fact that in multiple instances Oates spoke affirmatively of Freud as significantly contributing to the work of the pastor.[94] For instance, in Oates's doctoral dissertation, he admitted that any topic dealing with Freud was often associated with everything opposed to the Christian faith. Nonetheless, Oates sought to remove any "terminological objections by discovering the things-in-themselves that both Freud and Christian religion have in common."[95] Precluding that theory and method were mutually exclusive, Oates came to conclude, in part through the influence of his mentors and professors, that Freud's psychology most closely reflected a biblical psychology.[96] Through his complex theory of personality in which human nature was seen as the natural result of particular causes, Oates believed that Freud's contribution helped support and strengthens the doctrine of man, which was fundamentally religious, through a scientific approach.[97]

---

93. Curtis, "Role of Religion," 1. As mentioned in the first chapter, nearly every dissertation, thesis or major work devoted to exploring the impact of Oates on the field of pastoral counseling was written or compiled by individuals who had a largely positive and sympathetic view toward Oates's theological perspective.

94. In one of his last published books, Oates maintained that Freud's mostly positive contribution to pastoral care should not be neglected. See Oates, *Presence of God in Pastoral Counseling*, 127. See also Durst, "Theological Dimensions of Human Existence." Durst excuses Oates's interest in psychoanalytical theory in relation to Christian anthropology by stating that Oates was writing during a period in which Freud was extremely popular. He noted that Oates should not be criticized because he kept a "clinical adherence to biblical insight as revelation under the category of divine sovereignty over humanity" (Durst, "Theological Dimensions of Human Existence," 7).

95. Oates, "Significance of the Work of Sigmund Freud," 72. Speaking to Freud's anthropology, Oates stated, "In its origins he sees personality as a bundle of animal impulses; he sees solidified adult character, burdened with the sense of guilt, and torn by conflicting desires. Here is the source of all pathology in the spirit of man: the clash between his sense of demands of society, his sense of his own ideals, and his sense of need for instinctual satisfaction" (55). See Zilboorg, *Mind, Medicine, & Man*, 326; Freud, *The Ego and the Id*, 9.

96. Oates, "Significance of the Work of Sigmund Freud," iii–iv. The reader should be reminded of the direct influence of Gaines Dobbins, Ralph Bonacker, Olin Binkley, Anton Boisen, and Harrold Tribble in relation to this dissertation (Oates, "Significance of the Work of Sigmund Freud," v).

97. Oates, "Significance of the Work of Sigmund Freud," 25–26. See also Oates,

Ironically Oates viewed Freud's psychological theory of man, along with that of Darwin's theory of evolution, as greatly contributing to the humility of mankind. By suggesting that "man is not the master of his own soul and the captain of his own fate," Freud helped bring man's prideful nature back to a point of humility.[98] Even though Oates does not praise every aspect of Freud's psychology of man, any critiques offered focus upon surface-level discrepancies and ignore fundamental points of divergence between Freudian anthropology and a biblical anthropology.[99]

CONCLUSION

In an attempt to construct and outline the psychological anthropology of Wayne Edward Oates, it is important to first highlight in what ways secular psychology influenced his conception of pastoral counseling in its entirety. By revealing the therapeutic worldview that undergirds each of the major conceptual elements of his counseling, I have attempted to demonstrate the depth of Oates's reliance upon and active utilization of secular psychology leading to a view of humanity constructed primarily from these influences. In spite of the fact that Oates has been widely represented as espousing an anthropology derived from Scripture, it has been demonstrated that his commitments and conclusions tended to land him outside of the scope of theological orthodoxy.

Christian Pastor (1982), 246; Oates, *What Psychology Says*, 67, 92; Oates, *Behind the Masks*, 18; Rollo May, *Art of Counseling*, 145; Collins, "Pastoral Concern for Man," 68.

    98. Oates, "Significance of the Work of Sigmund Freud," 56.

    99. Oates, "Significance of the Work of Sigmund Freud," 226–27.

4

Pilgrimage of Personality

Understanding People in Process

THE SCIENTIFIC STUDY OF personality did not come into wide popularity within psychological theory until the early twentieth century in America. The early study of personality was more concerned with seeking to understand the nature and essence of persons as opposed to the current popular notions of personality as primarily a collection of character traits and personal preferences. While not becoming widespread until this time, the study of personality has intrigued theologians, philosophers, and scientists for centuries.[1] Until the seventeenth century, each of these groups approached the study of personality largely from a common anthropological position, that man was a creation of God and indebted to him in their very essence. However, with the dawn of the Enlightenment in the eighteenth century, personality began to be studied through the empirical lens of the modern sciences as these made formal breaks from organized religion.[2] By the time of Wilhelm Wundt's experiments at the University of Leipzig in the late 1800s, psychology formally broke from its philosophical and theological heritage and since then has systematically attempted to dispose of the soul because the immaterial refuses to be subjected to empirical tests and measures.[3]

---

1. Van Leeuwen, *Person in Psychology*, 210.
2. Oates, *Religious Dimensions of Personality*, 279–80.
3. Allport, *Becoming*, 56. See also Allport, "Ego in Contemporary Psychology," 451–78.

The study of personality was not only the object of interest for secular psychologists, but soon came into popular use by many pastoral theologians.[4] Historically, the concept of *self* was primarily thought of in negative terms as it was couched in a Calvinist theological anthropology highlighting, among other things, depravity, noetic effects of sin, and darkness of heart and mind. However, philosophers such as John Locke and other British empiricists opened the door to a reinterpretation of the self in humanistic terms. Holifield noted, "Implicit in the Lockean notion of selfhood were intimations of autonomy and individuality which could clearly dissolve the chain of being in a hierarchical cosmos. In that sense, it can be said that the seventeenth-century clergy lived in a world of souls, not of selves. Or at least they tried."[5] As the centuries progressed into the post-Enlightenment era, the perspective and purpose of pastoral counseling transitioned from the care of souls in redemption and sanctification toward the nurture of the self for the purposes of psychic wholeness.[6] As has been described in previous chapters, Oates believed the Christian faith could benefit from open dialogues with personality theorists and contemporary psychologists. He wrote, "Descriptive, naturalistic, supernaturalistic, and revelation perspectives of personality are inextricably interwoven in the Western Christian tradition. Therefore, historical wisdom is necessary for a Christian understanding of personality which is at the same time both related to and different from modern psychological estimates of man."[7]

OATES'S UNDERSTANDING OF SELF

As a pastoral counselor, Oates recognized the central pursuit for all people as being the quest for identity and discovery of meaning. Consequently, seeking to understand the nature of man is a major motif found throughout Oates's writings.[8] Early in his writing career, Oates explored the naturalistic

---

4. Oates, "Personality Theory and Pastoral Counseling," unpublished essay, Wayne E. Oates Papers, box 10: folder 7. Oates viewed the "shifting emphasis" of pastoral counseling toward the utilization of psychological data and research as something that would eventually become "an integrated body of clinical knowledge" for the church.

5. Holifield, *History of Pastoral Care*, 59.

6. Murvachik, *American Protestantism*, 39. See also Holifield, *History of Pastoral Care*, 97.

7. Oates, *Religious Dimensions of Personality*, 277. See also Durst, "Theological Dimensions of Human Existence," 118.

8. Bush, "Human Suffering," 10, 60–61. Mays went further to call his interest in selfhood as an overarching motif in his writings. See Mays, "Contemporary Theology and Pastoral Care," 52. Oates expresses this interest in the following volumes: *Bible in*

understanding of man and argued that this understanding could be corresponded to a Christian anthropological perspective because both Christian revelation and contemporary psychology sought to ask and answer the same inherent questions in corresponding fashion.[9] While pointing out differences in these two anthropological vantage points, Oates believed in the compatibility between a psychological and biblical understanding of selfhood.[10] Although many authors went to great lengths to affirm the theological and biblical orientation of his anthropology, they each conceded that his theology was perceived through a psychological lens.[11] According to Bush, Oates saw consistent overlaps in the psychological and theological conceptions of personality in that the psychiatrist and theologian sought for man to come to grips or terms with himself, while they may have slightly different emphases in getting him to that place.[12] Oates was convinced that the truths presented in reading a Christian anthropology into a secular framework could guide the pastor "in a more precise understanding of a more realistic participation with people struggling to 'put off the old man' and to 'put on Christ' in whom the Christian's life is hid with God."[13]

While there are those who have defended Oates on the grounds that his anthropology was biblical, many have also pointed to his eclectic use of psychology in informing his anthropology regarding the essence and nature of man. One of the most vocal defenders of the biblical nature of Oates's anthropology admitted that his theology was far from systematic and in fact was presented in generalities that were limited to a relatively narrow theological pool. Regarding his use of psychology, however, Oates engaged in selective borrowing of a wide range of psychological systems in which he included in his own system of thought. These qualities further detract from the supposition that Oates's anthropology was biblical in content and tone.[14] Faced with such a scathing critique, Oates denied this claim on the grounds

---

Pastoral Care, 71; *Protestant Pastoral Counseling*, 100; *Christ and Selfhood*, 185.

9. His first major work dealing with the nature of man was *The Religious Dimensions of Personality*, published in 1957. The book was revised and reprinted as *The Psychology of Religion* in 1973 and retained much of the same language and content.

10. Oates, *Religious Dimensions of Personality*, 282–83. The author's choice to use the terms *selfhood* and *personality* is due to the fact that these were Oates's terms of choice when referring to the inner identity, essence, and nature of man.

11. Collins, "Pastoral Concern for Man," 47; Curtis, "Role of Religion," 264; Mays, "Contemporary Theology and Pastoral Care," 22; Bush, "Human Suffering," 187.

12. Bush, "Human Suffering," 59. Oates, *Religious Dimensions of Personality*, 298–99.

13. Oates, *Christ and Selfhood*, 26. A later section of this chapter will demonstrate how a psychological and biblical anthropology differ from one another greatly.

14. Mays, "Contemporary Theology and Pastoral Care," 39.

that while he may have been informed by various psychotherapeutic methods and theories, he did not *center* his anthropology upon them. According to him, because God had not made any therapeutic model "common or unclean" and as long as his counseling theory was grounded in theology, then "God may reveal His Presence through any of them [psychological theories of man], even when a particular theorist may 'know it not.'"[15] As an implication of his eclectic use of psychological principles, Curtis, much like Bush and Collins, mentioned that "Oates is not entirely consistent in his perspective on religious experience, on the one hand judging it from the Christian absolute of revelational truth, or on the other hand evaluating it from the relativistic stance of does-it-help-the-person-to-function."[16]

Prelude to Selfhood

According to Oates, the "prelude to selfhood" was found in the "personal acknowledgement of God's ultimate sovereignty over human existence."[17] In what Oates identified as the "Person of the Ultimate Presence," one euphemism among several that Oates used for God, both Jews and Christians could find themselves confronted by the one who is "absolute reality itself, the living Being par excellence who communicates himself and makes himself . . . known to man in history."[18] In Bush's reading of Oates, seeing God in this way "compels humankind to seek meaning and fulfillment in life through the attainment of full selfhood."[19] While statements such as these suggest an alignment of Oates's understanding of the essence and nature of man with a biblical and theological understanding of God, key commitments regarding Oates's view of God demonstrate otherwise. The implication of this therapeutic view of God essentially presented a

---

15. Oates, *Presence of God in Pastoral Counseling*, 34. By stating that theology formed the groundwork of his anthropology, thus he could not be labeled eclectic in his use of psychology, Oates's argument is essentially a non sequitur fallacy. Oates himself noted the influence of psychoanalysis (Freud), interpersonal psychiatry (Sullivan), client-centered therapy (Rogers), and cognitive therapy (Beck) among others.

16. Curtis, "Role of Religion," 253.

17. Bush, "Human Suffering," 66; Oates, *Becoming Children of God*, 39; Oates, *Revelation of God*, 80.

18. Oates, *What Psychology Says about Religion*, 173. In addition to Jews and Christians, Oates included all religious peoples of the earth who acknowledge the "Ultimate Source of Being" in God. See also Bush, "Human Suffering," 61.

19. Bush, "Human Suffering," 91; see also Oates, *Revelation of God*, 72. In this volume, Oates used the life and ministry of Ezekiel to illustrate God's call to selfhood. This begs the question, is God's ultimate purpose and objective for mankind to achieve selfhood?

pragmatic and heuristic reduction of God, to what Oates often identified as a "God-consciousness" that served as a man-centered tool by which the counselor could best service the needs of his religious client.[20] This utilitarian approach to God carried with it the implication that one did not need to be a Christian in order to achieve selfhood. It only meant that Christ had revealed the "Ultimate Self of Being," another euphemism for God, and through him the image of true selfhood could be uncovered.[21] Bush relates the influence of Plato concerning the soul of man (e.g., preexistence of the soul, immortality without redemption) and how often his thought has been incorporated into Christian tradition often without any criticism of the antithesis of interpretation regarding the nature of man. With this connection, Bush noted the humanistic overtones of Platonic influence concerning man's natural goodness found in the personal achievements and "fulfillment of his natural potentialities . . . to improve himself."[22] By making a connection between Oates's view of God and secular thought, Bush inadvertently indicted Oates as purporting a man-centered theology and anthropology. Oates stated, "When we have taken into *account and given full credence* to all the *nourishing factors in personality development*, we still come face to face with the quiet reality that we are not quite able to avoid: Man decides upon faith whether or not it is better for him to grow or to remain as he is!"[23]

Pilgrimage to Personality

Oates saw the human lifespan in terms of a pilgrimage in which the individual underwent various developments and processes resulting in the formation of their final sense of self. For the most part, Oates utilized three terms to express what constituted personhood. These included the concepts of identity, selfhood, and personality.[24] For Oates, the term *identity* merely

---

20. Oates, *Protestant Pastoral Counseling*, 15. It is explained in this work, that the client's God-consciousness did not have to be centered on the Christian God. Oates borrowed this concept from Tillich who popularized this understanding of God from his existential psychology. See the following sections of this chapter for more on this. See also Bush, "Human Suffering," 60–61.

21. Oates, *Religious Dimensions of Personality*, 88; Oates, *What Psychology Says about Religion*, 94.

22. Bush, "Human Suffering," 63.

23. Oates, *Religious Dimensions of Personality*, 174–76. See also Oates, *Psychology of Religion*, 86.

24. Oates never expressed a singular theory of personality (or personhood) so that even the various uses of these terms, at times, is difficult to distinguish. However, there is general agreement that the topic of personality was of central importance to Oates by the fact that it can be found throughout his writings. See also Oates, "Significance of

described the characteristics of all humans. All people, whether they are Christians or not, have an identity which essentially involves "the choice of the kind of human being you intend to be, the way of life that is yours, the inner persuasion as to your own unique mystique" and is the sum total of one's commitments in life.[25] Identity is dependent upon circumstances, prone to existential threats, and is merely the initial stage in the developmental process leading toward self-maturation.[26] The next chain in this process is achieving *selfhood*. Selfhood differed from identity in that an individual had concentrated or focused their attentions upon a specific source of content by which the pattern of their life would be modeled. Oates defined selfhood as the "habitual center of focus of man's identity . . . [the] Christian assumes that the decisive factor in focusing man's identity is his encounter with Christ."[27] Curtis noted that while it was not necessary that one be a Christian in order to reach selfhood, there are those who had looked specifically to Jesus as their source of content.[28] Even so, selfhood was not the ultimate end goal of human development. While man's identity became "focused" in selfhood, it became fully organized in the *personality*. Maintaining balance was a goal of human development, according to Oates, due to the fact that a lack of balance often brought about neuroses and stunted personality growth and self-understanding. He noted, "Personality is unified around the central loyalty to which persons give themselves most wholeheartedly."[29] A major difference found in Oates's use of selfhood as opposed to personality is the role religion played in the life of the individual. Religion rightly understood by the individual, can be a key organizing factor which further grounds and orients an individual and brings them to a state of wholeness.[30] Speaking to pastors, Oates noted, "Both you and those whom you would

---

the Work of Sigmund Freud," 27.

25. Oates, "Defining Your Identity," 2, Wayne E. Oates Papers, box 12: folder 1.

26. Erikson, *Identity, Youth, and Crisis*, 20–21. See also Oates, *Religious Care*, 66; Collins, "Pastoral Concern for Man," 72. Collins noted that Erikson provided a developmental approach to man that coincided with Oates's anthropological considerations. Indeed Oates often referred to Erikson regarding this topic. Developmentalism will be covered in greater detail in a following section of this chapter.

27. Oates, *Christ and Selfhood*, 41.

28. Curtis, "Role of Religion," 181.

29. Oates, *Religious Dimensions of Personality*, 270. See also Oates, "Personality Theory and Pastoral Counseling," 6, Wayne E. Oates Papers, box 10: folder 7; Oates, "Some Psychological Implications," 3–12.

30. Oates, "Significance of the Work of Sigmund Freud," 44.

serve are on a pilgrimage of selfhood, the end result of which is either a self in Christ or a self apart from Christ."[31]

Christological Considerations

A perfunctory reading of Oates's writings concerning the nature and essence of man seems to demonstrate a commitment to a biblical Christology. According to Oates, the central objective of all pastoral care and personal counseling is that Christ is formed in the personality of the person who is seeking help.[32] It is to guide lost and wandering souls into a relationship with Christ that promises meaning in the face of an otherwise meaningless existence.[33] In illustrating this Oates stated, "Until man encounters God in Christ, his own efforts to understand himself and to define the nature of his own personality go unaided and is fraught with ambiguities and contradictions."[34] Oates claimed that the fullness of man's personality could only be determined through the revelation of God in Jesus Christ; in fact, by using terms such as "creation" and "fullness" he suggested that in the pre-Christian state man was an incomplete, divided, and destructive self and that only Christ could reconcile man with his inner-self and with God.[35] The decisive factor that made the difference between the old self and the new self was an encounter with Jesus Christ.[36] Oates's working hypothesis was that Jesus served as the center of true selfhood through the example of his life and through the power of his forgiveness. Man is called to act upon this forgiveness by reciprocally "accepting Christ's love as the organizing center of our identity, as the heart of our existence as a self."[37] Oates argued that

---

31. Oates, *Christian Pastor* (1982), 82.

32. Oates, *Christian Pastor* (1982), 77. The exact goal is expressed in the 1951 edition of this book. Oates makes mention that proper conversion results in the organization of the personality in which true selfhood is born.

33. Curtis, "Role of Religion," 112. Curtis draws direct lines of influence of Paul Tillich and Victor Frankl in that "meaningfulness" is an essential ingredient to human existence.

34. Oates, *Religious Dimensions of Personality*, 50.

35. Oates, *Christ and Selfhood*, 246.

36. Oates, *Christ and Selfhood*, 25. Oates's language tends to be ambiguous regarding the *ordo salutis* and the part this plays when selfhood and personality is achieved. For instance, at one point Oates suggested that Jesus' disciples' selfhood only came to "full-term birth" when they encountered the resurrected Christ (Oates, *Christ and Selfhood*, 31). This begs the question, where the disciples not true "selves" before the resurrection? In instances likes these, Oates's pilgrimage of personality often brings more confusion than clarity. See Isa 29:6, 44:2; 49:5; Ps 139:13; Jer 1:5.

37. Oates, *Christ and Selfhood*, 41.

Christ was not only a model for man in the organization of personality, but that he was also the vehicle by which true selfhood could be achieved.[38] It is not surprising from such commitments that Oates was generally affirmed for holding a strong christological emphasis as the key to his anthropology. As typical in the numerous reviews of *Christ and Selfhood*, C. R. Stinnette Jr. noted, "In choosing to center his study of the modes of selfhood within the focus of Christology Wayne Oates has made another important contribution to pastoral theology and to the reapproachment of theology and science."[39]

Psychological Interpretation

While there are instances when Oates identified the uniqueness of the Christian understanding of personality as being centered on the person and work of Jesus Christ, a study of related theological confessions within his writings revealed psychological influences which ultimately reinterpreted his understanding of the nature and essence of man in a perspective that emphasized man-centeredness.[40] Once again, this is problematic for anyone claiming a strong biblical theology as undergirding Oates's understanding of man. Oates believed that it was through the lens of secular psychology that best provided an understanding of Jesus as the model of selfhood to all humans. He stated,

> The pilgrimage of encounter with Christ on the part of the Christian community is in itself an historical treasure of psychological wisdom. The ways in which fluctuating psychological modes of life both have been shaped by and have exerted shaping influence upon the interpretation of the Person of Jesus Christ throw vivid light upon our knowledge of ourselves.[41]

Regarding the true beginning of the selfhood of Jesus, Oates stated, "Most of the answers to these questions and many others like them, stemming from Jesus' decisions as to his birthright and as to who his father was, must be answered from the silence of Scriptures, in other words, by logic and

---

38. Collins, "Pastoral Concern for Man," 47. Curtis takes as Oates thesis that "God in Christ enables us to develop our humanity to the fullest." See Curtis, "Role of Religion," vi.

39. Stinnette, original manuscript review of *Christ and Selfhood*, Wayne Oates Papers, box 3: folder 8. See also St. Amant, review of *Christ and Selfhood*, 215.

40. Oates, *Religious Dimensions of Personality*, 21, 302–4; Collins, "Pastoral Concern for Man," 28, 48–49.

41. Oates, *Christ and Selfhood*, 22.

surmise."⁴² Here Oates suggested that Jesus may not have been aware who his father was until he made the volitional decision that God was his father. In other words, Jesus agreed to his own concept of selfhood. The implications behind this unorthodox claim are multifaceted. According to this suggestion, Jesus was not aware of his identity as Messiah until after his baptism, further implying that there may have been a time where Jesus was not an organized self.⁴³ Oates extended this line of heretical thought by placing Jesus on the same soul-searching plane as the rest of humanity. He stated, "Jesus probed the Hebrew Scriptures for the meaning of his own existence. ... We find him choosing the prophesies of the Isaiahs as the working models of his identity ... as to the quality of selfhood he was affirm. He chose to be a Suffering Servant, a selfhood which had been prepared from him and awaited his affirmation."⁴⁴

To further draw out Oates's warped Christology, he claimed that God actualized himself in Jesus Christ so that his own identity became focused in the person of Christ and his selfhood became manifest. In turn, Jesus chose "fully to actualize his true selfhood in the flesh what he already had been from the foundation of the world: God."⁴⁵ Oates used the term *actualize* to describe the process by which Jesus rightly comprehended his own selfhood. The term *self-actualization* had become popular in the writing of personality and humanistic psychologist Abraham Maslow as the pinnacle of his theory of human motivation.⁴⁶ First coined by Kurt Goldstein,

---

42. Oates, *Christ and Selfhood*, 43.

43. Oates, *Christ and Selfhood*, 31. See also Rawlison, *New Testament Doctrine of Christ*, 30. Oates further explains that Mary may have raised Jesus in the teachings of the Scriptures that he was the Messiah. Oates added, "It is inconceivable that she [Mary] would not have instructed Jesus to a great extent along the lines of a prophetic interpretation of his calling in God, although to what extent we do not know" (Oates, *Christ and Selfhood*, 78). This speculation, however, contradicts the biblical account of Jesus' early awareness of his deity, to the point of teaching this truth to his own mother (Luke 2:41–52).

44. Oates, *Christ and Selfhood*, 44. Once again this interpretation flatly contradicts scriptural accounts of Jesus as the Word of God existing before the creation of the world and co-extant with God the Father (John 1:1; 10:30; Heb 1:1–3; Col 1:15–16).

45. Oates, *Christ and Selfhood*, 29. See also Oates, *Presence of God*, 16. Oates went on to state that Jesus' divinity was actualized through his substitutionary death. This begs the question, was Jesus any *less* divine before the incarnation or before his penal substitutionary death on the cross? The answer, of course, is no.

46. While Oates does not directly refer to Maslow in *Christ and Selfhood*, Curtis mentions a similarity between Maslow's anthropological stances and those of Oates in that man has a nature that expresses concreted needs, man's growth is tied to mental health and leads toward self-appreciation and esteem, and pathology is revealed when man's potential is threatened. See Curtis, "Role of Religion," 18.

Maslow's mentor, who was a philosophically minded neurologist, this term initially detailed the tendency within all life forms to develop into their best state via their unique inner potential.[47] Maslow repurposed the term to refer "to the highest level of human growth where one has reached one's fullest potential."[48] In short, Maslow's anthropological commitments and concept of actualization required that man was intrinsically good in both nature and essence.[49]

In capitalizing on the idea that the Messiah was the result of God actualizing himself, in addition to suggesting there may have been a time when Jesus was not an "organized self," Oates articulated a man-centered anthropology. This result was not entirely missed even by those who were largely uncritical of his "mostly orthodox" theology.[50] For instance, one critic noted that Oates offered an interpretation of Christology which reflected "an instance that man's own experience provides the necessary structure for understanding both the relevance and the uniqueness of that event [the incarnation]."[51] For Oates, self-acceptance and self-understanding were psychological concepts which provided the counselor the insight needed to understand his client and could lead an individual to achieve maturity in personality.[52] Curtis noted that "Oates begins with a definition of self as the

47. Goldstein, *Organism*, 13. Goldstein's work is briefly mentioned in Andras Angyal's work *Foundations for a Science of Personality*. This book is one of two which Oates identified as having an impact on his thinking and forming of *Christ and Selfhood* with the other being Sullivan's *Conceptions of Modern Psychiatry*. See Oates, *Christ and Selfhood*, 38; Tillich *Systematic Theology*, 3:30.

48. Waller, "Self-Actualization," in Anthony, *Evangelical Dictionary of Christian Education*, 620. Maslow's hierarchy of needs was first presented in print in 1943, nearly twenty years before the publishing of *Christ and Selfhood*. See Maslow, "Theory of Human Motivation," 370–96.

49. Gough, "Abraham Maslow," in Anthony, *Evangelical Dictionary of Christian Education*, 450. See also Maslow, *Motivation and Personality*, 3; Maslow, *Toward a Psychology of Being*, 3; and Ryckman, *Theories of Personality*, 374. Oates does refer to Maslow's work in *Psychology of Religion*, 27, and *On Becoming Children of God*, 27.

50. Elliott, review of *Christ and Selfhood*, photocopy in Wayne E. Oates Papers, box 3: folder 8.

51. Stinnette, original manuscript review of *Christ and Selfhood*, Wayne E. Oates Papers, box 3: folder 8. He later suggested, in the brief critique offered of the book, that in emphasizing the "personal mode of Christ," referring that Jesus actualized his own selfhood, Stinnette questions whether Oates had "fallen into the trap of picturing God as another person—with its attending danger of driving every other person into fragmentation" (93).

52. St. Clair, review of *Christ and Selfhood*, Wayne E. Oates Papers, box 3: folder 8; Oates, "Inner World," 16–18; Oates, "How Can a Minister Learn to Accept Himself?," *Tomorrow: A Brighter Day for the Baptist Ministry* (journal), 4–7, Wayne E. Oates Papers, box 6: folder 2; and Oates, "Improving Your Self-Image," *The Student*, November

center which is the focus of man's identity.... The self begins his pilgrimage, not initially in a state of alienation, but in a state of finitude."[53] Allport's influence was marked in Oates's belief that the center of man's being included his or her own "personal resolves, driving intentions, and personal commitments in life."[54] Ultimately, the problematic implications concerning a theory of personality as seen from Oates's writings, lead to an "earthen vessel view of man."[55] In this view, the great treasure of the Holy Spirit is excluded in favor of celebrating the temporary trappings of man.

CLINICAL UNDERSTANDING OF MAN

During the summer of 1925, Anton Boisen facilitated the first group of ministerial students engaged in a formal clinical pastoral training program. Boisen's therapeutically oriented anthropology informed his clinical methodology. For Boisen, the concerns of theology were man-centered and contributed toward self-realization. Optimal patient care depended greatly upon the patient's own self-perception.[56] Ultimately, Boisen communicated to his students a liberal theological perspective in which personal convictions were pliable and "should be changed when they do not take into account the facts of human experience."[57]

Under Boisen's influence, the early years of the CPE movement also saw the utilization of the behavioral sciences in the study of patients. Murvachik noted a trend leading toward the adoption of psychology in ministering to alienated patients. CPE provided a new perspective for Christian work at its inception as a modernist movement within mainline Protestantism.[58]

1978, 29–32, Wayne E. Oates Papers, box 32: folder 17.

53. Curtis, "Role of Religion," 11. See also Hall and Lindzey, *Theories of Personality*, 86.

54. Oates, *Becoming a Person*, 33.

55. Oates, *Religious Care*, 1–3; Oates, *On Becoming Children of God*, 39; Oates, *Behind the Masks*, 133. See 2 Cor 4:7; Rom 1:16ff.

56. Boisen, *Exploration of the Inner World*, 191.

57. Aden and Ellens, *Turning Points in Pastoral Care*, 168. Boisen studied under William Adams Brown at Union Theological Seminary. Brown, in turn, was trained under the liberal theology of William Newton Clarke of Colgate-Rochester Seminary and was influenced by the philosophy of William James at Harvard. Brown and Clarke's works were standard texts found in seminaries ranging from Union Theological Seminary to Southern Seminary, where Harold Tribble was to teach a young Wayne Oates. See Aden and Ellens, *Turning Points in Pastoral Care*, 21; Brown, *Christian Theology in Outline*, and Clarke, *Outline in Christian Theology*.

58. Muravchik, *American Protestantism*, 23. See also Thornton, *Professional Education for Ministry*. Helen Flanders Dunbar, an inaugural leader of the Council for the

Ministers and chaplains were taught that the ideas of their patients were "just as properly objects of empirical investigation as their pulse rate or their blood pressure."[59] Boisen's students also utilized professional interviewing techniques, note-taking skills, and constructed formal case studies in order to gather information about their patients and gain proficient experience in chaplaincy work. According to those in the movement, the responsible and effective minister of the modern century needed to be prepared and adequately trained in innovative methods that demonstrated scientific, technological, and psychological competency.[60]

Oates became an inheritor and propagator of not only this clinical approach to pastoral counseling and training, but also toward a clinical anthropology.[61] One of the tenants of the clinical understanding of man to which Oates subscribed rested on the belief that achieving insight regarding the personality conflicts of the client would lead the client gaining a measure of control over their situation. Modern theology, which was centered on an individual's pursuit of psychological wellness and sought to articulate the "dynamic understandings of persons," functionally replaced a theology which was once focused on the salvation of souls.[62] In this insight-driven approach, concepts such as repressed memories and the unconscious were elevated in a focused attempt to learn more about the nature and essence of man. While noting how helpful insight-oriented psychology was to the pastoral counseling task, Oates stated, "The acceptance, clarification, and balancing of contradictory needs in the lives of people is vital concerning their feelings towards God."[63] Oates agreed with Boisen that the insight and

---

Clinical Training of Theology Students, provided an image of the priest drinking deeply from the well of science in order to avoid becoming "suspect and ostracized from increasingly large social groups" (Thornton, *Professional Education*, 37). The minister would either partake of the psychological waters, or become a cultural and professional pariah.

59. Boisen, *Exploration of the Inner World*, 184. See also Boisen, *Religion in Crisis and Custom*, xi.

60. Aden and Ellens, *Turning Points in Pastoral Care*, 20. During the time of Boisen's work at Worcester State Hospital, science, evolutionary theory, technological advances, and business efficiency permeated American society and institutions of higher education. See Boisen, *Out of the Depths*, 151.

61. Oates, "Ecumenical Thrust of Clinical Pastoral Education," 2. Oates identified the "study of living human documents" as the standard of CPE. In an address to the Association of Clinical Pastoral Educators (ACPE) Oates stated, "Anyone [sic] of us worth his salt and not a complete phony would lay his job on the line any day if this value of the empirical testing of hypothesis by the clinical method was being subverted, set aside, or watered down."

62. Oglesby, *New Shape of Pastoral Theology*, 221.

63. Oates, *Christian Pastor* (1982), 246–47.

depth psychologies contributed greatly to the pastoral counseling task in that by bringing the unconscious to bear upon the behavior of the client, meaning and order was often brought forth from confusion and chaos.[64]

In addition to plumbing the depths of man's unconscious, a clinical understanding of man also necessitated a measure of empirical observation. Mays noted that Oates often turned to psychology and psychotherapy for "refinement and clarification," of his theological convictions, thus presenting a doctrine of man informed by secular perspectives.[65] Mays inadvertently described Oates's view of humanity in anthropocentric, existential, or therapeutic terms by noting that it was grounded upon the empirical study of mankind.[66] Durst also stressed that Oates viewed the "riches of empirical science" as a necessity in order to fulfill the commission of God for the pastor in the care of souls.[67] Inherent in Oates's purpose and direction for pastoral counseling was allowing individuals to make new discoveries and improve their own lives. Oates defined this task as the "systematic effort to apply inductive, clinical, and scientific method to the accepted function of the minister as he confers with persons about their personal problems and life destiny."[68]

Living Human Documents

Boisen's goal for his students was to first and foremost "learn to *read human documents* as well as books, particularly those revealing documents which are opened up at the inner day of judgment."[69] This clinical study of human behavior predated Boisen by several years as seen in William James's admission that *documents humanis* (human documents) made up the majority of his data and research which contributed to his study of religious experience. Oates followed what he considered to be James's "method of letting the

---

64. Oates, *Protestant Pastoral Counseling*, 63. See also Boisen, *Exploration of the Inner World*, 266.

65. Mays, "Contemporary Theology and Pastoral Care," 16.

66. Mays, "Contemporary Theology and Pastoral Care," 12. See also Oates, *Religious Dimensions of Personality*, 29; Oates, *Religious Factors in Mental Illness*, vii.

67. Durst, "Theological Dimensions of Human Existence," 218.

68. Oates, *Pastoral Counseling*, 56. See also *Christian Pastor* (1982), 191; Oates, *New Dimensions in Pastoral Care*, 5; Dillon, "Wayne E. Oates," 12, December 1, 1977, Wayne E. Oates Papers, box 37: folder 51.

69. Boisen, *Exploration of the Inner World*, 10, emphasis added. It should be noted that the phrase "living human documents" demonstrated reliance upon human understanding, reasoning, perception, and knowledge to the exclusion of the only *truly* living document, the Bible. See also Oates, *Christian Pastor*, 34; Oates, *New Dimensions*, 7.

autobiography of persons speak" in his quest to better understanding the inner workings of man.[70] As a pastoral counselor Oates was convinced that in order to identify the problems that people brought to him, it was vitally important that he "must first be a student of the person in the privacy of his own mind" before he could rightly interpret his difficulties, much less provide him with directive teaching or counsel.[71] With this conviction in mind, the concept of living human documents suggested a focus and emphasis on individualism in Oates's concept of self. Speaking of Oates's anthropological commitment to man's uniqueness, Collins stated, "Man is called to express his identity in his own special way."[72] Harkening back to Oates's conception of human nature, this end goal was ultimately realized through Jesus providing a sense of individualism, safety, and security in order for the person to create their own pathway to full selfhood. In essence, Jesus becomes a tool of individualistic personality development. Oates affirmed that Boisen had taught a generation of ministers that "the real laboratory for discovering the clearest revelation of the meaning of God in Christ was among the sick, the outcast, the distressed failures of life. These were, according to him [Boisen] the 'written living human documents of flesh and blood' where God was most certainly making himself known."[73] Oates's clinical training taught him not to expect the revelation of God to be relegated only to the Bible or "to be recorded in books and to be gathering dust upon library shelves" but to find God's revelation of himself in the dynamic, progressing, and messy lives of people in need.[74]

For Oates, everyday crises had psychological significance for the individual. Among the resources available to the counselor, the "literature of the Bible and that of Christian history" were helpful supplements to the

70. Oates, *Religious Dimensions of Personality*, ix. See also James, *Varieties of Religious Experience*, 3; Oates, "Personality Theory and Pastoral Counseling, 13, Wayne E. Oates Papers, box 10: folder 7.

71. Oates, *Christian Pastor* (1951), 34. See also Oates, *New Dimensions in Pastoral Care*. Many of the early leaders and influencers in modern pastoral counseling movements, including Boisen, Hiltner, Rauschenbusch, Fosdick, and Niebuhr, recognized the importance of clinical case history methodologies. Case histories were client-centered and often challenged, in their eyes, the "pat answers or preconceived theological formulas for ministers to the human condition" (Oates, *Christian Pastor* [1951], 7).

72. Collins, "Pastoral Concern for Man," 50. See also Oates, "Clinical Pastoral Training's Contribution to Theology," 4, Wayne E. Oates Papers, box 6: folder 24. In the clinical method, the patient as person becomes the focus of the care.

73. Oates, *Revelation of God in Pastoral Counseling*, 20.

74. Oates, *Revelation of God in Pastoral Counseling*, 20. Oates stated, "The central and living truth of the Scripture does not begin with a book, a theory of inspiration, but with an eye-opening encounter with the Resurrected Lord Jesus Christ" (Oates, *Presence of God in Pastoral Counseling*, 65).

study of living human documents.[75] Despite the fact that Oates did not hold to a view of Scripture as the sole and sufficient source for his anthropology, he has, nonetheless, been consistently described as Bible-centered regarding his approach to counseling.[76] Durst defended Boisen's influence on Oates regarding the focus on human documents as the primary source of information sought after by clinically trained pastors and counselors by relying upon a passage from 2 Corinthians for support.[77] Walter Jackson generally lauded Oates for his theological fundamentalism and orthodoxy and claimed that one of the only issues that some in the field of pastoral counseling took with Oates was that he was too biblical because "so many of his presuppositions, theoretical constructs, and practical procedures are expressed in biblical quotations."[78] Regarding his view of Scripture, Edgar affirmed that Oates assumed the "authority of Scripture" held in tandem with a more progressive view which subsumed the concerns of contemporary man while also noting that Oates's perception continued to progress until he had come to the conclusion that "all Scripture was written for our instruction, but all Scripture is not equally wise."[79] Collins noted that Oates saw the Bible as the norm of revelation and as the primary resources available to man concerning God's dealing with him.[80]

---

75. Oates, *Christian Pastor* (1982), 27. See also *The Bible in Pastoral Care* and *Psychology of Religion* for extended discussion related to the use of Scripture as a tool in the hands of counselors.

76. For the purposes of this book, I am defining the term *biblicist* as one who could be identified with theological conservatism, as opposed to theological liberalism, and points to the Bible as the sole authoritative source of anthropology, epistemology, metaphysics, etc., with all other resources being seen as either inferior or antithetical to Scripture.

77. Durst, "Theological Dimensions of Human Existence," 30. The verse used to support the biblical nature of "living human documents" is 2 Cor 3:2–3, which states, "You are our letter, written in our hearts, known and read by all men; being manifested that you are a letter of Christ, cared for by us, written not with ink but with the Spirit of the living God, not on tablets of stone but on tablets of human hearts."

78. Jackson, "Oates Agenda for Pastoral Care," 140. See also Durst, "Theological Dimensions of Human Existence," 45.

79. Edgar, "Pastoral Identity," 155. This was referred to by Oates in *The Christian Pastor* (1982), 98. See also Tillich, *New Being*, 70.

80. Collins, "Pastoral Concern for Man," 35. Oates's focus was on empirical findings which he believed provided a respectable knowledge of God that could be depended upon. There seems to be a neoorthodox emphasis and reliance upon the biblical events (e.g., incarnation, resurrection, etc.) as opposed to and distinctly separated from the biblical record itself (Collins, "Pastoral Concern for Man," 55).

Oates openly rejected the fundamentalist and biblicist labels because he did not consider himself an inerrantist.[81] Jackson conceded that Oates often made "use of higher critical methods of biblical studies and uses historical, textual, linguistic, and form-critical methods routinely. Freed by these disciplines, he is not enslaved to the literal text of the Bible and therefore does not deserve the 'biblicist' label."[82] While Oates never *overtly* rejected Scripture's validity, power, or benefit in leading those with psychological deficiencies toward the goal of the development of healthy personalities, his approach to the Bible reflected caution and in many occasions promoted a man-centered hermeneutic.[83] One note of caution Oates leveled against the approach of relying upon the Scriptures too heavily was their frequent misuse in the hands of pastors and the mentally ill. The more immature or psychologically insecure an individual was, the more likely they were to grossly misinterpret the Bible's message. Only the "secure, mature, and informed" pastor who had a strong grasp on the "psychodynamics of personality" could utilize Scripture appropriately.[84] This misuse, which Oates attributed to legalism, was considered grievous to the extent that it caused an inner disturbance to those seeking counsel.[85] In order to avoid a legalistic and static hermeneutic, and instead appropriately utilize the Bible as a resource designed to help men and women cope with their soulish needs, the pastor according to Oates should be clinically trained which provided the experience necessary to give a "life-centered interpretation" of the hurting person's problems.[86] Ultimately, Oates viewed the personal perspective of the patient or counseling client, depicted as the living human document, as standing at the center of a therapeutic encounter between the minister and

---

81. Oates, *Christ and Selfhood*, 33. Case in point, when referring to the biblical record as the source for understanding persons, Oates notes that the authors of the Bible "at no point claims . . . infallibility." However, he seems to ignore several passages in Scripture that attest to that fact (2 Tim 3:16–17; Heb 4:12; 2 Pet 3:15–16; 1 Tim 5:18).

82. Jackson, "Oates Agenda for Pastoral Care," 140.

83. Oates, *Bible in Pastoral Counseling*, 56. Oates depicts the Bible as a source of validation for the pastor. Oates seems at times to ascribe value to the Bible due to the authority it lends to the counseling relationship and its contribution to developing "a health-giving attitude in the pastoral use of the Bible" (Oates, *Bible in Pastoral Counseling*, 11). See also Oates, *Revelation of God*, 11.

84. Oates, *Bible in Pastoral Counseling*, 23.

85. Oates, "Legalism and the Use of the Bible," 38.

86. Oates, *Bible in Pastoral Counseling*, 31. Even so, Oates stated that even if the counselor "fundamentally" identifies the correct understanding of the client, if the client rejects this interpretation then it should be discarded (Oates, *Bible in Pastoral Counseling*, 88). For the reference that Oates makes to Roger's person-centered clinical approach, see Rogers, *Counseling and Psychotherapy*, 26–27.

the struggling individual.[87] While giving verbal affirmation of the Bible's usefulness in identifying the nature of man, Oates's anthropology functionally affirmed that through "detailed empirical studies of personality growth" counselors were enabled to more specifically grasp what maturity of selfhood looked like.[88]

DYNAMIC NATURE OF MAN

The final aspect of Oates's understanding of personality related to the dynamic nature of man.[89] In this section, Oates's eclectic use of various psychological theories can be clearly seen. From Oates's writings, the researcher identified three distinct, yet overlapping, streams of thought as represented by various psychologists and philosophers to whom Oates was indebted in the building of his anthropology. These include process theology, developmental psychology, and existential philosophy.[90]

Man in Process

The first stream of thought ascribed to by Oates was that of process theology. Based on the metaphysical system of philosophy expressed by Alfred North Whitehead, process theology contends that all of creation, and even God, undergoes processes leading to self-development. It is defined as a "contemporary theological movement based on a view of reality in which process, change, and evolution is just as fundamental as substance, permanence, and stability."[91] Oates adopted, taught, and made frequent references to process thought in relation to a dynamic view of human nature and existence and incorporated this philosophy into his view of ministry.[92] Trained initially

---

87. Bush, "Human Suffering," 199.

88. Oates, *What Psychology Says about Religion*, 61.

89. For the purposes of this book, the term *dynamic* refers to change, process, evolution, fluidity, development and any characteristic opposing the ideas of stability, consistency, or immutability.

90. Oates, *Psychology of Religion*, 13. The reader should take note that the overlap between these broad streams of thought is extensive; however, the purpose of this section is not to exhaustively relay to the reader each of these systems, but to highlight key aspects of each as used by Oates.

91. Davis, *Theology Primer*, 34. See also Whitehead, *Religion in the Making*, 98. Here Whitehead expressed God as a being who is constantly becoming and creation itself is eternally ongoing due to the process of God's self-realization. See also Hoggard-Creegan, "Process Theology," 958–59.

92. Collins, "Pastoral Concern for Man," 32, 142. See also Pittenger, *God in Process*, 98.

in mathematics and science, it was not until the final third of Whitehead's life that his writings explored the connections between religious experience and metaphysics. In general, his theology held to epistemological and axiological relativity in the context of a subjective reality. Indebted to the work of John Dewey and William James, Whitehead concluded that subjective experience was greater than objective essence. In his book *Process and Reality*, he claimed that the "ultimate metaphysical principle is the advance from disjunction to conjunction, creating a novel entity other than the entities given in disjunction."[93] In other words, the goal of reality is for individual entities or persons, to move from a place of disorganization and chaos to a place of organization and order. This is achieved primarily through personal experiences of transaction between the individual and the world around him. Ross supported the claim that Whitehead's conception of experience is the focus of his cosmology. He observed, "The emphasis on emotion, purpose, and valuation repeats the experiential theme of Whitehead's theory. . . . The paradigm of experience as the ground of unification is essential to Whitehead's theory."[94] Anthropologically speaking, the individual perspective was understood in terms of entities being directly tied to the ever changing universe for the purpose of accomplishing and achieving potentiality. Religion was formed for the purpose of aiding man in his attempt to achieve a sense of "individual worth of character."[95]

Gordon Allport was among the first psychologists to focus upon the human personality. In rejecting both a psychoanalytic and behavioristic approach to studying humans, Allport aimed to emphasize man's individuality and uniqueness against a backdrop of scientific uniformity.[96] As opposed to Wundt's positivist denial of the self and his establishment of a structural and soul-less anthropology, Allport was the first in a line of personality psychologists who attempted to retain the self while not reifying the concept.[97] Regarding the origins of the term *personality*, Allport

---

93. Whitehead, *Process and Reality*, 32. In his philosophy *entity* is a term used to describe the most fundamental building blocks of real things of which the world consists (Whitehead, *Process and Reality*, 27). See also Ross, *Perspectives in Whitehead's Metaphysics*, 85.

94. Ross, *Perspectives in Whitehead's Metaphysics*, 2–4; and also Shahan, *Whitehead's Theory of Experience*. Shahan states succinctly, "Process is the becoming of experience" (1). See Whitehead, *Process and Reality*, 252.

95. Whitehead, *Religion in the Making*, 17. See also Whitehead, *Modes of Thought*, 91.

96. Allport, *Personality*, vii.

97. Ryckman, *Theories of Personality*, 232. Allport identified Wundt's anthropology from a positivist perspective in that Wundt rejected the idea of an internal understanding of man due to it being inaccessible to scientific verification (Allport, *Personality*, 27).

pointed to the Latin word *persona* which was roughly translated mask or the person behind the mask.[98]

Allport's psychological approach to understanding man, which could be identified in an essentialist perspective, shared philosophical roots with Whitehead.[99] Allport defined personality as "the dynamic organization within the individual of those psychophysical systems that determine his characteristic behavior and thought."[100] Allport challenged the psychological field to see mankind's nature united with its purpose to preserve life and to make it full of meaning and worth. In this argument, he demonstrated an understanding of man reliant upon the development of individual personality in order to achieve satisfaction and ultimate meaning.[101]

Aspects of both Whitehead's and Allport's understanding of human nature were picked up by Oates pertaining to the shared experience of the pilgrimage of selfhood. He saw Whitehead's theology of God and man leading to a clearer understanding of how man encounters God, via religion, and that this interaction contributed to man becoming a more focused self.[102] In addition to this, personhood is not ultimately defined through "any unchanging essence or being;" instead it is a "self-caused becoming."[103] Humans are self-willed and pursue their own subjective aims which result in final causality. Oates was in agreement with Whitehead concerning selfhood in that "the essential question of vocation and calling in the person's life" becomes the guiding compass by which he has his "being and becoming."[104] Equally, in Allport, Oates affirmed that the process of becoming is a lifetime continuation and not tied to any particular stage of development.[105]

---

98. Allport, *Personality*, 26–27.

99. Allport, *Becoming*, 10. Allport, like Whitehead claimed that individuality was a major concern of human personality. He stated, "Personality is a less finished product than a transitive process. While it has the same stable features, it is at the same time continually undergoing change. It is this course of change, of becoming, of individualization that is now our special concern" (Allport, *Becoming*, 19).

100. Allport, *Personality*, 26–27.

101. Oates, *Psychology of Religion*, 27. See also Allport, *Becoming*, 98.

102. Oates, *Christ and Selfhood*, 23. See also Oates, *People in Pain*, 120; Whitehead, *Religion in the Making*, 16.

103. "Alfred North Whitehead," in Geisler, *Baker Encyclopedia*, 777.

104. Oates, *Christ and Selfhood*, 242. Whitehead, *Modes of Thoughts*, 228. Interestingly, Ross noted that some have criticized Whitehead unfairly by categorizing him as anthropocentric due to his emphasis and wide use of experience, humanity, and consciousness. See Ross, *Perspectives in Whitehead's Metaphysic*, 107; Allport, *Becoming*, 23.

105. Oates, *What Psychology Says about Religion*, 56. See also Allport, *Becoming*, 94–95, and Allport, *Individual and His Religion*, 142.

The second stream of thought encountered in Oates's view of man is that of developmental psychology. As one of the leading figures in the fields of human development and psychology, Erik Erikson's theory of human growth influenced Oates's own anthropological perspective. Trained as a psychoanalyst in Vienna under the tutelage of Anna Freud, Erikson immigrated to the United States in the early 1930s where he spent the rest of his life and career. Erikson became best known for his work on the eight stages of growth and change in the human personality. While a student of Freud, his theory differed in the fact that he believed personality was not fixed at childhood, but actually developed throughout the entire life cycle.[106] Oates named Erikson as being one of the psychologists who inspired him in this area of anthropology. Specifically, Oates valued Erikson's contributions to pastors in that through a study of human growth and development, the value of "spiritual becoming" is also intrinsically highlighted and this helps pastors better understand persons in ministry to them.[107] In one of Oates's early works, instead of offering a scriptural defense, he preferred to use Erikson's terminologies and the language of developmental psychology to describe the innate desires of man.[108]

While not initially thought of in terms of developmental psychology, in many ways Horace Bushnell was the proverbial voice in the wilderness that predated two distinct fields: developmental psychology and the new theology of modernism.[109] The publication of Bushnell's seminal work, *Christian Nurture*, in 1846 served as a milestone for the intersection of modern psychology, religion, and education. Bushnell stressed the reality of religious *experience* in order to more adequately delineate Christian faith. While his thesis was initially rejected and vigorously opposed by some Christians, in

---

106. Headrick, "Erik Homberg Erikson," 253. See also Erikson, *Identity in the Life Cycle*, 98; Oates, "Clinical Pastoral Training's Contribution to Theology," 10, Wayne E. Oates Papers, box 6: folder 24.

107. Oates, *Christian Pastor* (1982), 23. See Erikson's influence in *On Becoming Children of God* and *Spiritual Dimensions of Religion*. The following section will provide more details regarding the application of Erikson's theory in Oates's anthropology. See Collins, "Pastoral Concern for Man," 72.

108. Oates, *Religious Dimensions of Personality*, 101. See also Niebuhr, *Self and the Dramas of History*, 95.

109. It is interesting to note that Bushnell's successors included a host of theologians which were the founders of the "new theology" which sought to integrate historic Christianity with secular theories concerning human development (e.g., Darwinian evolution, etc.). Many of these men, including Washington Gladden, William Newton Clarke, William Adams Brown, and Walter Rauschenbusch, were read by Oates while in college and seminary. See Smith, *Conceptions of Sin*, 164–206; Oates, *Religious Dimensions of Personality*, 281.

the end it "has been the guiding light of all modern religious education."[110] This controversial book was viewed as countering the Calvinistic ethic of the day, which emphasized original sin and the need for repentance and salvation, in favor for a "sane and balanced view of the situation" which encouraged Christian parents to simply model Christian practice and raise their children as if they had always been Christians. Christian belief, according to Bushnell and his followers, was to be couched in experience and behavior.[111] Reed and Prevost noted, "Bushnell's educational philosophy was saturated with experimental and naturalistic thought. He proposed that proper education could solve human problems, even religious problems and claimed that morally good parents nearly always produced morally good children."[112] Oates defended Bushnell as a misunderstood figure who did assume the inherent corruption of human nature, but "felt that it was wisest to undertake the remedy of corruption at once in the very earliest stages of human life."[113] Oates naturally connected with Bushnell due to their shared vocation as pastors; in fact, it was Bushnell's "profound psychological concern for developmental problems in Christian nurture" that influenced some of his own sermons on related matters.[114]

Rollo May started his academic career at Union Theological Seminary, but eventually abandoned ministerial preparation and transferred to nearby Columbia University. He also earned the first PhD in clinical psychology in the United States under the mentorship and direction of Paul Tillich.[115] In one of his earlier works, May identified man's capacity for objective self-understanding as a distinguishing mark of personality and self-concept. According to May, developmentalism, as the psychological and physiological

---

110. Miller, *Education for Christian Living*, 29–30. This book was viewed as being so radical that Bushnell had to rewrite and tone down large sections in order for it to be considered for subsequent publications.

111. Miller, *Education for Christian Living*, 29. Miller pointed out, "Horace Bushnell's *Christian Nurture*, is the most significant book of the nineteenth century in Christian education" (11).

112. Reed and Prevost, *History of Christian Education*, 320. See Smith, *Changing Conceptions*, 148–50.

113. Oates, *Psychology of Religion*, 71. For his part, Oates identified *Christian Nurture* as a "prophetic document in the field of development of personality in much the same way that the writings of Walter Rauschenbusch were prophetic in the field of social relationships." See also Oates, *What Psychology Says about Religion*, 53; Oates, *Revelation of God*, 78; Bushnell, "Kingdom of Heaven," 41–42.

114. Oates, *Revelation of God*, 9. See also William Powell Tuck, ed., *Pastoral Prophet: Sermons and Prayers of Wayne E. Oates*.

115. See Edgar, "Pastoral Identity," 44–45; Cooper, *Paul Tillich and Psychology*, 16; May, *Man's Search for Himself*, 92; May, *Art of Counseling*, 207–24.

maturation of humans through the various life-stages leading to the birth of the self-awareness, was the "continuum of differentiation from the 'mass' toward freedom as an individual."[116] This anthropocentric view of reality led to May's concept of *Einfühlen*, which reinforced an empathy-centered approach to counseling. Regarding this concept utilized in his counseling, Oates commented, "This orientation implied that a pastor seeks to enter into the 'internal frame of reference' of the person whom he is seeking to help. He tries to create a psychological climate of understanding and warmth."[117] For May, the implication of an empathetic relationship was that there was no room for the counselor's personality, thought, and presuppositions. These represented "egocentricity" in counseling, which May identified as the opposite of empathy.[118] The presence of an identifiable and healthy personal territory was also central to May's developmental theory. For him, when an individual does not have a clearly defined "territory," what May thought of as the "decisive self which stands apart from both [biological environment and interpersonal milieu] as one's own private intellect," he is likely to develop a psychological disorder.[119] This group of developmental psychologists uniquely reflected Oates's own eclecticism; however, the similarities shared by Tillich, Bushnell, and May articulate an understanding of man's nature in the form of stages designed biologically and socially to lead to personality growth and development.

The final stream of thought utilized by Oates deals with existential philosophy. While this philosophy has already been discussed, in part regarding its influence in Oates's phenomenological method, existentialism also influenced his anthropology and worked in tandem with the key tenants of process theology and developmental psychology in a dynamic understanding of man's nature.[120] Existential philosophy is essentially anthropocentric and touts teaching methods which "begin and end with the learner's situation."[121] Paul Tillich, once again, represents this stream of

---

116. May, *Man's Search from Himself*, 119. May's conclusions are not surprising as he studied the work of the early depth psychologists, and he studied with Adler personally. See also May, *Art of Counseling*, 7.

117. Oates, *New Dimensions of Pastoral Care*, 8–9. See also May, *Art of Counseling*, 145; Oates, "Significance of the Work of Sigmund Freud," 217.

118. May, *Art of Counseling*, 82. See chapter 3 on the discussion related to phenomenology in Oates's pastoral counseling method.

119. Oates, *When Religion Gets Sick*, 102. See also May, *Existence*, 64–65.

120. Oates, "Personality Theory and Pastoral Counseling," unpublished essay, 17, Wayne E. Oates Papers, box 10: folder 7. Oates stated, "This is true historically, in that some of the same thinkers who philosophically influenced the development of existentialism have also been patron saints of these psychological theorists about personality."

121. Wilson, "Existentialism," 274.

thought that influenced Oates's conception of man. Oates directly adopted Tillich's perspective particularly in terms of what it meant for man to be and become a person.[122] Tillich saw existential philosophy as a "natural ally of Christianity" in that it provided a framework by which man's state could be clearly identified. According to Tillich, "Existentialism gives an analysis of what it means to exist."[123] The ultimate concern for man is about his being and meaning. These two concerns make up for each individual the whole of reality and are the aim of existence.[124] Oates affirmed Tillich's framework as a helpful tool that helped the pastoral counselor to sort out the anxieties of men which are characteristics of personality that threatened depersonalization."[125]

Another existential thinker who influenced Oates's views on human nature was Martin Buber. Buber, a Jewish philosopher and sociologist, was most widely known for his concept of "I-Thou" in which he claimed that "in one's own life with nature, with other persons, and with spiritual existences, a person can become an 'I' only when the object with which one has to do is seen as a 'Thou' rather than as an impersonal 'it.' In and through such relational events there is a meeting with the absolute Other, the eternal Thou, God."[126] This theory made a wide-ranging impact within modern theological circles, being utilized by Emil Brunner, Karl Barth, Richard Niebuhr, and Paul Tillich.[127] In essence, man is man as he relates to others, himself and Buber's conception of God. He noted:

> Human life and humanity come into being in genuine meetings. There man learns not merely that he is limited by man, cast upon his own finitude . . . but his own relation to truth is heightened by the other's different relation to the same truth—different in

---

122. Bush, "Human Suffering," 72.

123. Tillich, *Systematic Theology*, 2:25. This state was either in estrangement from or reconciliation to his ground of being. This will be explored in the next chapter.

124. Tillich, *Systematic Theology*, 1:14. See also Tillich, *Systematic Theology*, vol. 3, where he states that inherent in the process of becoming there is self-integration, self-creation, and self-transcendence (32).

125. Oates, "Personality Theory and Pastoral Counseling," unpublished essay, 18, Wayne E. Oates Papers, box 10: folder 7.

126. Obitts, "Martin Buber," 191. Buber's conception of the "Eternal Thou" deemphasized God as a person and stressed the relational aspect. See Buber, *I-Thou*, 63; Cohen and Halverson, *Handbook of Christian Theology*, 175.

127. Cohen and Halverson, *Handbook of Christian Theology*, 173. Tillich went as a far as to call the *I-Thou* construct the "common good of the Protestant world."

accordance with his individuation and destined to take seed and grow differently.[128]

Buber's anthropology could be summarized by the phrase, "man in relation" in that only through interpersonal and intrapersonal relationships can the human personality accept other "selves" and thus become healthy and unified.[129] Oates viewed Buber's theology as "psychologically relevant" in portraying the "self in dialogue with itself and with God in a personal encounter."[130]

Often in his writings when Oates mentioned Buber, the work of Harry Stack Sullivan would be referenced due to their common themes shared by both theorists. In itself, Sullivan's work was a major source for Oates's anthropology.[131] Oates noted that many pastoral counselors in America turned to Sullivan's theory of personality due to the fact that it avoided "complicated gnostic nomenclature," which was characteristic of theorists including Carl Jung, and through its emphasis on the "more interpersonal interpretation of the ways in which human experience is organized in different modes of relationships in terms of a living self's power to communicate with his significant community."[132] Sullivan, who was a trained psychoanalyst, provided great understanding of personality development that gave "the religious educator and the theologian insight into the approximate meaning of theological truth to the growing person."[133] Sullivan was one of the leaders in American psychiatry who promoted a psychosocial approach to personality. Viewing humans as social organisms across the lifespan, psychiatry had to be focused upon how interpersonal relationships played a fundamental role in individuals becoming persons.[134] Sullivan's psychiatry

128. Buber, *Knowledge of Man*, 69.

129. Oates, *When Religion Gets Sick*, 102; Buber, *I-Thou*, 64–65; Oates, *Religious Dimensions of Personality*, 289–91.

130. Oates, *What Psychology Says about Religion*, 101; Buber, *Knowledge of Man*, 173. Oates pointed to New Testament passages (e.g., Matt 6:16; Gal 2:11; 2 Cor 5:12; Luke 9:51) that he believed depicted genuine religion in the terms used by Buber. See Oates, *Psychology of Religion*, 21.

131. Mays, "Contemporary Theology and Pastoral Care," 44; Oates, "Personality Theory and Pastoral Counseling," unpublished essay, 18, Wayne E. Oates Papers, box 10: folder 7. Oates noted Sullivan's influence in the third edition of *The Christian Pastor* (26), *On Becoming Children of God* (7), and *Christ and Selfhood* (21).

132. Oates, "Personality Theory and Pastoral Counseling," unpublished essay, 7, Wayne E. Oates Papers, box 10: folder 7.

133. Oates, *Psychology of Religion*, 81. See Sullivan, *Interpersonal Theory of Psychiatry*, 33–34. It is interesting to note that before Sullivan studied psychiatry, he was a hospitalized schizophrenic. This story has similarities to Boisen's psychiatric history. See Oates, *Minister's Own Mental Health*, 6–7.

134. Corsinsi and Marsalla, *Personality Theorists*, 342–43. See also Sullivan,

can be considered dynamic because he saw humanity as being in a constant state of flux. Also by tracing the development of humans, he could arrive at conclusions that explained the etiologies of mental disorders. Information regarding personality disorders could only be found in the active participation of the psychiatrist in relation to his client, not in static data.[135] The works of Tillich, Buber, and Sullivan added "reflective, philosophical richness" to Oates's own therapeutic approach. As a Christian pastor, he found that existential issues regarding being, death, rebirth, and general considerations of humanity were consistent themes in his ministry.[136]

Anthropological Implications

There are several anthropological considerations drawn from Oates's writings that best summarize the confluence of these influential streams of thought. Oates was committed to the fact that man and his world (concerning anthropological and metaphysical concerns) were constantly in a state of process. Utilizing a psychological frame of reference, man's nature and personhood was "at its core the emergence of a dynamic self in the unfolding pilgrimage of a meaningful existence in relation to the purpose of God for the individual in the universe."[137] He observed the tension between being (actual persons) and becoming (potential persons) that man experiences through his natural life. It is the responsibility of the pastoral counselor to pay attention to the struggles man encounters in seeking to become a unified personality in order to provide therapy necessary to see this goal achieved.[138]

Man, in particular, is in the process of becoming an individual, what he called a unified personality. Oates saw the role of Christian pastors,

---

Interpersonal Theory of Psychiatry. Sullivan's anthropology was steeped in evolutionary thoughts. He unequivocally affirmed, "Man is born an animal" (20).

135. Sullivan, *Interpersonal Theory of Psychiatry*, 13–15. Oates mentioned that both Sullivan and Buber had influence in pastoral counseling circles due to their role in transitioning counseling from a passive to a more active process. Oates's book *Protestant Pastoral Counseling* is based on Sullivan's general approach. See Oates, *Protestant Pastoral Counseling*, 65; Collins, "Pastoral Concern for Man," 71.

136. Oates, "Existential Psychotherapy," personal notes, 1, Wayne E. Oates Papers, box 30: folder 19. Oates identified Tillich and Buber specifically as philosophical grandparents of existential psychotherapy.

137. Oates, *Bible in Pastoral Care*, 65. See also Oates, *Protestant Pastoral Counseling*, 217; Durst, "Theological Dimensions," 42; Sherrill, *Struggle of the Soul*. In *Psychology of Religion*, Oates stated, "Anthropologically, reality is centered in the patient's perception of his own world and 'field of events'" (Oates, *Bible in Pastoral Care*, 37).

138. Oates, *Religious Dimensions*, 53–54. See also Murphy, *Personality*, 82.

counselors, and teachers as guiding young people in the "process of becoming a person in his [or her] own right before God."[139] One anthropological implication behind this developmental process in Oates's thought is that apart from existence, many people are in various stages of incompleteness. Regarding children, Oates viewed them as "incomplete" and suggested that parents were responsible, in part, for the co-creation of their child's personality and were called to lead them to completeness.[140] Needs were identified according to how they would contribute to the personality development of the individual and are defined accordingly.[141] Of all of the "needs" that young people required in order to achieve personhood, Oates capitalized on the need to establish healthy trusting relationships. This concept is borrowed by Oates from Erik Erikson's psychology in which the need to establish trust within the life cycle was essential for proper development. When individuals mistrust others it was inevitably due to the fact that their parents did not place trust in them. Failure on the parts of parents to establish these types of relationships may cause irreparable harm to their children and create barriers to them becoming full persons.[142] Utilizing John 1:12 as proof for this developmental understanding of man's nature, Oates defended his position that an infant required his parents' belief and trust in order to empower him to believe that he can grow and learn new things. If a parent deprives his child of the opportunity to "do something he thinks he can do for himself" the parent can spoil the entire process of becoming.[143] The spiritual implications of this were even starker than any psychosocial consequences. Oates defined faith as the "confidence in others, oneself and God."[144] By relating

---

139. Oates, *Becoming Children of God*, 23; Allport, *Pattern and Growth*, 112; Sherrill, *Struggle of the Soul*, 23–24.

140. Oates, *Christian Pastor* (1982), 32. See also Oates, *Becoming Children of God*, 35. In this work, Oates is more explicit when he states, "In the toddler the sense of selfhood is incomplete but well begun." He later categorizes human infants along with other "lower animals" (15). See also Sullivan, *Interpersonal Theory of Psychiatry*, 158; Allport, *Becoming*, 64.

141. Oates, *Religious Dimensions of Personality*, 255. Sullivan identified a need as anything element that would maintain equilibrium in the inner life of an individual and would counter unnecessary tension. Essentially, needs were defined and tied to pragmatic value as related to personality growth. See Sullivan, *Interpersonal Theory of Psychiatry*, 37.

142. Oates, *Christian Pastor* (1982), 237. See also Erikson, *Identity in the Life Cycle*, 56, 64–65.

143. Oates, *On Becoming Children of God*, 37. See also *Christian Pastor* (1982), 78. Here Oates relates this anthropological assumption to the relationship between the counselor and his client. When a client trusts his counselor's motives, they will confide in him. Oates calls this the relationship of trusted motive.

144. Oates, *On Becoming Children of God*, 16; Oates, *Psychology of Religion*, 275.

the concepts of trust and faith within a development and process-oriented framework, he essentially identified faith as a resource of personhood. If this is accurate, would it be possible for infants to be considered persons? Oates answered this conundrum by implying that infants could indeed inherit faith from their parents. He stated, "The infant child partakes of the deposit of faith vicariously through the commitment of father and mother to God in the context of the commitment of the larger family of God, the church."[145] While this conclusion has difficulty enough being defended on scriptural grounds, it should also be stated that even Oates's conceptualization of faith itself was depicted in self-serving and heuristic terms.[146]

People become defined personalities within a context of others who accept them as being the person they understand themselves to be.[147] Oates affirmed that self-knowledge was key to understanding man's nature. He stated, "Through self-searching, one gains new knowledge into himself. The experience continues as the person accepts himself in the light of the knowledge and insight he has received and finally realizes 'that God also accepts him as he is.'"[148] For Allport, the task of the psychology of religion was to increase man's self-awareness and self-knowledge which enabled man to firmly bind himself to the greater process of creation.[149] Spiritual maturity, understood by Oates as the conditioned or unified personality, could only be reached through personal experience and careful counseling.[150] Oates noted, "Being a self in our own right, having a sense of integrity and personhood in relationship to God, in turn, is the prelude to spiritual communion with God."[151]

ANTHROPOLOGICAL CRITIQUE FROM SCRIPTURE

In considering the various conclusions made by Oates regarding man's nature and identity, and how these are rooted in secular psychological and developmental theories, it is necessary to summarize and critique these views

---

145. Oates, *On Becoming Children of God*, 33.

146. Oates, *Psychology of Religion*, 277.

147. Oates, *On Becoming Children of God*, 35; Oates, *Protestant Pastoral Counseling*, 190; Collins, "Pastoral Concern for Man," 71; Oates, *What Psychology Says about Religion*, 101.

148. Oates, *Religious Dimensions of Personality*, 228; Mays, "Contemporary Theology and Pastoral Care," 31.

149. Allport, *Individual and His Religion*, 8–9, 98; Oates, *Psychology of Religion*, 54.

150. Oates, *Bible in Pastoral Care*, 58. See also Murphy, *Personality*, 579; Oates, *Revelation of God*, 53–54.

151. Oates, *Revelation of God*, 80.

from a biblical vantage point. This will be done in order to demonstrate to what extent Oates's understanding of man differed from biblical teaching.

The first conclusion to be summarized is Oates's conviction that the central task in life for man is self-clarification and personality development. The Bible, however, contains a conflicting message regarding man's central purpose. Ecclesiastes 12:13–14 states, "The conclusion, when all has been heard, is fear God and keep His commandments, because this applies to every person. For God will bring every act to judgment, everything which is hidden, whether it is good or evil."[152] Man is ultimately beholden to God, not himself, for his purpose in life. The Apostle Paul taught that even man's very body was not his own. He stated, "Or do you not know that your body is a temple of the Holy Spirit who is in you, whom you have from God, and that you are not your own?" (1 Cor 6:19). Paul expanded the implication of this teaching to include the fact that not only does God own man's physical body, but that it is incumbent upon man to present his body, soul, and mind as a "sacrifice, acceptable to God" (Rom 12:1–2).[153] As the Lord over all creation, man owes God his worship, devotion, and obedience (Exod 9:16; 1 Cor 10:31; Col 3:17). As opposed to Oates's conclusion that man's own purposes of self-development should be the central drive of his life, the Bible teaches that it is indeed God's purposes and plans that should be man's overarching concern (Eph 1:11–12).

The second implication of Oates's anthropology is related to the first in that it is inevitably up to man to navigate his own life and that the purposes, plans, and thoughts of God hold only peripheral value. A biblical anthropology, however, demonstrates that man is neither a self-sustaining nor independent creature, but one that is wholly reliant upon God for his life. In no place in Scripture is this made more evident than in the Psalms. Asaph wrote, "My flesh and my heart may fail, But God is the strength of my heart and my portion forever" (Ps 73:26). In speaking on how God is the author of man's prosperity and perseverance, Solomon added, "Unless the Lord builds the house, They labor in vain who build it; Unless the Lord guards the city, The watchman watches in vain" (Ps 127:1). As noted by Leslie Allen, within the wisdom of ancient Israel the "will of God was ignored at man's peril, not only in the realms of military activity (2 Sam 2:1), national internal policy (Hos 8:4) and foreign policy (Isa 30:1), but also in the ordinary life of the individual believer."[154] In general, all life, not just man's life, is sustained and preserved

---

152. See also Mic 6:8.

153. Bruce, *Letter of Paul to the Romans*, 212–13. See also Sanday and Hedlam, *Critical and Exegetical Commentary*, 352.

154. Allen, *Psalms 101–150*, 180.

by God's direction, design, and dominion (Jer 10:12; Matt 5:45; Col 1:17). It is folly to assume that man can self-direct any aspect of creation or his own life outside of God's presence, guidance, strength, and power (Ps 104:10–32; Matt 19:26; John 15:5; 1 Cor 8:6; Phil 4:13). Also, God's understanding is higher and greater than man's and this once again speaks to the impossibly of man being able to direct his own life successfully (Jas 1:5–8). Solomon urged, "Trust in the Lord with all of your heart and do not lean on your own understanding. In all of your ways acknowledge Him, and He will make your paths straight" (Prov 3:5–6). Regarding this command, Duane Garrett noted that to trust God with all of one's heart implies total commitment. He stated, "The prohibition against depending on one's own understanding and against intellectual pride (vv. 5b, 7a) implicitly reject a 'secular' search for wisdom and look back to the thesis of the book (1:7)."[155] The Hebrew word for trust (בָּטַח) in this verse denotes a reliance and confidence upon God instead of one's self. Human understanding is unreliable and cannot be depended upon.[156] In a commentary regarding the futility of idolatry, the prophet Jeremiah noted, "I know, O Lord, that a man's way is not in himself, nor is it in a man who walks to direct his steps" (Jer 10:23). As has been shown, the Bible contains numerous teachings that point to the fact that man is *not* in control.

Third, Oates seemed to demonstrate that a study of human behavior alone can bring about an adequate source of knowledge about man's nature and identity. Oates was convinced that a study of man vis-à-vis empirical methods was sufficient to discover and correct human problems. In addition to this, Oates viewed the Bible as not being sufficient to speak to the human problem.[157] As has been touched on previously, a biblical anthropology demonstrates that man has no knowledge outside of God, and any such study of man that does not begin and end with theology proper misses the mark. In Eccl 3:11, the Preacher (קֹהֶלֶת) speaks of the eternality and wisdom of God as it relates to humanity. He noted, "He [God] has made everything appropriate in its time. He has also set eternity in their [man's] heart, yet so that man will not find out the work which God has done from the beginning even to the end."[158] In short, in an effort to understand man, a close study of God should take preeminence. An empirical study of man cannot serve as the foundation of any anthropology, psychology, or theology in the very fact that man as a creature is limited and finite (Jas 4:14–15). Instead it is God who fully

---

155. Garrett, *Proverbs, Ecclesiastes, and Song of Songs*, 80–81. See also Prov 16:9; Ps 37:23–24.

156. Longman and Garland, *Proverbs–Isaiah*, 64–65.

157. Oates, *Bible in Pastoral Care*, 27.

158. Garrett, *Proverbs, Ecclesiastes, and Song of Songs*, 299.

searches and understands and knows the heart of man (Pss 94:11; 139:23). Surrounded by the sins of the people of Judah, Jeremiah proclaimed, "Thus says the Lord, 'Cursed is the man who trusts in mankind and makes flesh his strength, and whose heart turns away from the Lord'" (Jer 17:5). The Bible is clear that there is no confidence in the flesh; therefore, it can be argued from Scripture any study that centers on man to the exclusion of God as his ultimate Creator and Sustainer is ultimately fruitless.[159]

The final conclusion from Oates's understanding of human nature assumes that man is always in a process of becoming and is somehow never complete as he progresses through various developmental stages of physical maturation. Relying upon Erikson's psychosocial stages of development as an influencing framework, Oates equated man's subjective sense of self with his actual status as a created being.[160] The Bible, on the other hand, does not depict man as being in the process of creation, but fully formed even before physical birth. King David spoke to this important aspect of anthropology when he noted:

> For You formed my inward parts; You wove me in my mother's womb. I will give thanks to You, for I am fearfully and wonderfully made; wonderful are Your works, and my soul knows it very well. My frame was not hidden from You, When I was made in secret, and skillfully wrought in the depths of the earth; Your eyes have seen my unformed substance; and in Your book were all written the days that were ordained for me, when as yet there was not one of them. (Ps 139:13–16)

As expressed by the Hebrew scholar, Franz Delitzsch in his *Biblical Commentary on the Psalms*, the very life of man is "manifest to God even to the very root of his being and on every side" and a "miracle of God's omniscient and omnipresent omnipotence."[161] In another place in Scripture, the implication behind the fact that humans are created and formed complete while still in the womb is implied in the Old Testament law concerning personal injuries. If a man intentionally or accidently injured a woman who was pregnant, the man could lose his life if the unborn baby died (Exod 21:22–23).[162] Humans are not in a constant state of "becoming," but are in many respects complete, though sin-sick and marred, creations before a holy God.

---

159. Prov 1:9; 2:6; Job 28:28; Jer 10:14–15; 17:9; Ps 118:8–9; 146:3; Mic 7:5.
160. Oates, *Becoming Children of God*, 35.
161. Delitzsch, *Biblical Commentary on the Psalms*, 350.
162. Durham, *Exodus*, 323.

NEGLECTING THE TRUTH OF HUMAN NATURE

This chapter represents an effort to present Oates's comprehensive commitments regarding his view of human nature in order to expose its *unbiblical* foundations. While claiming theological orthodoxy and Christ-centered aims, Oates's theory of personhood is built upon a concept of selfhood interpreted through the lens of modern psychology which affirms the supremacy of man over God. Another faulty assumption, which has hampered biblical efforts of soul care within the church, is in Oates's clinical approach to counseling. The clinical and therapeutic lens places humans as both the gold-standard for what to strive toward and as the central reference-point in the counseling task overall. Modern psychology is built upon the unspoken rule that observation is objective and value free. In reality, these "sciences" of human motivation and behavior are laden with anti-biblical presuppositions. As a result, God's self-revelation within Scripture is relegated as a "supplementary" resource and necessarily viewed as an insufficient and unauthoritative resource in understanding the human condition. This chapter concluded by presenting three streams of thought which influenced Oates's understanding of man's dynamic and evolving nature. Utilized as they were by Oates, these influences contributed to the overarching belief that human nature is fundamentally tied to the *process* of becoming a unified whole and is best defined as being man centered, experience driven, and developmentally focused. As noted, even a brief survey of Scripture seriously challenges the validity and veracity of Oates's anthropological claims.

5

Disordered Personality

Identifying Threats to Healthy Selfhood

IN THE PREVIOUS CHAPTER, I presented the first major component of Wayne Oates's anthropology. The second component of his anthropology necessarily proceeds from the first. Regarding man's nature as in a constant state of development, beginning as a loosely defined identity and leading to a unified and centered personality, Oates's approach to pastoral counseling led him to consider the psychological and spiritual problems that could hinder man from reaching his intended goals. Throughout his writings, Oates identified certain threats which could potentially serve as roadblocks in keeping individuals from proper spiritual growth, development, and maturation. In this chapter, the author will outline these problems within the context of the literature and draw connections to psychological influences while also providing an accounting of Oates's commitments to the scriptural account.

USES AND MISUSES OF RELIGION

The concept of religion is a common and important theme found throughout Oates's writings. In one of his earlier books, *Religious Factors in Mental Illness*, he described the value religion had to those considered mentally ill in that it provided an interpretive framework to explain what "goes on within him and between him and his spiritual community."¹ The utilitarian view of religious experience as a grid for interpreting psychologically afflicted persons preceded Oates in the work of one of his mentors, Anton Boisen. Over the course of his life, Boisen had five psychotic episodes. After his most severe episode, which led to his hospitalization, negative experiences in the psychiatric ward led him to a new perspective concerning mental illness. For Boisen, mental illness, not therapy, provided a context through which a person could find healing and wholeness. He equated mental illness "in some respects to religious experience, an experience of radical upheaval and spiritual healing."² The only difference between a psychotic episode and a religious experience lay in the outcome.

Through his own experience as a patient and his many years working closely with mental patients, Boisen concluded that their "inner world had come crashing down" and that part of this internal conflict was due to misguided religious understandings or difficulties.³ For those within the clinical pastoral education movement, including Boisen and Oates, the framework of religious experience was an analytical tool in the work of finding the "sense hidden in the nonsense of the [psychiatric] patient."⁴ This heuristic view of religion was also espoused by modern pastoral theologians such as William Adams Brown who saw that in Christianity "no other religion meets so completely and in so satisfying a way the permanent needs of mankind."⁵

Of course, the very terms *religion* and *religious experience* were recognized by Oates as ambiguous and even confusing concepts that required clarity in order to be useful.⁶ Oates defined religion as "an individual's discovery of eternal and satisfying relatedness in his universal field of interpersonal relationships, whereby he lives with courage and sensitivity without morbid defensiveness and loss of feeling."⁷ Allport's concept of religion offers a clearer context for comprehending the thrust of Oates's definition. For Allport, religion was personal in that it was all about man binding himself to the Creator in an attempt to further develop his own sense of self and

---

1. Oates, *Religious Factors in Mental Illness*, vii.
2. Aden and Ellens, *Turning Points in Pastoral Care*, 11–12. See also Holifield, *History of Pastoral Care*, 231–49; and Thornton, *Professional Education for Ministry*, 55–71.
3. Boisen, *Exploration of the Inner World*, 5.
4. Oates, *Religious Factors in Mental Illness*, 34.
5. Brown, *Modern Theology*, 23.
6. Oates, *When Religion Gets Sick*, 16.
7. Oates, *Religious Factors in Mental Illness*, 114.

personality.[8] This person-centered leaning is clearly echoed in Oates's own definition. Oates offered another definition of religion in his book *Religious Care of the Psychiatric Patient*. In this context religion meant "the patient's need for freedom from bondage to fear, hate, and despair. The patient's *need* for love, forgiveness, and hope . . . the patient's *need* for a sense of serenity in the face of change and the process of aging . . . the patient's *need* for a personally chosen set of ethical standards."[9] Oates's person-centered and needs-oriented definition was borrowed from Allport. Allport is not the only psychologist referred to by Oates regarding his notion of religion. The psychology of religion long held to a conception of religion that was pragmatic, functional, and utilitarian. William James defined religion as the "feelings, acts and experiences of individual men in their solitude, so far as they apprehend themselves to stand in relation to whatever they may consider divine."[10] Even earlier than James, Leuba offered an even more explicitly man-centered definition of religion as "that part of human experience in which man feels himself in relation with powers of psychic nature, usually personal powers, and makes use of them."[11]

Defined in pragmatic terms, religion could be construed as either helpful or harmful depending on is interpretation and how it was utilized.[12] Oates noted that when the concept of religion was used positively in the Bible it referred to the open, honest, and personal experiences of a person's inner life and character before God.[13] This idea of religion was affirmed by Oates so much so that he characterized it in terms of redemption. An individual's relatedness to his faith community and to God was the decisive

---

8. Allport, *Individual and His Religion*, 142; Oates, *Religious Factors in Mental Illness*, 114. Similarly, Freud taught that the purpose of religion is for the development of the self-concept. See Oates, *Christ and Selfhood*, 94.

9. Oates, *Religious Care*, 16, emphasis added. See also Bush, "Human Suffering," 179; Clarke, *Outline of Christian Theology*, 4. Notice the common themes of experience, personal affections, and self-will in the definitions given.

10. James, *Varieties of Religious Experience*, 41. See also Stolz, *Psychology of Religious Living*, 30. Stolz's book was widely used in colleges and seminaries in the early 1930s. Binkley used this as his classroom text at Wake Forest College between the years of 1938 and 1944. During this period, Oates took this class with Binkley and was exposed to Leuba's and James's ideas about religion.

11. Leuba, *Psychological Study of Religion*, 52. See also Coe, *Psychology of Religion*, 63.

12. Oates, *Religious Factors in Mental Illness*, 2–3; see also Tillich, "Communicating the Gospel," 3–10.

13. Oates, *Psychology of Religion*, 19. Oates also refers to this as a "maskless" experience. The use of this description harkens back to the definition of personality given by many theorists and even Oates himself.

factor that distinguished between someone who was spiritually and psychologically healthy and someone who could be considered diseased.[14]

While religion could indeed be depicted as increasing empathetic understanding and community, it could also be utilized to alienate and estrange.[15] Religion that was "sick" could be the cause of mental illness and psychological distress when it was used as a punitive tool. Oates even stated that religion could develop into an emotional disorder in cases where it tied a bereaved or grieving person too much to the past. In describing this, Oates noted:

> Therefore, the pastoral care and counseling, the emotional therapy of the bereaved, is a vital part of both preventing and treating the mentally ill . . . religion becomes sick when it is the vehicle for maintaining a constricted territory for a growing person. The need for one's own place in life is a matter of life and breath. To be denied it in the name of religion adds insult to injury in the wounding of the mental stability of a person.[16]

Sick religion hinders the basic functions of life, what Oates identifies as elements leading to individual growth and development in one's personality. The person consequently becomes malfunctioned. The sick elements of religion referred to "specific situations in which particular people suffer major failures of functioning in the conduct of their lives because of religious preoccupations and stumbling blocks."[17] An instance of such stumbling blocks was provided by Oates regarding the parent-child relationship. Oates suggested that religion could be harmful and hinder growth and mental health if one's parents had been overly strict in their religious observance. The implication behind any attempt by parents to transmit, or "project," their religious beliefs onto their children, could potentially cause mental instability or illness.[18] In general, Oates saw the use of religion as a tool of dominance, power, manipulation, legalism, or restriction which threatened or outright

---

14. Oates, *Religious Factors in Mental Illness*, 120.

15. Oates, *Psychology of Religion*, 41.

16. Oates, *Psychology of Religion*, 268–69. Oates explores the relationship between pathology and religion at length in *Religious Factors in Mental Illness* and *When Religion Gets Sick*.

17. Oates, *When Religion Gets Sick*, 20–21. It is important to note that Oates does not use the word "false" to describe religion that is sick. A survey of the literature also showed a lack of a sin-concept in this discussion.

18. Oates, *Religious Factors in Mental Illness*, 18; Oates, *Behind the Masks*, 88. Concerning developmentalism, Rollo May defined it as the psychological and physiological maturity of a human through the lifespan leading to the birth of self. It is the "continuum of differentiation from the 'mass' toward freedom as an individual" (May, *Man's Search for Himself*, 119).

denied a person's self-image, or private self, as a misuse that served as a problem in the overall aim of becoming an organized personality.[19]

THREATS TO SELFHOOD

While an unhealthy view of religion and religious experience could certainly hinder growth and development, Oates also identified existential threats that could lead to despair, deconstruction of one's self-concept, and personality disorder. Oates identified human suffering as a potential catalyst for bringing these threats to fruition. According to him, suffering was a broad concept and included the "intrusion of any affliction confronting humanity, both individually and corporately, which interferes with physical, emotional, and spiritual health of people."[20] Suffering was a problem that hindered personal growth and kept people from achieving "wholeness" and could cause "emotional starvation" in which the self-image was threatened. This could especially be seen in the life of vulnerable individuals, including children.[21] This type of suffering involved conflict and uprooted people from sources of stability in their lives. This ultimately served to interrupt the end goal of maintaining equilibrium in life. As in the previous section, sick religion itself could be a contributing factor to suffering.[22] In this understanding of suffering, Oates's anthropocentrism is demonstrated in man becoming a victim to his problems, both internal and external. Consequently, his personal goals are elevated, and inherent sin, guilt, and responsibility are rarely mentioned.[23]

For Oates, the problems of man could be clarified, understood, and interpreted best through a modern psychological lens. Instead of primarily portraying man as a transgressor of God's law, he was depicted as a destructive self and victim to "separation, estrangement, alienation, bondage, and

---

19. Oates, *When Religion Gets Sick*, 120.
20. Oates, *Where to Go for Help*, 11; see also Bush, "Human Suffering," 55.
21. Bush, "Human Suffering," 42–44. See Oates, *Revelation of God*, 69.
22. Oates, *Religious Factors in Mental Illness*, 135. Oates did believe that suffering could contribute to growth and maturity and not always hinder it. Personality development required the soul to struggle, overcome fear, and at times risk suffering. See Oates, *On Becoming Children of God*, 18; Bush, "Human Suffering," 53; Sherrill, *Struggle of the Soul*, 23–24.
23. Oates, *Christ and Selfhood*, 26. See also Bush, "Human Suffering," 53; Tillich, *Courage to Be* (nonbeing); Oates, *Religious Dimensions of Personality*, 249. Regarding suffering, Bush observed that Oates never provided a definitive reason behind human suffering in general, and instead only focused on the effects of suffering. A review of the literature centered on this topic reveals that sin was rarely explicitly mentioned as a source of suffering.

despair."[24] While Oates did mention sin in his writings, he typically avoided any emphasis on man's inherent sinfulness and guilt, preferring instead the therapeutic emphasis of the pastor's role, the need for empathetic approaches to people's past history of sin, and looking toward building redemptive communities for the purpose of acceptance. Man's struggle with sin was depicted as an inner struggle for "integration and self-consistency." For the most part, Oates viewed the counselee's struggle with a "desperation for acceptance, forgiveness, personal worthiness, and self-esteem" as the inherent problem that needed to be addressed in counseling.[25]

Alienation

One of the hindrances to man's personality development identified by Oates was the threat of alienation. According to Collins, Oates's affirmation of man as sinful was expressed in terms of his disunity and alienation from his Creator.[26] Curtis also identified alienation as a major dilemma faced by men within Oates's anthropological structure. However, where traditional theology would clearly identify sin as man's central problem, Curtis noted that Oates most often did not utilize this concept as much as he did psychological concepts.[27] In his natural state, man found himself as an alienated identity with no relationship to God, thus having no connection to the "Ground of Being." In this state, man is constantly threatened with "condemnation, meaninglessness, and death."[28] In *The Presence of God in Pastoral Counseling*, Oates identified the problem that must be addressed as the need people have for a community of faith and a sense of belonging. In order to move away from alienation, an identity must be discovered that "enables them who are not a people to become the people of God."[29] Notably, not once in this volume does Oates mention sin and its role in his anthropological paradigm. He concluded, "God's attitude toward the lost is that of separation and alienation, but not one of rejection and hostility."[30] In not one instance

---

24. Oates, *Christ and Selfhood*, 26.

25. Oates, *Presence of God in Pastoral Counseling*, 71.

26. Collins, "Pastoral Concern for Man," 28.

27. Curtis, "Role of Religion," 96. See also Tillich, *Systematic Theology*, 2:49; Oates, *Religious Dimensions of Personality*, 83.

28. Oates, *Christ and Selfhood*, 37. Tillich was a major influence on Oates's conception of anthropology as it relates to hamartiology and soteriology. See Cooper, *Paul Tillich and Psychology*, 18.

29. Oates, *Presence of God of Pastoral Counseling*, 18.

30. Oates, *Christ and Selfhood*, 28. See also Collins, "Pastoral Concern for Man," 48.

in this entire volume did Oates write of the lost sinner as being an enemy of God or in rebellion against him.[31]

Estrangement

Another threat to man becoming an organized personality was demonstrated not only in man's alienation from God, but in his estrangement from a community of other selves. When characterizing the nature of evil, Boisen described it as the "sense of isolation or estrangement" that accompanied inner conflict and mental stress.[32] According to Tillich, estrangement also characterized the natural state of man's existence, and while it was not a biblical term, he argued that it did retain biblical overtures regarding man's predicament.[33] May used the term *loneliness* to describe this particular threat in which one's positive sense of self-esteem and worth was attacked when individuals found themselves alone. He noted, "The more basic reason [for loneliness] is that the human being gets his original experiences of being a self out of his relatedness to other persons, and when he is alone, without other persons, he is afraid he will lose this experience of being a self."[34] Estrangement, thus, was considered an ontological threat to personality in which self-acceptance was not possible unless one was accepted in person-to-person relationships.[35] Oates depicted the struggle of self-preservation as being a crux concern to pastoral counseling. In his attempt to stay connected to meaningful communities and affirm the presence of threats such as estrangement, man may continue in his process of becoming.[36]

Tillich noted, "Emptiness and loss of meaning are . . . implied in man's finitude and actualized by man's estrangement."[37] Oates believed that a vital aspect in the process of becoming was meaning. If man did not have meaning, he would be directionless and fail to grow and mature. Men must accept

---

31. Rom 5:10; Col 1:21; Jas 4:4.

32. Boisen, *Exploration of the Inner World*, 268.

33. Tillich, *Systematic Theology*, 2:44–45; Tillich, *Courage to Be*, xxi. Cooper noted that Tillich used this term to coincide with the theological concept of total depravity and he believed that existentialism and psychotherapy contributed to theology in finding a remedy for this problem. See Cooper, *Paul Tillich and Psychology*, 65.

34. May, *Man's Search for Meaning*, 28.

35. Oates, *Behind the Masks*, 29; Oates, *When Religion Gets Sick*, 102; Rogers, *On Becoming a Person*, 18, 21; Buber, *Knowledge of Man*, 69.

36. Oates, *Religious Dimensions of Personality*, 69. See also Tillich, *Courage to Be*, 164.

37. Tillich, *Courage to Be*, 48. See also Oates, *Psychology of Religion*, 54; Bush, "Human Suffering," 10.

responsibility and avoid "boredom" which could halt any forward motion on their way to developing as a unified personality. As an existential crisis, meaninglessness can have symptoms with examples including everything from adultery and alcoholism to mental disorders and depression.[38] Curtis noted, "For Oates, man is a time-oriented creature which means that his dilemma spans the spectrum of past, present, and future. The dilemma of his past is sin and guilt over alienation from God; the dilemma of the present is absence of meaning in the face of impersonal social roles; the dilemma of the future is the unalterable reality of death."[39] As part of the helping team the pastoral counselor, according to Oates, was tasked with saving people from the fate of meaninglessness brought on by the dual threats of alienation and estrangement.[40] When the pastor accepts the presence of God as the center of the counseling relationship, the threat of meaninglessness, condemnation, and death are gone away with.[41] Throughout his works, Oates suggested that due to the estrangement of the sinner from himself and others and alienation of man from his ground of being in God, self-acceptance and a sense of personhood can be lost. The result is a psychological anxiety over sin (i.e., guilt) leading to despair and disorder.[42]

ANXIETY AND PERSONALITY DISORDER

Resulting from the problems listed above, man's personality could risk becoming jeopardized and disordered. In fact, much of what Oates viewed as personality disorders, mental illnesses, and psychological neuroses resulted from these problems. May identified the root of humanity's malady as the loss of self-dignity and a sense of personal worth.[43] Oates, in unity with the psychologists whose influence is recognized in his work, quantified the malady that resulted from sick religion and threats to selfhood as anxiety. He defined anxiety as a "reaction of tension to threats to selfhood of an individual or to the groups to which he belongs and for which he feels

---

38. Oates, *Religious Dimensions of Personality*, 251. See also Hiltner, *Self-Understanding*.

39. Curtis, "Role of Religion," 120. See Oates, *Religious Dimensions of Personality*, 301; Oates, *Anxiety in Christian Experience*, 120.

40. Oates, *Bible in Pastoral Care*, 62.

41. Oates, *Presence of God in Pastoral Counseling*, 32. Oates mentions that the presence of God is found in "living conversations with persons."

42. Oates, *Anxiety in Christian Experience*, 68. See also Sullivan, *Interpersonal Theory of Psychiatry*, 42; May, *Man's Search for Himself*, 14.

43. May, *Man's Search for Himself*, 55.

responsible."[44] For Oates, this anxiety was existential in that it centered on the subjective experiences of individuals. Anxiety corresponded with the basic tenets of Christianity in that both were "vital, alive, and never static and their process is never written on tablets of stone, but always on tablets of human hearts."[45] This understanding revealed a focus of self-reliance in Oates's thinking concerning the ultimate goal of defeating threats to self.[46]

Oates shaped his understanding of anxiety from psychologists who have influenced other facets of this anthropology. May conceptualized anxiety as the human right to protect what he values against those things which would threaten his existence. He equates selfhood, personal freedom, self-esteem, dignity, and mental health with existence. He stated, "Anxiety, like a torpedo, strikes underneath at the deepest level . . . and it is on this level that we experience ourselves as persons, as subjects who can act in a world of objects. Thus anxiety in greater or lesser degrees tends to destroy our consciousness of ourselves."[47] He also referenced the work of James in his formulation of anxiety. James noted that the main source of anxiety for man was the threat of separation which removed man from relationships that nourished one's self-concept.[48]

Understanding of Sin

From a wide cross-section study of his writings, Oates often referred to sin in ambiguous terms. This is not to say that Oates outright ignored or rejected the concept of sin; however, as Collins noted, there was not "much talk about the origin of sin. Oates is more concerned with sin as it manifests itself in life."[49] When he did refer to sin, most often it was described in terms

---

44. Oates, *Anxiety in Christian Experience*, 9. Like suffering, anxiety could be for the benefit or detriment of the individual. This result depended on how the individual reacted and responded to the threats against selfhood. In this Oates unequivocally advocated for Tillich's book *Courage to Be*, which he believed could not be undervalued in the discussion of anxiety as a potential source of courage (Oates, *Anxiety in Christian Experience*, 132).

45. Oates, *Anxiety in Christian Experience*, 10. See Sherrill, *Struggle of the Soul* and Paul Tillich, *Shaking the Foundations*, 178.

46. Oates, *Behind the Masks*, 18. See also Fromm, *Man for Himself*, 65–66; Curtis noted in his dissertation that while Oates was a Christian and Fromm was an atheistic humanist, there were several points of comparison between these two regarding their anthropology. See Curtis, "Role of Religion," 296–97.

47. May, *Man's Search for Himself*, 43–44, 160.

48. Oates, *Christ and Selfhood*, 112; Oates, *Religious Factors in Mental Illness*, 196; see James, *Varieties of Religious Experience*, 199.

49. Collins, "Pastoral Concern for Man," 40. See also Oates, *Psychology of Religion*,

borrowed from psychological theorists. For Oates, sin had been described as an "interpersonal maladjustment."[50] Also, it was the struggle of the soul and even resulted in self-elevation.[51]

In providing a more specific definition of sin, Oates related this theological concept within a psychological framework for anxiety. He defined sin as "that guilt for which one must needs accept personal responsibility. . . . At the risk of total destruction, the sinner bears his heart before God and enters the forgiveness which reveals to him that he is acceptable to God *though unacceptable even to himself.* This is the anxiety of sin."[52] In this, anxiety acted as a barometer which measured the actual motives of the sinner.[53] In an address given to the Medical College of Virginia in 1978, Oates presented an unpublished essay entitled "The Concept of Sin and Forgiveness in Patient Care," in which he sought to interpret these biblical concepts in light of modern psychological terms of health and illness.[54] After explicating seven different facets of sin, all of which were undergirded by various psychological consequences, Oates summarized his understanding of sin:

> All of this points to the most common meaning—simply missing the mark of God's intention for us as human beings. Bad aim. Low shot. Cheap shot. Poor shot. Missing the mark. We miss the mark of the intention of God in creation and therefore are alienated from ourselves and others as well as God. We miss the mark of our own sense of calling and destiny.[55]

Through the subtle influences of a psychological perspective, Oates suggested that the ultimate intention God had for humanity was for them to continue in the struggle to be human, to protect themselves from those

---

203; Oates, *Religious Factors in Mental Illness*, 95.

50. Collins, "Pastoral Concern for Man," 41. See Oates, *Religious Dimensions of Personality*, 21; Sullivan, *Interpersonal Theory of Psychiatry*, 44; Thelan, *Man as a Sinner*, 32.

51. Oates, *Christian Pastor* (1982), 25. Sherrill, *Struggle of the Soul*; Niebuhr, *Nature and Destiny*, 1:250–51. Thomas Oden made connections between Oates's and Rogers's anthropologies regarding the "psychological paradigm of the fall. See Oden, *Kerygma and Counseling*, 89–93; Rogers, *On Becoming a Person*, 522.

52. Oates, *Anxiety in Christian Experience*, 64. The capacity to sin, according to Oates, "represents a relatively high state of moral development and the anxiety of sin is a normal type of anxiety."

53. Oates, *Anxiety in Christian Experience*, 67.

54. Oates, "Concept of Sin and Forgiveness in Patient Care," 1, Wayne E. Oates Papers, box 33: folder 28. At this point in his career, Oates had already left Southern Seminary and had taken a post as the Professor of Psychiatry and Behavioral Sciences at The University of Louisville.

55. Oates, "Concept of Sin and Forgiveness," 11–12.

threats that would essentially de-humanize them. It is through a "distinctively human existence" that God is brought the most glory.[56] Interestingly, Oates did not provide biblical support for his definition of sin, nor did he define sin as missing the mark as it relates to rebellion against a holy and righteous God.[57] Oates's concept of sin was in line with other definitions by his mentors within the modern pastoral counseling tradition. Hiltner defined sin as "that part of man's alienation from God (and from his own true being) for which he himself is responsible."[58] Boisen saw the biblical definition of sin as outmoded and unacceptable for use in clinical settings. His redefinition encapsulated a new meaning within an anthropocentric context as the "rupture of one's supreme loyalties as represented in the idea of God."[59] Going back even further, to the beginnings of the psychology of religion movement, James Leuba viewed sin not as a fall, but as a "rise to a higher mental life involving a clearer consciousness of right and wrong—a consciousness already dimly present in the higher animals."[60]

For Oates, the ultimate consequence of leaving God out of one's life led to "total personality disintegration and disorder."[61] Personality disorders were merely shadows and "semblances of sanity," and authentic living. For him, pastoral counselors were to be concerned with "humanely, gently, but persistently unmasking these ways of life. Such persons have a pseudo self overlaying the image of God in them. Our prayer in relation to each of these masking life-styles is that we may enable the real person to emerge."[62]

---

56. Oates, "Concept of Sin and Forgiveness," 12. See also Curtis, "Role of Religion," 102.

57. Hab 1:13; 1 John 1:5; 3:5; Deut 25:16; 32:4; Josh 24:19; Isa 6:3; 53:9; Ps 139:1–4; Heb 4:13.

58. Hiltner, *Preface to Pastoral Theology*, 94. This work served as a cornerstone text in the field and was appreciated and utilized by Oates. Toward the end of the work, Hiltner made special mention of the work of Carl Rogers and affirmed his nondirective and client-centered approach.

59. Boisen, *Exploration of the Inner World*, 209.

60. Leuba, *Reformation in the Churches*, 96. Leuba saw Christ's atoning sacrifice as superfluous and total depravity as a myth. Oates did not seem to go as far as Leuba in his conclusions; however, he did regularly approve of psychological definitions of conversion, which de-emphasized these former affirmations. See also Oates, *Religious Dimensions of Personality*, 108; Oates, *Religious Factors in Mental Illness*, 196; James, *Varieties of the Religious Experience*, 189.

61. Oates, *Bible in Pastoral Care*, 37; *Behind the Masks*, 22.

62. Oates, *Behind the Masks*, 14. See also Hervey Cleckley, *Mask of Sanity*. Oates also mentions that the Diagnostic and Statistical Manual III (DSM-III) had been a definitive guide for his work and "indispensable" to him in explicating man's problems.

ANTHROPOLOGICAL CRITIQUE FROM SCRIPTURE

Anthropological conclusions made by Oates regarding the ontological and existential problems faced by mankind are formed and articulated primarily from a modern psychological perspective which greatly differed from biblical teaching. Oates's anthropological commitments related to the doctrine of sin, in many cases, react against clear hamartiological teachings found within Scripture.

The first conclusion made by Oates in attempting to negotiate human problems is that religion primarily fills a utilitarian need. Throughout a majority of his writings, Oates regarded religion as potentially troublesome and as the source of conflict in many people's lives. However, according to Scripture, true religion is not only a blessing, but it is actually a normal outward expression of all that God has taught and provided for mankind. James 1:23–25 outlines what true religion looks like. At its core, its basic requirement is that one "looks intently at the perfect law, the law of liberty" and obeys it (Gal 2:20; Matt 16:24; 8:34). James goes on to say that true and pure religion is evidenced in one's service to others in the name of Jesus Christ and in maintaining a position of personal holiness that requires self-denial (Jas 1:27).[63] In a similar vein, the Old Testament speaks to the requirement for believers to both understand and know the commands and expectations of God, and at the same time walk in obedience to these commands (Mic 6:8). In both of these instances, there is no room for self-centeredness or encouragement to drive toward meeting one's own felt and unmet needs. As believers are built up in the faith, the Christian religion is depicted as being opposed to the "philosophy and empty deception" of the world which is based on the "tradition of men" instead of on the confession, identity, and substitutionary atonement of Jesus Christ (Col 2:8–9). In capitalizing on the notion that organized religion has some helpful purposes, Oates ignores the importance of this key doctrine.

The second conclusion reached by Oates in his attempt to outline the spiritual ailments of man is the understanding that suffering is almost exclusively a hindrance to proper growth, development, and formation of an independent personality. Interestingly, there are several instances where the Bible contains teaching about the fruitful nature and purpose of suffering. First, the purpose of God for his children who suffer is that they have the opportunity to develop Christ-honoring character and hope in the face of their trials (Rom 5:6–12; 12:-13; 8:28–29; Jas 1:2–8. 12). Suffering, as an act of refining, can also be used by God to teach and instruct. Proverbs

---

63. Martin, *James*, 52–53.

17:3 states, "The refining pot is for silver and the furnace for gold, but the Lord tests hearts."[64] In the New Testament, the Apostle Paul uses suffering to encourage and give hope to those who were living in difficulty (Acts 14:22).

Third, Oates came to the conclusion that problems in the life of man culminated in the loss of dignity, personal esteem, and self-worth, thus revealing these as key characteristics and objectives to be pursued and obtained in his anthropology. The Bible, however, presents a stark contrast to this observation. The consequence of sin leads to more than existential alienation or psychological detachment, but to spiritual death itself (Rom 3:23; 6:23–24; Jas 1:15). Regarding the implication of spiritual death, the prophet Isaiah noted, "But your iniquities have made a separation between you and your God, and your sins have hidden His face from you so that He does not hear" (Isa 59:2). In speaking of the results of sin, no word more clearly contrasts with Oates's conclusion than the words of Jesus himself. He noted that "everyone who commits sin is a slave to sin" and that only through commitment to him in trust and faith would one become truly free (John 8:34–36).

The final point that can be summarized from Oates's anthropology concerning the problems of man is his characterization of sin as a personal and psychological maladjustment instead of defining it as a state of rebellion before God leading to disobedience, evil, and death (Jas 3:16–17). Anxiety, as the disordered way of relating to persons, oneself, and God, functionally displaces the biblical understanding of sin within Oates's anthropology. Instead of man dealing with the consequences of sin against God and living under that judgment, discipline, or condemnation, Oates replaced sin with existential anxiety and repackaged spiritual consequences with psychological concepts. He stated, "The definable personality disorders bear psychological markers of the person's lack of insight, lack of foresight, and unwillingness to appoint or ordain any other person as his or her teacher."[65]

While Oates refrained from capitalizing on both the personal sinfulness and corporate guilt of man, the Bible contains clear teachings that highlight sin as *the* problem of man that must be addressed. The heart of man is wicked and is compromised in sin (Jer 17:5–9; Pro 4:23). In fact, the Bible teaches that sin is so pervasive within the human condition that anyone claiming not to have sin is deceptive and untruthful (Luke 6:43–45; Rom 1:28; 3:23–24; 5:12; Jas 1:14–15; 1 John 1:8; 3:4; 5:17). In the Apocalypse of John, the apostle noted that those who engage in wicked deeds in their sin are inheritors of "the lake of fire that burns with fire and brimstone, which is

---

64. Ps 66:10–12.
65. Oates, *Behind the Masks*, 125–26.

the second death" (Rev 21:8). Thus, those who are yet to be transformed by the power of Christ's blood are considered enemies of God (Rom 5:10; Jas 4:4; Phil 3:18; 1 John 4:3).

MISSING THE MARK OF MAN'S PROBLEMS

There are several unfortunate casualties in Oates's view of the problems that people face. As has been noted in this chapter, his thinking centered on "sick" religion as being the major contribution to personality development. While a "healthy" understanding of religion is characterized as one in which the self is supported, encouraged, and belongs, and contributes positively to personality development, sick religion presented a legalistic, restrictive perspective which only hinders growth. This use of religion, adopted from many who would not even consider themselves religious, much less Christian, not only takes the focus away from the egregious reality of sin and its consequences, but it only serves to further misconceptions of what good, faithful, and true religion looks like. Second, Oates's views of threats to selfhood, including alienation and estrangement, did reference a relationship with God; however, these derivatives of psychological theory have little to do with God. Instead they focus on fostering our sense of security, self-esteem, and self-worth. These are indeed problems and threats, but not in the way that they are depicted by Oates. The very pursuits are actually the very things that draw our naturally self-worshipping hearts away from our sovereign Lord. The end goal of personality growth is of such importance that even the biblical concept of sin, as an affront to a righteous God, is itself recast in a therapeutic light. Unfortunately, the result of this therapeutic approach to the problems we face as human beings focuses on how to avoid inconveniences in order to foster a sense of self-centeredness.

6

Reorganized Personality

Utilizing Tools to Achieve Self-Acceptance

THE FIRST TWO COMPONENTS of Oates's anthropology which relate to the nature of man and the ailments that create barriers to man's personality growth and development naturally lead into the final component dealing with the solutions to such problems. In essence, this aspect of Oates's anthropology runs parallel to the larger framework and purpose of Oates's pastoral counseling theory and method as a whole. Oates noted that the counseling task had as its aim the facilitation of personality development and as offering "help to persons to modify life patterns with which they have become increasingly unhappy, and to provide comradeship and wisdom for persons facing inevitable losses and disappointments in life."[1]

Oates seemed to position problem-solving as the very center of the counseling task. Claiming psychological insights as an aid to understanding the problems of man, Oates's solution to these problems was approached in like manner. He noted, "The needs of anxious persons focus the message of Biblical [sic] and psychological truth, on the one hand, with the theory and practice of pastoral counseling, on the other hand, in what may be called a 'bifocal' view of what Christian experience in fact and process really is."[2] In

---

1. Oates, *Pastoral Counseling*, 9.

2. Oates, *Anxiety in Christian Experience*, 10. Oates claimed that "three lines of insight and discipline converge" upon the better understanding of the nature, causes, and

a succinct manner, Oates's perspective can be easily seen to be informed by the psychology of Christian experience rather than on the authority of the Bible. The multifaceted and integrated approach in seeking to answer man's essential problems is depicted through the establishment of redemptive relationships, maintaining unconditional acceptance, expanding the boundaries of salvation which will ultimately lead to the therapeutic organization of one's selfhood.

REDEMPTIVE RELATIONSHIPS

Oates's anthropology reflected therapeutic and phenomenological qualities, coming from familiar sources including Boisen, May, Sullivan, Rogers, and Hiltner. Manifested as a prescription to the existential, psychological, and spiritual problems encountered by man, Oates emphasized these qualities in the context of establishing an empathetic relationship between the counselor and the client and also fostering these relationships between the client and others.[3] The redemptive presence of the counselor was touted as being effective enough on its own as to become an actual "aid to recovery" for those who are hurting.[4]

In establishing redemptive relationships, Oates sought to address the loss of identity which often resulted from a lack of self-esteem. For instance, the empathetic approach to passive-aggressive people was to "develop confidence and continuity in a skill within the manifest capabilities of this person . . . and encourage them to believe in themselves."[5] Essentially, the minister was tasked with uncovering the real selves of his clients or parishioners. By avoiding a judgmental and biased perspective, the pastor can exercise empathetic wisdom in understanding the struggles which threaten his counselee.[6] According to Oates, the pastor was to avoid becoming a tyrant

---

solutions to existential anxiety. These insights may include the Bible, but they necessitate modern psychotherapeutic interventions and the "clinical experience of pastoral counselors" (Oates, *Anxiety in Christian Experience*, 9). See also Oates, *Bible in Pastoral Care*, 10.

3. Jeane, "Analysis of Wayne Edward Oates' Phenomenological Method," 34.

4. Oates, *Christian Pastor* (1982), 54. Within the literature, this bond is called the "relationship of trusted motive" which highlights as its chief end for the counselor to win the confidence of the one whom he is providing counsel. Rollo May, of whom Oates relied upon for this thought among others, noted that it was necessary for caregivers to portray accurate empathy, nonpossessive warmth, and inherent genuineness (May, *Existence*, 64–56.).

5. Oates, *Behind the Masks*, 80.

6. Oates, *Christian Pastor* (1982), 71. See also Thurneysen, *Theology of Pastoral Care*, 132; Oates, *Psychology of Religion*, 39.

or conqueror at all costs. Instead, he should be seen as part of a collaborative effort along with the parishioner as he enters their psychological territory of being. Oates noted, "This orientation implied that a pastor seeks to enter into the 'internal frame of reference' of the person whom he is seeking to help. He tries to create a psychological climate of understanding and warmth."[7]

As the reader may notice, Oates's prescription for addressing man's psycho-spiritual pathology through establishing redemptive relationships is rooted in phenomenological psychology. While phenomenological presuppositions undergirded Oates's counseling methodology, as outlined in chapter 3, these also equally undergirded this particular component of his anthropological structure. Redemptive relationships had as their goal to understand the core of a person's being in order to identify, clarify, and nurture their self-concept without, in turn, losing the individual's own sense of self. Thus, a person can remain open-minded, mutually learn, lower threats to self, and move toward change.[8] The anthropocentric nature of this prescription to man's ailments is not only seen through an empathetic, value-free, and man-centered emphasis, but more drastically demonstrated by the lack of God-talk. As Oates stated, counseling conversations and relationships may or may not be centered on "God or Christ, the church, or the Holy Spirit. However, when such a specific God consciousness comes to pass in the fullness of time, the relationship itself is the exegesis, the witness, the concrete instances of what God is about in the world."[9] In brief, the central focus of the redemptive relationship was not primarily on the God of the Bible, but on the individuals who made up the relationship as manifested in their purposes and personal objectives.

These counseling relationships were to be established not only to clarify an individual's sense of personality in the midst of turmoil and struggle, but also to help them avoid personality disorder. Oates suggested that a common trait held by those who have personality disorders is that they were unable to form lasting relationships.[10] Oates considered those who rejected interpersonal grounding relationships as being detached or

---

7. Oates, *New Dimensions of Pastoral Counseling*, 9. This concept was borrowed from Rollo May's *Einfühlen* (i.e., to have sympathetic understanding). See also Oates, *When Religion Gets Sick*, 103, 114.

8. Oates, *Psychology of Religion*, 36. See also Steere, *On Listening to Another*, 1–2.

9. Oates, *Christian Pastor* (1982), 172. See also Oates, *Behind the Masks*, 130. See also Oates, *Anxiety in Christian Experience*, 124–25.

10. Oates, *Behind the Masks*, 134. Durability denoted a lasting and secure interpersonal relationship as used by Harry Stack Sullivan in *Interpersonal Theory of Psychiatry*, 308–10. Here Oates relies upon Hiltner, *Pastoral Counseling*, 32, and Rogers, *Client-Centered Therapy*. See also Oates, *Presence of God*, 25; Oates, *New Dimensions of Pastoral Care*, 59.

disoriented selves. In turn, these individuals were exposed to self-destruction through separation, alienation, estrangement and a host of other threats to personality development.[11] In order to avoid isolation and meaninglessness, a vacuum in which a healthy personality could never develop properly, one must obtain faith which he summed up in the context of relationships.[12] Infusing counseling relationships with spiritual meaning, Oates correlated these secure relationships, designed to see those in need become "real persons," with the theological concepts of conversion and regeneration. He argued that people who go through pastoral counseling should perceive their experience "as both a theological experience of redemption and an emotional experience of healing."[13]

Oates mentioned that while durable relationships are the crux of the success of one's interpersonal life, they are also were prone to falter. In these scenarios, it is important to seek out the durable relationship found in the "Eternal Presence of God."[14] While this assertion seemed to place man-centered, human relationships as secondary to a spiritual relationship with God, Oates stressed that the end goal of all counseling was that people have reconciled to others in a covenant of mutual trust and support. Toward this end, the counselor must become partners with his counselee in getting them to listen to their inner selves and others.[15]

By the end of the 1950s, Hiltner had published three books that reflected his notion of pastoral counseling as it related to the overall shepherding role of the minister. *Pastoral Counseling* (1949), *The Counselor in Counseling* (1952), and *The Christian Shepherd* (1959) were published during a time when many in the church, including pastors, were embracing humanistic counseling theories and reacting against directive and authority-based

---

11. Oates, *Christ and Selfhood*, 92–93. Oates provides an example of this from the Bible in Matt 19:16–20 (cf. Mark 10:17–31 and Luke 18:18–20) when the rich young ruler rejected the durability that Jesus could offer him.

12. Collins, "Pastoral Concern for Man," 73. While the concept of faith will be explored later in this chapter, it is important to note that Oates defined it as a means to defend oneself against threats to personality and secondarily as expressed in human relationships. These definitions, however, represent an unbiblical understanding and use of faith as seen from the perspectives of James 1 and Hebrews 11.

13. Oates, *Anxiety in Christian Experience*, 125. See also Oates, *Christian Pastor* (1982), 192.

14. Oates, *Presence of God in Pastoral Counseling*, 27. Oates remains vague about what exactly the "Presence of God" is. Early in this volume, Oates does make it clear that pastoral counselors can become too dependent upon the Bible as the only source of this understanding. He draws his own understanding of the presence of God from both Judeo-Christian teachings while attempting not to "disparage" any other interpretation from other religious traditions (Oates, *Presence of God in Pastoral Counseling*, 9–13).

15. Oates, *Presence of God in Pastoral Counseling*, 80.

counseling.[16] For Hiltner, the aim of pastoral counseling was centered on the "attempt by a pastor to help people help themselves through the process of gaining understanding of their inner conflicts. Counseling is sometimes referred to as emotional reeducation, for in addition to its attempt to help people with a problem immediately confronting them, it should teach people how to help themselves with other problems."[17] In this approach, the pastor-shepherd served as a facilitator and avoided making inadvertent moral judgments of the client. Counseling should not be coercive but clarifying. Responsible pastoral counseling cautiously avoided blatant pronouncements in favor of the client coming to conclusions on his or her own.[18]

In like manner, as a chaplain, Boisen had as his goal to help the patient organize the chaos of his or her inner world, only then could they experience a positive sense of success and spiritual freedom.[19] Successful care resulted in the actualization of the patient's "better self" so he or she could overcome any personal struggles and inconveniences resulting from inner personality conflict.[20] The perspective and purpose of ministry and counseling was viewed "not so much as a quest to guide souls toward salvation but rather to nurture psyches toward wholeness."[21] Oates agreed that counseling which did not provide the counselee with the keys to his own healing did more to engender emotional and psychological confusion and would actually hamper the personality development of the counselee. Oates desired to stimulate the proper initiative within those seeking his counsel so that they

16. Aden and Ellens, *Turning Points in Pastoral Care*, 175. While at the University of Chicago, many of Hiltner's students came into direct contact with Rogers's client-centered psychotherapy while they conducted internships at his counseling center, which operated on campus.

17. Hiltner, *Pastoral Counseling*, 20.

18. Hiltner, *Pastoral Counseling*, 22. See also Hiltner, *Christian Shepherd*, 40. In the act of clarifying and judging, the pastoral counselor makes sure that any judgment has a positive perspective in an attempt to avoid negativity or self-domination. At all costs, "inferiority feelings" on behalf of the client should be guarded carefully against.

19. Boisen, *Exploration of the Inner World*, 5. For Boisen, salvation was equated with proper inner reorganization (204). Richard Cabot and Russell Dicks identified the concern for the minister as the "growth of souls." This was, according to them "the production of novelty within the range of a purpose without dominant self-destruction." The gospel is not mentioned as a factor. (Cabot and Dicksm, *Art of Ministering*, 376).

20. Boisen, *Exploration of the Inner World*, 266. Nearly fifty years after Boisen inaugurated the first CPE trial, Abraham Maslow's humanistic psychology touted self-actualization as the answer for all of mankind's ills.

21. Muravchik, *American Protestantism*, 39. For a perspective on the classical forms of pastoral care that stand in stark contrast to the psychologized and clinical approach, see Oden and Browning, *Care of Souls in the Classic Tradition*, and Purves, *Pastoral Theology in the Classical Tradition*.

would become concerned about their own fate and take their future into their own hands.[22] Oates was committed to the idea that for the counselee to begin the journey of healing psychological wounds, the counselor must be willing to participate in the spiritual pilgrimage of their counselee. Thus, the pastoral counselor joined "upon a search with the seeker after life much more often than he gives pat 'answers' to deep life issues, thereby relieving the person of the anxiety of asking and seeking."[23]

SELF-CLARIFYING ACCEPTANCE

Regarding unconditional acceptance, Oates maintained that any educated and useful pastoral counselor should be aware and familiar with the key literature within the field of psychotherapy, of which he included the work of Rogers and Tillich.[24] Oates's indebtedness to Rogers is seen through his affirmation of Rogers as a psychological pioneer in applying a client-centered therapy "to areas such as personality growth and development, teaching, and human relations encounter groups."[25] Regarding theological acceptance, Tillich claimed that self-love was important in the process of working through life issues. He argued that there could be no lasting change without some measure of self-acceptance and that this was the first step in uncritically accepting others.[26] Self-affirmation according to Tillich was "affirmation in one's own essential being, and the knowledge of one's essential being is mediated through reason, the power of the soul to have adequate ideas."[27] By providing atmospheres of unconditional acceptance, Oates affirmed that organized selfhood could be achieved by those who struggled with a lack of self-identity.[28]

22. Oates, *Protestant Pastoral Counseling*, 154.

23. Oates, *Religious Dimensions of Personality*, 253.

24. Oates, *Christian Pastor* (1951), 114. Rogers highlighted unconditional acceptance as the rudimentary basis for all counseling.

25. Oates, *Behind the Masks*, 27. Key goals of Rogerian psychotherapy included the establishment of a nonthreatening environment, operating from a humanistic worldview, investing confidence in the client's innate value, and avoiding responsibility for the client's life. See also Oates, *Bible in Pastoral Care*, 72.

26. Cooper, *Paul Tillich and Psychology*, 3–4.

27. Tillich, *Courage to Be*, 21. For Tillich, self-affirmation referred to "the paradox of participation in something which transcends the self" and not necessarily countered against low self-esteem (165). This is consistent with writings from Boisen, Hiltner, and Oates.

28. Jeane, "Analysis of Wayne Edward Oates' Phenomenological Method," 23. See also Oates, *Protestant Pastoral Care*, 32–34; Sherrill, *Guilt and Redemption*, 142–44, and Rogers, *Counseling and Psychotherapy*, 18.

Reconciliation between man and God, man and others, and man with himself could be accomplished through relationships built on trust and empathy. The concept of trust and faith were synonymous in Oates's writing. He depicted these theological concepts as "working through love" where the shepherd remained "permissive" and loved the sheep and avoided dominating and ruling the flock.[29] Christians must know each other and accept one another at a subjective and experiential level—in this, forgiveness, trust, and love become actualized and the healthy personality develops.[30] This emphasis in counseling was capitalized upon in Hiltner's work. He argued that counseling should not be coercive, but clarifying, and that the counselee should not encounter moral judgement on behalf of the counselor which would potentially threaten him.[31] Any counselor who seeks to offer directives, according to Hiltner, should be purposed to offer a positive perspective in an attempt to avoid unnecessary negativity or domination. At all costs, according to Hiltner and his contemporaries, the "inferiority feelings" of the client should be guarded carefully so as to not upset him.[32] Thus, the counselee was encouraged to come to his own conclusions in order to address his internal disorganization. Roberts, in like manner, noted the therapeutic value of self-acceptance and unconditional acceptance, believing it to be the very cornerstone of the therapeutic ministry. He wrote, "Therapy has a moral purpose because it rests on the assumption that internal harmony and a capacity for personal growth and responsibility are better than emotional conflict, anxiety, and self-enslavement."[33] Oates, having taken his cue from these men, viewed the function of therapy as the effort on the part of the pastor "to decode the communication in such a way that the patient is not only understood but perceives that he is both understood and accepted."[34]

Oates saw no philosophical or theological conflict between personal self-worth as gleaned from the works of psychologists and the objective grounding of the *imago Dei* within man.[35] In fact, he argued that self-ac-

29. Oates, *Christian Pastor* (1982), 78.

30. Oates, *Christian Pastor* (1982), 81. Oates quoted Phil 1:9 to support this theory. However, this verse does not refer to the perfect knowledge of man as a pre-requisite to reconciliation, but a perfect knowledge of God as informing Christian maturity and spiritual growth.

31. Hiltner, *Pastoral Counseling*, 22.

32. Hiltner, *Christian Shepherd*, 40.

33. Roberts, *Psychotherapy*, 40. Roberts defined acceptance as a "noncondemnatory [sic] attitude" (38). See also Hiltner, *Christian Shepherd*, 30, and Rogers, *On Becoming a Person*, 47.

34. Oates, *Religious Factors in Mental Illness*, 59.

35. Oates, *Presence of God in Pastoral Counseling*, 39. Oates suggested that the

ceptance and self-worth were actually purchased by Christ's death.[36] May identified man's ability and capacity to see himself from the outside as a distinguishing mark of a healthy personality. In referencing May, Oates made a connection between his understanding of self with the concept as promoted by existential philosophy and personality psychology in that, as May put it, "the more self-awareness a person has, the more alive he is."[37] Oates saw it as the church's mission to nurture and foster a sense of self-esteem and unconditional acceptance in all of those who struggled with "the low sense of self-esteem that specifically underlies the dependent, the passive-aggressive, the asocial, and the avoidant personality disorders and that underlies the rest of them more generally."[38]

For Oates, forgiveness had an important role in the resolutions to man's problems, especially as this concept related to the avoidance of threats to selfhood. Oates relied heavily on Tillich's theological-psychological correlation paradigm for this notion of forgiveness.[39] For Tillich, being forgiven and being able to accept and love oneself is virtually the same thing. In his work *The New Being*, Tillich noted, "One accepts one's self as something which is eternally important, eternally loved, eternally accepted. The disgust of one's self, the hatred of one's self has disappeared. There is a center, a direction, a meaning for life."[40] As mentioned in the previous chapter, ex-

---

source of counsel came from the value of man in the *imago Dei*. However, I question how the Bible fits into this essentially epistemological statement. For more on this, see the anthropological critique at the end of this chapter.

36. Oates, *What Psychology Says about Religion*, 101–2. Oates traces psychology from the ancient Greek maxim: "Know Thyself" to the motto of the Age of Enlightenment "Be Thyself," to the Christian commandment of "Give Thyself." *Christ and Selfhood* more explicitly states that Christ's death afforded man the gift of grace resulting in self-acceptance. However, the researcher questions whether the death and resurrection of Christ was meant to culminate in self-acceptance or self-denial as several New Testament passages seem to point to the nature of Christ renewing the self instead of emphasizing *self*-in-Christ. See Luke 9:23–25; Rom 6:5–6; 2 Cor 5:16–17; Eph 4:21–24; Col 3:9–11.

37. May, *Man's Search for Himself*, 116.

38. Oates, *Behind the Masks*, 133. Commenting on Oates's stance here, Collins noted, "In an atmosphere of acceptance and forgiveness man is able to accept himself as he really is and does not have to defend or to deceive himself" (Oates, *Behind the Masks*, 49). This in effect, is the product of healthy religion.

39. It should be noted that Tillich's correlational method was not without its detractors. As put by Terry Cooper, some noted that Tillich had no right to conflate the doctrine of justification with psychological acceptance.

40 Tillich, *New Being*, 22; Tillich, *Systematic Theology*, 3:224–25. This concept, as understood by Tillich, is strongly connected to the psychological concept of self-actualization. See also Tillich, "Impact of Pastoral Psychology," in *Ministry and Mental Health*, 16, and Curtis, "Role of Religion," 268.

istential anxiety was identified by many pastoral psychologists as a barrier to personality development. For both Tillich and Oates, the only way to escape and to have ultimate victory from the existential despair faced by a modern generation was to have the "courage to accept oneself as accepted in spite of being unacceptable."[41] Oates saw self-acceptance as essential to turn away threats of anxiety, meaninglessness, and isolation which often led to despondency. One could only truly accept oneself, however, once he received forgiveness from both God *and* his trusted community.[42]

Explaining his understanding of forgiveness and its function in the spiritual and psychological health of personality, Oates stated:

> Meeting him [Jesus] in forgiveness has enabled us to face with courage the threat of our condemning histories of sin. We have been empowered through faith to accept our history and our heritage as our own and the threat of dissociating ourselves from our real identity has been transcended in the encounter with the Love known as Christ.[43]

Collins contextualized Oates's view of forgiveness with the ideas of the therapeutic Jesus who offered to man a religious experience that promised to help spiritually and psychologically unify those who suffered with a disorganized and displaced sense of identity.[44] Jesus Christ, having interposed himself as a sacrifice for man, provided redemption for the self. No longer would the self be exposed to threats of destruction and the "absurdities of the cycle of life itself," instead the inherent integrity of the self could finally be restored.[45] Oates argued that man's greatest need was for a "durable and lasting selfhood . . . for an individuality which is not the pawn of natural law. . . for a covenant and a fellowship which cannot be taken be broken or separated."[46]

---

41. Tillich, *Courage to Be*, 164. Tillich equates the "courage to be" with the Apostle Paul's concept of justification by faith. It seems that Tillich's understanding of faith is in man, while Paul's is clearly in the God of Scripture.

42. Oates, *Anxiety in Christian Experience*, 72. Self-acceptance on the part of the client necessarily precluded an uncritical posture of acceptance on behalf of the counselor toward the client.

43. Oates, *Christ and Selfhood*, 90. According to Oates, the history of man's sin demonstrates his incapability of loving and accepting himself. This is man's fate apart from Christ (Oates, *Christ and Selfhood*, 50). See Pauck, *Introduction to Christ and Adam*, 8.

44. Collins, "Pastoral Concern for Man," 49.

45. Collins, "Pastoral Concern for Man," 119.

46. Oates, *Christ and Selfhood*, 126. This need for self-affirmation is echoed throughout the work of Tillich as well. Tillich's theology placed his concept of God as the source of self-affirmation and self-love in the face of self-doubt. See Tillich,

REORGANIZATION OF PERSONALITY

A major problem faced by man was that of a lack of self-confidence and Oates saw the pastoral counselor as the one who should infuse and invest confidence within selves that were lacking that particular quality. For Oates the problem of ill-defined or dependent personalities was that they expected God to do everything for them "without *exerting faith in themselves* and in God in order to rise up and be persons in their own right."[47] While Oates and Tillich stressed the importance of God's acceptance, they did so with the caveat that a measure of self-acceptance or reflection was required.[48] The man-centered implication behind Oates's understanding of faith as self-acceptance was further stressed by Curtis who noted, "Oates, then, sees faith as the beginning of being a person. Faith begins as a good feeling about oneself and his world."[49]

For Oates, faith was ultimately expressed in the conversion of the self from a place of disorganization and culminated in the focused self or fully organized personality.[50] This implied that man could have an active part to play in achieving his own healing, thus being rescued from the problems that plagued him.[51] As has been mentioned previously, Oates utilized William James's understanding of conversion, which centered upon the frame of reference of the individual rather than on the supernatural action of the God of Scripture.[52] Oates saw James as revolutionary in the way he applied the "function of conversion in the 'empirical me' of the human being" in order to "overcome [psychological] division within the self."[53] Taking a cue from theorists including James, Starbuck, Coe and Leuba, Oates saw conversion as the vehicle by which the study of the psychology of religion was grounded. The objectivity and empirical nature of Oates's conception of conversion is clearly seen by his statement, "Conversion is an observable,

---

Systematic Theology, 2:12.

47. Oates, *Behind the Masks*, 27, emphasis added.
48. Oates, *When Religion Gets Sick*, 125.
49. Curtis, "Role of Religion," 265.
50. Conversion and salvation are used synonymously unless stated elsewhere.
51. Collins, "Pastoral Concern for Man," 49.
52. Collins, "Pastoral Concern for Man," 79. See James, *Varieties of Religious Experience*, 157, and Oates, *Psychology of Religion*, 94–95.
53. Oates, "Conversion and Mental Health," 43. Oates not only refers to the positive contributions of William James in the discussion of how conversion could be understood within the context of the mental health field, but also made mention of several other of his influencers, including E. D. Starbuck, Sigmund Freud, Gordon Allport, Anton Boisen, Erik Erikson, and Paul Tillich.

behavioral phenomenon. It can be spoken of in both a sacred and secular manner" and it was also an "abrupt change toward an enthusiastic religious attitude, with the highly emotional features being conspicuously evident, whether they are lasting or not."[54] Oates contextualized his understanding of conversion and salvation not with theological or biblical terms, but instead through anthropocentric language which shows the overt psychological influence on his thinking.[55]

Oates saw conversion as making a positive contribution to the psychological health of a personality.[56] He referred to religion as being either healthy or unhealthy. In explicating the characteristics of healthy religion among those who suffered from psychological problems, Oates relied upon the economic and pragmatic value of religion. He stated, "In essence, healthy religion binds people together in such a way that their individuality is enabled both to be realized and to be consecrated to the total community of relationships to which they belong."[57] Collins noted that more than anything else, conversion provided internal and external unity for the divided self. In addition, he noted that Oates equated theologically oriented concepts, including salvation, conversion, and redemption, with psychological development. At one point, Oates stated that "the redemption of man from sin and the emergence of a free self in man, respectively, are inseparably tied up with a struggle of the soul in the process of time and becoming."[58]

At the point of conversion, Oates believed that man's personality went through a recreation. The divided, estranged, and destructive self now

---

54. Oates, *Psychology of Religion*, 92. See also Roberts, *Psychotherapy*, 129. As an influential writer referenced by Oates, David Roberts spoke of the dynamic nature of salvation which "implies that its saving purpose is to give men a faith and a mode of life which will make them no longer ashamed of themselves. It cures guilt, not by putting forward ideas which assure men willy-nilly that they are 'all right,' but by releasing a power which removes the causes of guilt" (Roberts, *Psychotherapy*, 129).

55. Oates, *Psychology of Religion*, 93. See Oates, *Anxiety in Christian Experience*, 12–25; James, *Varieties of Religious Experience*, 41, 157; Boisen, *Exploration of the Inner World*, 191, 205; Maslow, *Toward a Psychology of Being*, 126; Tiebout, "Conversion as a Psychological Phenomenon," 28–34.

56. It should be noted that Oates also recognized ways that conversion could be considered psychologically harmful. These conceptions usually included unhealthy religious ideations within the minds of psychotic patients that "increase the unhappiness and lack of unity in the person" (Oates, *Psychology of Religion*, 17).

57. Oates, *Religious Factors*, 113. See also Bush, "Human Suffering," 179.

58. Collins, "Pastoral Concern for Man," 74–75; as quoted in Oates, *Religious Dimensions of Personality*, 162–63. See also Tillich, *Systematic Theology*, 2:167. Tillich believed that salvation was the saving from "ultimate negativity" which is in itself the condemnation to eternal death; however, he believed that there was saving power apart from Jesus.

could become reconciled and resurrected in a new form.⁵⁹ It is important to note that it was primarily in the incarnation in which Oates believed man was saved from alienation and estrangement and brought to a place of empowerment to accept himself.⁶⁰ Curtis made an interesting, if somewhat controversial, statement related to Oates's understanding of man's redemption. He stated,

> If guilt is ontological, forgiveness is also ontological, for acceptance proceeds from the life of God. Oates returns to the centrality of Jesus Christ for this issue, for Jesus is the declaration of God to man that he is forgiven. Forgiveness is the declaration of a historical act, the Incarnation of Jesus. Significantly enough, Oates relates forgiveness to the Incarnation of Jesus, not to the Atonement of Jesus. Forgiveness is rooted in his life more than his death. Jesus came to be the real man, thus with the authenticity of his decision he won a selfhood that is the model for following selves.⁶¹

A focus on the incarnation of Jesus, rather than on his death and resurrection related to the atonement, as the primary event leading to man's redemption is a major departure from traditional Christian emphases in theological studies and reflects influences from modernism which seek to reinterpret biblical doctrine from a man-centered perspective.⁶² This humanistic perspective related to soteriology combined with a man-centered anthropology exposes Oates's methodological goals.

According to Oates and the psychologically oriented sources he utilized, the panacea, or cure-all, for man includes an escape from the external and internal threats to personality development and concludes in the rediscovery of the self. As stated by May, the answer to man's loss of inner selfhood is to "rediscover the sources of strength and integrity within ourselves. This, of course, goes hand in hand with the discovery and affirmation of values in ourselves and in our society which will serve as the core of unity."⁶³ Roberts viewed psychotherapy as the only valid context in which to foster a healthy sense of self. He argued that the integration of the self,

---

59. Oates, *Christ and Selfhood*, 128. See also Boisen, *Exploration of the Inner World*, 204; Starbuck, *Psychology of Religion*, ix, 21; Coe, *Psychology of Religion*, 152–53, 171.

60. Oates, *Christ and Selfhood*, 246.

61. Curtis, *Role of Religion*, 269–70. See Oates, *Christ and Selfhood*, 52; Tillich, *Courage to Be*, 2.

62. Cohen and Halverson, *Handbook of Christian Theology*, 233, 258. See also Oates, *Religious Care*, 3; Oates, *Christ and Selfhood*, 41.

63. May, *Man's Search for Himself*, 79.

which was the goal of mental health services, involved the "adequacy to cope with ongoing processes and situations . . . whereby the individual may continue to move forward in self-understanding and in the understanding of others."[64] Conversion and salvation also referred to psychological healing which led to an individual's sense of wholeness. As an anchor in the field of pastoral counseling, Hiltner conceived of healing as the process by which one was restored to "functional wholeness" in the face of physical or psychological impairment.[65] Hiltner also believed that healing could come through various avenues or sources, whether sacred or profane, and that pastors at times must avoid "exclusive concentration on alleged Christian means and modes of healing" which "may impede healing in the Christian sense."[66] Throughout *The Exploration of the Inner World*, Boisen argued that the ultimate goal of clinical pastoral education was reorganizing the inner world of the patient in such a way that their personality could be saved, clarified, and made healthy. This understanding of the therapeutic organization of selfhood directly influenced Oates's anthropology.[67] For Oates, the task of the pastoral counselor could be summed up in the work of crisis ministry. In *The Christian Pastor*, Oates stated, "The straitening anxieties of these times of crisis call for a reorganization of the total personality of an individual and his family, and the result may easily be disorganization. These crises either strengthen or weaken an individual personality."[68] Thus, as a member of the "helping team" who utilized the therapeutic resources of psychology, Oates saw it as his unique responsibility and privilege to help the disordered personality achieve unity of being and inner coherence.[69]

---

64. Roberts, *Psychotherapy and the Christian View of Man*, 34. Interestingly, Roberts admitted that "perfect integration" of the self as the "harmonious awareness of all the forces that are at work in the self" was difficult to reach at best.

65. Hiltner, *Preface to Pastoral Theology*, 89. See also Hiltner, *Christian Shepherd*, 19–20; Rogers, *Client-Centered Therapy*, 159–72, and Tillich, "Relation to Religion and Health," 16–52.

66. Hiltner, *Preface to Pastoral Theology*, 101. See also Tillich, *Systematic Theology*, 2:167–68.

67. Jeane, "Analysis," 34. See also Oates, *Religious Factors in Mental Illness*, xii; Oates, *Revelation of God*, 20; and Oates, "Protestant Principles and Pastoral Care," 19.

68. Oates, *Christian Pastor* (1951), 13. The language used by Oates is parallel to that of Boisen and Hiltner.

69. Oates, *Psychology of Religion*, 58; Oates, *Religious Dimensions of Personality*, 128.

ANTHROPOLOGICAL CRITIQUE FROM SCRIPTURE

Oates's anthropological commitments related to the doctrine of salvation, in many cases, oppose clear soteriological teachings found within the Bible. The first conclusion made by Oates is that man's sense of peace and inner tranquility was to be secured primarily through empathetic and healthy interpersonal relationships. While humans are called to care and be concerned for one another in love (Rom 15:14; 1 Thess 5:14–15; 2 Tim 4:1–5; Heb 10:24–25; Eph 4:14–16; Exod 18:17ff.), true spiritual peace is not generated nor granted from these relationships, but they are gifts from God (1 Cor 14:33; 2 Cor 13:11; Jas 1:17; Phil 4:9; 1 Thess 5:23; Heb 13:20; 2 John 1:3). It is through Jesus Christ alone that man is reconciled from his sin-state unto God. Romans 5:1 states that Christians "have peace with God through our Lord Jesus Christ." The peace of God is said to surpass (ὑπερέχω) the limited comprehension of man in that it originates from God himself (Phil 4:7).[70] While worldly peace is temporary and dependent upon circumstances, the peace from God is a gift that does not trouble the heart of man and produces spiritual characteristics that bring glory to God (John 14:27; Gal 5:22–26; Titus 2:11–12).

Oates noted that the end goal of counseling should ultimately be about the formation of dependable and supportive relationships. Once again, this anthropological paradigm fails to highlight the importance and necessity of one being reconciled to God first (2 Cor 5:18, 20; Rom 5:9–11). Jesus explicitly stated that the greatest commandment was for man to first love God and then love his neighbor (Matt 22:37–39). The implication here is that without being reconciled to God in a relationship of grace, it is impossible to truly love one's fellow man.[71] Biblical reconciliation goes beyond simply establishing or forming relationships between two parties, but it refers to restitution, reformation, and a renewal of a bond that was once broken but now has been made perfectly whole.[72] According to Paul, all things on this earth and in heaven will be reconciled to God in Jesus Christ through the "blood of His cross" (Col 1:20–22). No human relationship can attempt to substitute what is accomplished only through the death and resurrection of God's son (Eph 2:16; 2 Pet 3:9).

Another conclusion drawn out of Oates's anthropological commitments is that self-acceptance was the key to true healing. In this, faith is essentially reimagined and refers more to self-confidence than confidence in

---

70. Vine, *Expository Dictionary*, 55.
71. MacArthur, *Matthew 16–23*, 339–40.
72. Vine, *Expository Dictionary*, 260–62.

Christ. In truth, biblical faith has more to do with the realization that man is not sufficient in himself (Rom 5:8; 8:34; 2 Cor 5:14; 1 Pet 3:18). In teaching his followers what was required in order to be considered a faithful disciple, Jesus stated, "If anyone wishes to come after Me, he must deny himself, and take up his cross daily and follow Me. For whoever wishes to save his life will lose it, but whoever loses his life for My sake, he is the one will save it" (Luke 9:23–24).[73] As a theme found throughout Oates's anthropology, the concept of *self* communicates a focus on an individual's personal happiness and fulfillment at the expense of the care and concern for others (Phil 2:3; Jas 2:1–10).[74] Instead, Christians are called to abandon self interest in order to "lay down our lives for our brethren" (1 John 3:16).

The final anthropological conclusion that can be construed from this aspect of Oates's thought suggests that the nature, source, and effects of salvation are primarily internal and not external. As has been previously stated, the inner thoughts and heart of man is wicked and evil. To attempt to argue that man can, in essence, save himself goes against the very core of a biblical anthropology (Gen 6:5; Jas 4:1–4). Titus 3:5 states that it was God who saved man from unrighteousness and sin. Through God's mercy and the "washing of regeneration and renewing by the Holy Spirit" in the work of Jesus Christ was man justified and declared righteous in his sight. In one of his pastoral epistles, Paul gave full credit to God for man's salvation, being sure to emphasize it as a gift of God that could never be earned by man (Ps 37:39; John 3:16–17; Acts 4:12; Eph 2:4–9). Indeed, it is man who is fully dependent upon God for his salvation (Acts 16:30–33; Rom 10:9–10).

SEEING PAST THE REAL SOLUTION

This chapter outlines the key conclusions held by Oates regarding the solutions to man's problems. Prescribed solutions to what Oates perceived was the main problem that plagued all people in life are informed explicitly by a human-centered anthropology. While Oates confessed a reliance on the Bible in his descriptions of these solutions, the biblical terms he most often utilized, including redemption, conversion, salvation, and reconciliation, were often derived from and corresponded with anti-Christian principles and contradicted conservative theological positions and interpretations. These principles are self-serving in nature and hold in common that the answer to man's problems can be found within themselves. Problems, in and of themselves, are also depicted in ways that reject objective and external

---

73. Luke 14:33.
74. Rieff, *Triumph of the Therapeutic*, 51.

authority. Through emphasizing the importance of establishing relationships, which were sensitive to the emotional needs of the individual, and by relating self-acceptance as a prerequisite to forming a healthy relationship with God, Oates's pastoral counseling functionally places man-centered solutions at the center of spiritual problems. As a result, Oates's prescribed solutions to man's problems characterize the development of a healthy personality as the ultimate goal and purpose of human existence virtually ignoring, and in many instances, contradicting the biblical account.

7

Looking Back to Look Ahead

As an influencer within the field of pastoral counseling throughout much of the twentieth century, the impact of Wayne Edwards Oates's legacy has been felt within broader American Protestantism. Within the Southern Baptist Convention, Oates did more than most to shape the approach, tone, understanding, and application of pastoral counseling through his extensive writing and teaching career at The Southern Baptist Theological Seminary. Through his connections and work with a variety of secular and denominational entities, Oates utilized multiple platforms to disseminate his therapeutic counseling theory and method.

Wayne Oates passed away over twenty years ago, but it was through his books, articles, personal letters, and the words of others who knew him well that I became acquainted with a man who was determined to overcome the difficulties of his early life and build a career that he hoped would help meet the needs of others. While Oates and I would find ourselves on opposite ends of the spectrum regarding our understanding of the nature and purpose of counseling, I find myself appreciating the fervor by which he pursued his goals. I dare say if I approached life with an ounce of vigor that Oates did, I might surprise myself with what I could accomplish.

Like many of us, Oates was impacted by those who came before him. As I have attempted to demonstrate throughout this book, a point at which

Oates and I stand distinctly apart has to do with our understanding of the sufficiency of Scripture. We would not necessarily disagree that the Bible is sufficient for matters of *faith and practice*, but we would part ways concerning *exactly* what that involves. As I attempted to outline in this book, many of Oates's formative influences, including several mentors, teachers, colleagues, and friends, did *not* view the Bible as an adequate or sufficient source to address modern man, the problems he may encounter, and the solutions to those problems. In the place of the biblical sufficiency-vacuum came descriptions and prescriptions of the behavioral sciences, efficacy claims of clinical methodology, and ultimately a psychologized anthropology. It was this commitment to a therapeutically oriented anthropology that I have attempted to carefully excavate out from under the shallow earth of biblical references and theological jargon used by Oates in much of his work. Interestingly, there are several academic essays and dissertations that have focused on various aspects of Oates's writings; however, very few have approached his contributions critically and none have attempted to expose a comprehensive anthropology. By constructing the key anthropological components above, I have shown not only that Oates's anthropology is therapeutically oriented, being shaped by concepts and principles derived from secular psychological influences, but that the subtle implications of this anthropological shift not only contradict the authority of the Bible, but its sufficiency as well.

From his early years, Oates pursued a sense of self-esteem in order to escape what he considered to be limited and less than desirable situations. With a determination to overcome, he poured himself into his education and work (living up to a label he coined—workaholic) in order to reinvent himself. Professors including Olin T. Binkley, Harrold W. Tribble, and Gaines S. Dobbins were each shown to have provided Oates with resources and tools which introduced him to modern psychology and secular philosophy. With the additional influence of two other men, Anton Boisen and Seward Hiltner, Oates joined the broad CPE movement and further assimilated psychological presuppositions and principles into his theological thinking as he popularized clinical and psychotherapeutic pastoral counseling models. This newly formed psychological framework would serve as the bedrock of his anthropology.

This book also sought to expose the philosophical framework which informed Oates's conception of pastoral counseling theory and method. Oates's philosophical commitments included an approach to ministry that was closely connected with mental health professionals and sought ways to incorporate the behavioral sciences into his counseling. As a pastoral psychologist, Oates was shown to have been ultimately concerned about meeting the felt needs of his clients. In order to do this, he adopted a therapeutic mindset which emphasized a man-centered and humanistic approach to counseling which contradicts a biblical counseling approach. By conceiving of pastoral counseling as a psychological-scientific pursuit, Oates subsumed presuppositions consistent with a secular worldview by correlating atheistic concepts with ideas found in Scripture.

After providing biographical, historical, and conceptual foundations the specific components within Oates's anthropology were explored. The first component concerns the nature of man. For Oates, the general focus is on man as a developing self. Terms used by Oates to refer to the "self" were shown to be linked to key figures within the field of personality psychology. Many of these individuals, most notably Gordon Allport, Rollo May, and Harry Stack Sullivan, were referenced by Oates in multiple published and unpublished works spanning his forty-year career. Other theorists, including Erik Erikson, Carl Rogers, Paul Tillich, and Alfred North Whitehead, were shown to also have influenced the way Oates conceived of human nature, growth, and development. Analyzing Oates's wide and eclectic use of these psychological resources demonstrated an anthropocentric understanding of man which emphasizes man's innate value and sense of identity as the penultimate concern.

The second component identified the problems of man as expressed throughout Oates's writings. It was demonstrated that while Oates did not neglect theological language in referencing the spiritual problems faced by all people; he often correlated these various concepts, including ideas of religion, sin, and guilt, with modern psychological contexts. Oates identified various threats to selfhood as the most common problem of man. According to him, threats including anxiety, alienation, and estrangement hindered healthy personality development and could cause permanent psychological damage. The works of Paul Tillich, Rollo May, and Anton Boisen that once again were directly utilized by Oates in this aspect of his anthropology mirrored his convictions. Ultimately, through a presentation of these existential threats, the therapeutic attempts of fostering a sense of self-esteem, security, and personality were shown to be self-serving and humanistic goals of Oates's counseling. Once more, the Bible was shown to not be a contributing factor in Oates's anthropological considerations.

The final component of Oates's anthropology that was studied involved his answers to the aforementioned problems. Oates's psychological conception of pastoral counseling manifested in methodology. Through establishing redemptive and durable relationships with clients, he was convinced that the client could overcome any existential threats to his or her personality. These relationships pointed to the client as the source of authority and relegated the counselor to that of a facilitator. The implication here is that "salvation" can come by means of societal and relational intervention or of one's on inner durability. The work of Seward Hiltner and Carl Rogers was compared with Oates's own conclusions and demonstrated to have been referenced by him in his writings on related subjects. The counseling relationship was seen to culminate in the total reorganization of the personality from that of an unhealthy and chaotic inner-life to that of one who was self-accepting, assured, and confident in their own selfhood. Once again, it was shown that these principles and conclusions were directly informed from a therapeutic and psychological worldview and not from the Bible.

UNSETTLING IMPLICATIONS

What could I hope to address or accomplish in spending years studying the writings of one seminary professor? Why decide to focus on his anthropological views? Why should you (or any of us) care? These questions speak to relevancy, and relevancy most often references the present and future. So why look back to the past? I am a firm believer that there is much that we can, and should, learn from the past in order to best prepare us for engaging in Christian ministry in the future. As I look at the current state of affairs in both broader Evangelicalism and more specifically in Protestant theological education and training, what I am *really* looking at is the result of subtle influences of the past. There are important implications that can be drawn from the conclusions made in this book. It is my hope that these will serve as both a warning and an encouragement to those of us who seek to minister the Scriptures faithfully in and for the church.

By showing how and why secular thought so pervasively penetrated Oates's anthropology, I have sought to reveal how dangerous psychological thinking found a safe harbor in one of the largest Protestant institutions and denominations in the world. Today, a large majority of pastors and church members alike have a general idea of counseling that looks more therapeutic, clinical, and professional than theological, personal, and pastoral. There is more attention brought to understanding personality types, meeting felt needs, or learning their "love language" than biblically seeking to align a wayward heart into conformity with Jesus Christ. By contributing to a growing number of works expressing related concerns, it is my hope to see the church turn away from "worldly philosophies" that only serve to take our eyes away from studying Scripture, in order to practice counseling that is uniquely biblical in principle and method. It is time once more for the Christian church to be known as people of the Bible in confession, creed, and counseling. We must remain vigilant in order to protect commitments to biblical sufficiency, authority, and inerrancy, especially as these relate to the task of soul care.

Through the lens of Oates's life as a seminary professor and through the history surrounding his time at Southern Seminary, it has been shown how liberal theological commitments, which limit scriptural authority and sufficiency, have impacted ministerial preparation and training for generations of pastors. This era of subterfuge in influencing young pastors-in-training with secular psychological principles relating to care and counseling in the church is unsettling. While at a cursory reading, Oates's language is often orthodox, the *meaning* behind his words and his commitments and methods largely do *not* reflect a reliance on faithful biblicism relating to anthropology. Anthropology is key. For Oates, it was anthropology that formed the very root of his pastoral counseling. What I have attempted to bring forth for the reader's consideration is the common theme we find in many places within Scripture. If and when the root is poisoned or diseased, the fruit will necessarily suffer harm. A view of human nature that is derived from what God has to say about who we are as people, what plagues our souls, and where we find our true hope and healing has *everything* to do with counseling. When these questions are disconnected from the truth of Scripture, the drift necessarily leads the content and method of our counsel astray. We must remain vigilant in order to protect commitments to biblical sufficiency, authority, and inerrancy, especially as these relate to vital task of the church.

RECOMMENDATIONS FOR FUTURE STUDY

In the course of this research, several topics of relevance and interest were touched upon; however, due to the restraints of this particular thesis and the limitations of this study, these could not be explored in their fullness. Among these areas of interest, there were four that particularly stood out as potential subjects of further research. I encourage anyone reading this to consider making their own contribution to these ongoing and important conversations.

In the study of the various influences that left their mark on Oates, strong links between various liberal theological perspectives and his eclectic use of modern psychology were uncovered. While I was unable to exhaustively outline the various liberal theological commitments related to Oates's anthropology or trace the connections between specific liberal theologians, individuals including Ludwig Feuerbach, Friedrich Schleiermacher, William

Newton Clarke, and William Adams Brown, a further study of these individuals and connections should be conducted especially in relation to their subtle influences within related theological fields.

As can be gathered even from a cursory reading of this book, the influence of Paul Tillich on Oates's psychological and theological understanding of man cannot be missed. With the expectation that many today may be unaware of the scope of Tillich's impact within the Evangelical church, I would encourage interested researchers to explore the lasting legacy of Tillich on the idea of Protestant pastoral counseling. While this thesis did allow some exploration of Tillich's views on secular psychology and theology as it directly influenced Oates's anthropological commitments, an in-depth study of Tillich's formative theological influences, relationships with influential psychologists, and academic career and legacy could serve to demonstrate how pastoral counselors and counseling within Evangelical circles came to be dominated by psychology instead of classical ideas of soul care throughout the twentieth century and beyond.

In conjunction with the preceding topic, further research should be done on the misappropriation of theological language, as demonstrated by Tillich, Oates and others, within discussions of Christian ministry and counseling. With the rise of influence of theological liberalism through the nineteenth and twentieth centuries, the researcher discovered that many who held to unorthodox convictions continued to use orthodox language in their books, lectures, and other writings. Study should be conducted to explore the reasoning behind this and the implication of this practice especially within theological institutions.

The final suggested topic of study is an examination of the early work and thought of James Leuba and his unique contribution to the psychology of religion. While peripherally influential to Oates's anthropology, Leuba's work within secular psychology, and his focus in religious psychology in particular, was intriguing especially due to the fact that he was a committed atheist. Due to his strong connection with G. Stanley Hall at Clark University, along with an association with major philosophical and psychological influencers in America, including E. D. Starbuck, G. A. Coe and William James, the work of Leuba should be explored further to outline his influences and his role in shaping the psychology of religion as an empirically based field of study.

Bibliography

Ackerly, Spafford. "The Teaching of Psychiatry to Undergraduate Medical Students." *Journal of Medical Education* 18 (1943) 167.
Adams, James Luther, and Seward Hiltner. *Pastoral Care in the Liberal Churches*. Nashville: Abingdon, 1970.
Adams, Jay E. *Christ and Your Problems*. Phillipsburg, NJ: P&R, 1971.
———. *The Christian Counselor's Manual*. Grand Rapids: Baker, 1973.
———. *Competent to Counsel: Introduction to Nouthetic Counseling*. Grand Rapids: Baker, 1986.
———. *Handbook of Church Discipline*. Jay Adams Library. Grand Rapids: Ministry Resources Library, 1986.
———. *Ready to Restore*. Grand Rapids: Baker, 1981.
———. *Shepherding God's Flock: A Handbook on Pastoral Ministry, Counseling, and Leadership*. Grand Rapids: Ministry Resources Library, 1986.
Aden, LeRoy, and J. H. Ellens. *Turning Points in Pastoral Care: The Legacy of Anton Boisen and Seward Hiltner*. Grand Rapids: Baker, 1990.
Aden, LeRoy, et al. *Christian Perspectives on Human Development*. Grand Rapids: Baker, 1992.
Adler, Mortimer Jerome. *What Man Has Made of Man*. New York: Ungar, 1957.
Allport, Gordon W. *Becoming: Basic Considerations for a Psychology of Personality*. New Haven: Yale University, 1955.
———. "Behavioral Science, Religion, and Mental Health." *Journal of Religion and Health* 3 (1963) 187–97.
———. *The Individual and His Religion: A Psychological Interpretation*. New York: Macmillan, 1950.
———. *Pattern and Growth in Personality*. New York: Holt, Rinehart and Winston, 1961.
———. *Personality: A Psychological Interpretation*. New York: H. Holt, 1937.
———. "The Roots of Religion." *Pastoral Psychology* 5 (1954) 13–24.
Ames, Edward Scribner. *Experiments in Personal Religion*. Chicago: American Institute of Sacred Literature, 1928.

Angyal, Andras. "Convergence of Psychotherapy and Religion." *Journal of Pastoral Care* 5 (1951) 4–14.

———. *Foundations for a Science of Personality*. New York: Commonwealth Fund, 1941.

Anthony, Michael J., et al., eds. *Evangelical Dictionary of Christian Education*. Grand Rapids: Baker Academic, 2001.

Ashbrook, James B. "The Functional Meaning of the Soul in the Christian Tradition." *Journal of Pastoral Care* 12 (1958) 1–16.

Bain, Homer A. "The Greatest Influence on My Pastoral Counseling." *American Journal of Pastoral Counseling* 7 (2004) 73–77.

Barb, Marion L., and Ernest E. Bruder. *Clinical Education for the Pastoral Ministry: Proceedings of the Fifth National Conference on Clinical Pastoral Education*. Washington, DC: Advisory Committee on Clinical Pastoral Education, 1958.

———. *A Survey of Ten Years of Clinical Pastoral Training*. Washington, DC: Saint Elizabeth's Hospital, Chaplain Services Branch, 1956.

Barnes, William Wright. *The Southern Baptist Convention: 1845–1953*. Nashville: Broadman, 1954.

Barth, Karl. *Church Dogmatics*. Edinburgh: T. & T. Clark, 1936.

———. *The Doctrine of the Word of God*. Edinburgh: T. & T. Clark, 1936.

Baxter, Richard. *The Reformed Pastor*. Carlisle, PA: Banner of Truth Trust, 1999.

Benner, David G., and Peter C. Hill. *Baker Encyclopedia of Psychology & Counseling*. Grand Rapids: Baker, 1999.

Binkley, Olin T. "Christian Ethics and Social Policy." *Review & Expositor* 44 (1947) 209–10.

———. *The Churches and the Social Conscience*. Indianapolis: National Foundation, 1948.

———. "Education of Ministers in Contemporary Society." *Theological Education* 3 (1967) 265–69.

———. *From Victory unto Victory*. Nashville: Broadman, 1945.

———. *Frontiers for Christian Youth*. Nashville: Broadman, 1941.

———. "The Minister's Moral Task." *Review & Expositor* 43 (1946) 369.

———. "Southern Baptist Perspective." *Theological Education* 12 (1975) 52–56.

———. "Southern Baptist Seminaries." *Christian Century* 80 (1963) 774–75.

———. "The Task of the Church." *Pastoral Psychology* 10 (1959) 9.

Binkley, Olin T., and Mavis Allen. *How to Study the Bible*. Nashville: Convention, 1969.

Bobgan, Martin, and Deidre Bobgan. *Psychoheresy: The Psychological Seduction of Christianity*. Santa Barbara, CA: EastGate, 1987.

Boisen, Anton T. *The Exploration of the Inner World: A Study of Mental Disorder and Religious Experience*. 2nd ed. Philadelphia: University of Pennsylvania Press, 1971.

———. *Out of the Depths: An Autobiographical Study of Mental Disorder and Religious Experience*. New York: Harper, 1960.

———. *Problems in Religion and Life*. New York: Abingdon-Cokesbury, 1946.

———. *Religion in Crisis and Custom: A Sociological and Psychological Study*. 3rd ed. Westport, CT: Greenwood, 1973.

Bonnell, John Sutherland. *Pastoral Psychiatry*. New York: Harper, 1938.

———. *Psychology for Pastor and People: A Book on Spiritual Counseling*. New York: Harper, 1948.

Bookman, Douglas. "The Scriptures and Biblical Counseling." In *Introduction to Biblical Counseling: A Basic Guide to the Principles and Practice of Counseling*, edited by John MacArthur and Wayne A. Mack, 63–97. Dallas: Word, 1994.

Booth, Howard John. "Edwin Diller Starbuck: Pioneer in the Psychology of Religion." PhD diss., University of Iowa, 1972.

Borchert, Gerald L., and Andrew D. Lester. *Spiritual Dimensions of Pastoral Care: Witness to the Ministry of Wayne E. Oates*. Philadelphia: Westminster, 1985.

Boyce, James Petigru. *Abstract of Systematic Theology*. Philadelphia: American Baptist Publication Society, 1887.

Boyers, Robert. *Psychological Man*. New York: Harper & Row, 1975.

Bremer, David H. "George Albert Coe's Contribution to the Psychology of Religion." PhD diss., Boston University School of Theology, 1949.

Brister, C. W. Review of *Christ and Selfhood*, by Wayne Oates. *Southwestern Journal of Theology* 4 (1962) 120–21.

Brown, William Adams. *Christian Theology in Outline*. New York: Scribner, 1906.

———. *God at Work: A Study of the Supernatural*. New York: Scribner, 1933.

———. "The Old Theology and the New." *Harvard Theological Review* 4 (1911) 1–24.

Browning, Don S. "Analogy, Symbol, and Pastoral Theology in Tillich's Thought." *Pastoral Psychology* 19 (1968) 41–54.

———. "New Trends in Pastoral Care: The Search for Method in Religious Living." *Christian Century* 90 (1973) 849–51.

Bruder, Ernest E. "Clinical Pastoral Training in Preparation for the Pastoral Ministry." *Journal of Pastoral Care* 16 (1962) 25–33.

———. "Some Theological Considerations in Clinical Pastoral Education." *Journal of Pastoral Care* 8 (1954) 135–46.

Brunner, Emil. *The Christian Doctrine of Creation and Redemption*. Philadelphia: Westminster, 1952.

Brunner, Emil, and D. S. Cairns. *God and Man: Four Essays on the Nature of Personality*. London: Student Christian Movement, 1936.

Brunner, Emil, and Olive Wyon. *The Mediator: A Study of the Central Doctrine of the Christian Faith*. New York: Macmillan, 1934.

Buber, Martin. *Between Man and Man*. New York: Macmillan, 1948.

———. *I and Thou*. 2nd ed. Translated by Ronald Gregory Smith. New York: Scribner, 1958.

———. *The Knowledge of Man: Selected Essays*. Edited by Maurice Friedman. Translated by Maurice Friedman and Ronald Gregor Smith. New York: Harper & Row, 1965.

Bulkley, Ed. *Why Christians Can't Trust Psychology*. Eugene, OR: Harvest, 1993.

Bush, L. R., and Tom J. Nettles. *Baptists and the Bible: The Baptist Doctrines of Biblical Inspiration and Religious Authority in Historical Perspective*. Chicago: Moody, 1980.

Bush, Theodore Andrew. "Human Suffering in the Theology of Wayne E. Oates." PhD diss., Aquinas Institute of Philosophy and Theology, 1980.

Bushnell, Horace. *Christian Nurture*. New York: Scribner, Armstrong, 1876.

Cabot, Richard C. "Adventures on the Borderland of Ethics: A Plea for a Clinical Year in the Course of Theological Study." *Survey* 55 (1924) 275–79.

Cabot, Richard C., and Russell L. Dicks. *The Art of Ministering to the Sick*. New York: Macmillan, 1936.

Calvin, John. *Institutes of the Christian Religion*. Rev. ed. Peabody: Hendrickson, 2008.

Campbell, Alastair V. *A Dictionary of Pastoral Care*. New York: Crossroad, 1987.

Cattell, Raymond B. *An Introduction to Personality Study*. London: Hutchinson's University Library, 1950.
Clarke, William Newton. *An Outline of Christian Theology*. New York: Scribner, 1898.
———. *The Christian Doctrine of God*. New York: Scribner, 1909.
———. *Sixty Years with the Bible: A Record of Experience*. New York: Scribner, 1909.
———. *The Use of the Scriptures in Theology*. New York: Scribner, 1905.
Clebsch, William A., and Charles R. Jaekle. *Pastoral Care in Historical Perspective: An Essay with Exhibits*. Englewood Cliffs, NJ: Prentice-Hall, 1964.
Clinebell, Howard John. *Basic Types of Pastoral Counseling*. Nashville: Abingdon, 1966.
Clymer, Wayne K. "Can the Counselor be a Prophet." *Journal of Pastoral Care* 10 (1956) 150–60.
Cobb, John. "The God of Process Theology." *Tikkun* 29 (2014) 43–45.
Coe, George Albert. *The Motives of Men*. New York: Scribner, 1928.
———. *The Psychology of Religion*. Chicago: University of Chicago Press, 1916.
———. *The Spiritual Life: Studies in the Science of Religion*. New York: Eaton & Mains, 1900.
Cogan, Morris. "Toward a Definition of Profession." *Harvard Educational Review* 23 (1953) 35–50.
Collins, Gary R. *Can You Trust Psychology? Exposing the Facts & the Fictions*. Downers Grove: InterVarsity, 1988.
Collins, J. C. "The Pastoral Concern for Man in the Thought of Wayne Edward Oates." PhD diss., Southwestern Baptist Theological Seminary, 1974.
Conver, Leigh E. "Care of the Soul: The Repurchase of a Stolen Birthright." *Review & Expositor* 94 (1997) 107–30.
Cooper, Ilene. "God of Becoming and Relationship: The Dynamic Nature of Process Theology." *Booklist* 110 (2013) 12.
Cooper, John W. *Body, Soul, and Life Everlasting: Biblical Anthropology and the Monism-Dualism Debate*. Grand Rapids: Eerdmans, 1989.
Cooper, Terry D. *Paul Tillich and Psychology: Historic and Contemporary Explorations in Theology, Psychotherapy, and Ethics*. Macon, GA: Mercer University Press, 2006.
Corsini, Raymond J. *Encyclopedia of Psychology*. 2nd ed. Vol. 4. New York: Wiley, 1994.
Corsini, Raymond J., and Anthony J. Marsella. *Personality Theories, Research, & Assessment*. Itasca, IL: Peacock, 1983.
Crouch, Kevin Michael. "The Influence of William James on E. Y. Mullins and the Changing Nature of Pastoral Ministry Instruction at Southern Seminary in the Early Twentieth Century." PhD diss., Southwestern Baptist Theological Seminary, 2014.
Curtis, Oliver B., Jr. "The Role of Religion in Selfhood: An Examination of Humanistic Psychoanalysis in Erich Fromm and Christian Selfhood in Wayne Oates." PhD. diss., Baylor University, 1972.
Davis, John Jefferson. *Theology Primer: Resources for the Theological Student*. Baker, 1981.
Deckard, Mark. *Helpful Truth in Past Places: The Puritan Practice of Biblical Counseling*. Scotland: Christian Focus Publications, 2010.
Deinhardt, Carol I., and Heather J. Rochon. "Is Our Truth God's Truth?" *Didaskalia* 12 (2000) 1–24.
Dicks, Russell L. *Pastoral Work and Personal Counseling: An Introduction to Pastoral Care*. Rev. ed. New York: Macmillan, 1949.

Dobbins, Austin C. *Gaines S. Dobbins: Pioneer in Religious Education*. Nashville: Broadman, 1981.
Dodd, C. H. *The Authority of the Bible*. 2nd ed. London: Nisbet, 1938.
Douglas, J. D. *The New International Dictionary of the Christian Church*. Grand Rapids: Zondervan, 1974.
Douglas, William. "Psychology in Theological Education." In *The Ministry and Mental Health*, edited by Hans Hofmann, 85–100. New York: Association, 1960.
Drakeford, John W. *Psychology in Search of a Soul*. Nashville: Broadman, 1964.
Draper, Edgar. "On the Diagnostic Value of Religious Ideation." *Archives of General Psychiatry* (1965) 202–7.
Duke McCall Papers, 1951–2013, James P. Boyce Centennial Library Archives and Special Collections, Southern Baptist Theological Seminary, Louisville, Kentucky.
Durst, Rodrick Karl. "The Theological Dimension of Human Existence: An Analysis of the Theology of Wayne Edward Oates." PhD diss., Golden Gate Baptist Theological Seminary, 1988.
Edgar, John Henry. "Pastoral Identity in the Thought of Wayne E. Oates (Ministry, Care, Counseling)." PhD diss., Southern Baptist Theological Seminary, 1985.
Eliason, Leland Virgil. "A Critique of Approaches to Integrating Psychology and Theology within Selected Evangelical Seminaries." ThD diss., Boston University School of Theology, 1983.
Elwell, Walter A., ed. *Evangelical Dictionary of Theology*. 2nd ed. Grand Rapids: Baker, 2001.
English, Horace B., and Ava Champney English. *A Comprehensive Dictionary of Psychological and Psychoanalytical Terms*. New York: Longmans, Green, 1958.
Erickson, Millard J. *Christian Theology*. Grand Rapids: Baker, 1998.
Erikson, Erik. *Childhood and Society*. New York: Norton, 1950.
———. *Identity in the Life Cycle*. New York: International Universities, 1959.
———. *Identity, Youth, and Crisis*. New York: Norton, 1968.
Farley, Edward. *Theologia: The Fragmentation and Unity of Theological Education*. Philadelphia: Fortress, 1983.
Feilding, Charles Rudolph. *Education for Ministry*. Dayton, OH: American Association of Theological Schools, 1966.
Feuerbach, Ludwig. *The Essence of Christianity*. New York: Harper, 1957.
Foucault, Michel. *Madness: The Invention of an Idea*. New York: Harper Perennial, 2011.
Fowler, James W. *Faith Development and Pastoral Care*. Theology and Pastoral Care Series. Philadelphia: Fortress, 1986.
Freud, Sigmund. *The Ego and the Id*. 1st ed. New York: Norton, 1961.
———. *A General Introduction to Psychoanalysis*. New York: Pocket, 1935.
Freud, Sigmund, and A. A. Brill. *Totem and Taboo: Resemblances between the Psychic Lives of Savages and Neurotics*. New York: Vintage, 1946.
Freud, Sigmund, and Katherine Jones. *Moses and Monotheism*. New York: Vintage, 1967.
Freud, Sigmund, and James Strachey. *Civilization and Its Discontents*. New York: Norton, 2010.
Freud, Sigmund, et al. *Freud: A Dictionary of Psychoanalysis*. 2nd ed. Greenwich, CT: Fawcett, 1963.
Fromm, Erich. *Man for Himself: An Inquiry into the Psychology of Ethics*. New York: Rinehart, 1947.

Fuller, Ellis, et al. A Tenth-Year Report: Curriculum Development, Department of Psychology of Religion and Pastoral Care. Southern Baptist Theological Seminary, Louisville, Kentucky, November 1953.

Fuller, Robert C. "The Emmanuel Movement: The Origins of Group Treatment and the Assault on Lay Psychotherapy." *Journal of the History of the Behavioral Sciences* 35 (1999) 328–29.

Gaebelein, Frank Ely. *The Pattern of God's Truth: Problems of Integration in Christian Education*. New York: Oxford University Press, 1954.

Gambrell, Mary Latimer. *Ministerial Training in 18th-Century New England*. New York: Columbia University Press, 1937.

Ganz, Richard. "Nouthetic Counseling Defended." *Journal of Psychology & Theology* 4 (1976) 193–205.

———. *Psychobabble: The Failure of Modern Psychology and the Biblical Alternative*. Wheaton: Crossway, 1993.

Geisler, Norman L. *Baker Encyclopedia of Christian Apologetics*. Grand Rapids: Baker, 1999.

———. *Christian Apologetics*. Grand Rapids: Baker, 1988.

Gladden, Washington. *The Christian Pastor and the Working Church*. New York: Scribner, 1898.

Glasse, James D. *Profession: Minister*. Nashville: Abingdon, 1968.

Goode, William. "Encroachment, Charlatanism, and the Emerging Profession." *American Sociological Review* 25 (1960) 902–33.

Grenz, Stanley J., and John R. Franke. *Beyond Foundationalism: Shaping Theology in a Postmodern Context*. 1st ed. Louisville: Westminster John Knox, 2001.

Grudem, Wayne A. *Systematic Theology: An Introduction to Biblical Doctrine*. Grand Rapids: Zondervan, 2000.

Hall, David D. *The Faithful Shepherd: A History of the New England Ministry in the Seventeenth Century*. Cambridge: Harvard University Press, 2006.

Hall, G. S. *Adolescence: It's Psychology and Its Relations to Physiology, Anthropology, Sociology, Sex, Crime, Religion and Education*. 2nd ed. New York: Appleton, 1915.

———. *Founders of Modern Psychology*. New York: Appleton, 1912.

———. *Jesus, the Christ, in the Light of Psychology*. Garden City: Doubleday, 1917.

Halverson, Marvin, and Arthur Allen Cohen. *A Handbook of Christian Theology*. New York: New American Library, 1974.

Hammett, Hugh B. "Gordon W. Allport—in Memorium." *Pastoral Psychology* (1968) 65–66.

———. "Historical Context of the Origins of CPE." *Journal of Pastoral Care* 29 (1975) 76–85.

———. "Planning as a Profession." *Journal of the American Institute of Planners* 23 (1957) 162.

———. "Religion and Psychoanalysis." *Journal of Pastoral Care* 4 (1950) 32–42.

Hammett, John S. *Biblical Foundations for Baptist Churches: A Contemporary Ecclesiology*. Grand Rapids: Kregel, 2005.

Harold Wayland Tribble Papers (MS 291). Z. Smith Reynolds Library Special Collections and Archives, Wake Forest University, Winston-Salem, North Carolina.

Henlee Barnette Papers (MS 474). Z. Smith Reynolds Library Special Collections and Archives, Wake Forest University, Winston-Salem, North Carolina.

Hiltner, Seward. *The Christian Shepherd: Some Aspects of Pastoral Care*. New York: Abingdon, 1959.
———. *Clinical Pastoral Training*. New York: Commission on Religion and Health, Federal Council of the Churches of Christ in America, 1945.
———. *The Counselor in Counseling: Case Notes in Pastoral Counseling*. New York: Abingdon-Cokesbury, 1952.
———. *Ferment in the Ministry*. Nashville: Abingdon, 1969.
———. *Pastoral Counseling*. New York: Abingdon-Cokesbury, 1949.
———. *Preface to Pastoral Theology*. New York: Abingdon, 1958.
———. *Protestant Religious Work in Mental Hospitals*. Evansville, IN: American Protestant Hospital Association, 1944.
———. *Self-Understanding through Psychology and Religion*. New York: Scribner, 1951.
Hiltner, Seward, and Lowell G. Colston. *The Context of Pastoral Counseling*. New York: Abingdon, 1961.
Hiltner, Seward, and Jesse H. Ziegler. "Clinical Pastoral Education and the Theological Schools." *Journal of Pastoral Care* 15 (1961) 129–43.
Hiltner, Seward, et al. "'Credentials' for Pastoral Counseling?" *Pastoral Psychology* 11 (1961) 45–58.
Hoekema, Anthony A. *Created in God's Image*. Grand Rapids: Eerdmans, 1994.
Hofmann, Hans F. *The Ministry and Mental Health*. New York: Association, 1960.
Holifield, E. B. *A History of Pastoral Care in America: From Salvation to Self-Realization*. Eugene, OR: Wipf & Stock, 2003.
Horney, Karen. *Neurosis and Human Growth*. New York: Norton, 1950.
Hull, William E. *Seminary in Crisis: The Strategic Response of the Southern Baptist Theological Seminary to the SBC Controversy*. Atlanta: Baptist History and Heritage Society, 2010.
Hulme, William Edward. *Counseling and Theology*. Philadelphia: Muhlenberg, 1956.
———. *Pastoral Care and Counseling*. Minneapolis: Augsburg, 1981.
Hunter, Rodney J., ed. *Dictionary of Pastoral Care and Counseling*. Nashville: Abingdon, 1990.
Husserl, Edmund, and William Ralph Boyce Gibson. *Ideas: General Introduction to Pure Phenomenology*. London: Allen & Unwin, 1931.
Jackson, Walter C. "A Brief History of Theological Education Including a Description of the Contribution of Wayne E. Oates." *Review & Expositor* 94 (1997) 503–20.
James, William. *The Principles of Psychology*. New York: Holt, 1890.
———. *Talks to Teachers on Psychology: And to Students on Some of Life's Ideals*. London: Longmans & Green, 1899.
———. *Varieties of Religious Experience: A Study in Human Nature; Being the Gifford Lectures on Natural Religion Delivered at Edinburgh in 1901–1902*. New York: Modern Library, 1902.
Jansma, Theodore. "The Pastoral Counseling Movement." *Reformed Journal* 10 (1960) 15–18.
———. "A Psychiatrist's 'Challenge' Challenged." *Pastoral Psychology* 11 (1960) 52–56.
Jeane, Martin Keller. "An Analysis of Wayne Edward Oates' Phenomenological Method of Diagnosis in Pastoral Counseling." PhD diss., Southwestern Baptist Theological Seminary, 1986.
Johnson, Eric L., and David G. Myers. *Psychology & Christianity: Five Views*. 2nd ed. Downers Grove: IVP Academic, 2010.

Johnson, Paul Emanuel. "Fifty Years of Clinical Pastoral Education." *Journal of Pastoral Care* 22 (1968) 223–31.

Johnson, Tommy Dale, Jr. "The Professionalization of Pastoral Care within the Southern Baptist Convention: Gaines Dobbins and the Psychology of Religion." PhD diss., Southwestern Baptist Theological Seminary, 2014.

Kelly, Robert. *Theological Education in America: A Study of One Hundred Sixty-One Theological Schools in the United States.* New York: Doran, 1924.

Kemp, Charles F. *Physicians of the Soul: A History of Pastoral Counseling.* New York: Macmillan, 1947.

Kierkegaard, Søren. *The Sickness unto Death.* Princeton: Princeton University Press, 1968.

Klink, Thomas W. *Depth Perspectives in Pastoral Work.* Englewood Cliffs, NJ: Prentice Hall, 1965.

Lambert, Heath. *A Theology of Biblical Counseling: The Doctrinal Foundations of Counseling Ministry.* Grand Rapids: Zondervan, 2016.

Leuba, James H. *A Psychological Study of Religion.* New York: Macmillan, 1912.

Lionni, Paolo, and Lance J. Klass. *The Leipzig Connection: The Systematic Destruction of American Education.* Basics in Education. Portland, OR: Heron, 1980.

MacArthur, John. *Matthew 16–23.* MacArthur New Testament Commentary. Chicago: Moody, 1988.

———. *Our Sufficiency in Christ.* Wheaton, IL: Crossway, 1998.

Maclaren, Ian. *The Cure of Souls: Lyman Beecher Lectures on Preaching at Yale University.* New York: Dodd, Mead, 1896.

Maddi, Salvatore R., and Paul T. Costa. *Humanism in Personology: Allport, Maslow, and Murray.* Chicago: Aldine Atherton, 1972.

Maslow, Abraham H. "Eupsychia—The Good Society." *Journal of Humanistic Psychology* 1 (1961) 1–11.

———. *Motivation and Personality.* 2nd ed. New York: Harper & Row, 1970.

———. "A Theory of Human Motivation." *Psychological Review* 50 (1943) 370–96.

———. *Toward a Psychology of Being.* 2nd ed. Princeton: Van Nostrand, 1968.

Maves, Paul B. *The Church and Mental Health.* New York: Scribner, 1953.

May, Rollo. *The Art of Counseling: How to Gain and Give Mental Health.* Nashville: Abingdon-Cokesbury, 1939.

———. *Existence: A New Dimension in Psychiatry and Psychology.* New York: Basic, 1958.

———. *Man's Search for Himself.* New York: Norton, 1953.

Mays, William C. "Contemporary Theology and Pastoral Care: A Study of the Writings of Wayne E. Oates." STM thesis, Divinity School of Vanderbilt University, 1968.

McMinn, Mark R., and Timothy R. Phillips. *Care for the Soul: Exploring the Intersection of Psychology & Theology.* Downers Grove: InterVarsity, 2001.

Meador, Keith G. "The Christian Century and Psychology's Secularizing of American Protestantism." In *The Secular Revolution: Power, Interests, and Conflict in the Secularization of American Public Life*, edited by Christian Smith, 269–309. Berkeley: University of California Press, 2003.

Mena, Danilo J. "Freud and American Liberal Protestantism: A Study of the Religion and Health Movement in the United States the Twentieth Century." EdD diss., Teachers College, Columbia University, 2002.

Menon, Sangeetha, et al. *Interdisciplinary Perspectives on Consciousness and the Self.* New York: Springer, 2014.
McNeill, John T. *A History of the Cure of Souls.* New York: Harper, 1951.
Miller, Samuel Howard. "Exploring the Boundary between Religion and Psychiatry." *Journal of Pastoral Care* 6 (1952) 1–11.
Mitchell, Kenneth R. "Do Pastoral Counselors Bring a New Consciousness to the Health Professions?" *Journal of Pastoral Care* 26 (1972) 245–57.
Moreland, J. P., and Scott B. Rae. *Body and Soul: Human Nature and the Crisis in Ethics.* Downers Grove: IVP Academic, 2000.
Moroney, Stephen K. *The Noetic Effects of Sin: A Historical and Contemporary Exploration of How Sin Affects Our Thinking.* Lanham, MD: Lexington, 2000.
Mowrer, O. Hobart. *The Crisis in Psychiatry and Religion.* Princeton: Van Nostrand, 1961.
———. "Some Philosophical Problems in Psychological Counseling." *Journal of Counseling Psychology* 4 (1957) 103–11.
Muravchik, Stephanie. *American Protestantism in the Age of Psychology.* New York: Cambridge University Press, 2011.
Murphy, Gardner. *Personality: A Biosocial Approach to Origins and Structure.* New York: Harper & Row, 1947.
Narramore, Bruce. "Psychology and Theology: Twenty-Five Years of Theoretical Integration." *Journal of Psychology & Theology* 25 (1997) 6–10.
Niebuhr, H. R. *Beyond Tragedy: Essays on the Christian Interpretation of History.* New York: Scribner, 1937.
———. *The Purpose of the Church and Its Ministry: Reflections on the Aims of Theological Education.* New York: Harper, 1956.
———. *The Self and the Dramas of History.* New York: Scribner, 1955.
Niebuhr, H. R., et al. *The Advancement of Theological Education.* New York: Harper, 1957.
North, Gary. *Foundations of Christian Scholarship: Essays in the Van Til Perspective.* Vallecito, CA: Ross, 1976.
Oates, Wayne Edward. *Anxiety in Christian Experience.* Philadelphia: Westminster, 1955.
———. "Association of Pastoral Counselors: It's Values and Its Dangers." *Pastoral Psychology* 15 (1964) 5–7.
———. *Behind the Masks: Personality Disorders in Religious Behavior.* Louisville: Westminster, 1987.
———. *The Bible in Pastoral Care.* Philadelphia: Westminster, 1953.
———. *The Care of Troublesome People.* Bethesda, MD: Alban Institute, 1994.
———. *Christ and Selfhood.* New York: Association, 1961.
———. *The Christian Pastor.* Philadelphia: Westminster, 1951.
———. *The Christian Pastor.* 3rd ed. Philadelphia: Westminster, 1982
———. "Conception of Ministry in the Pastoral Epistles." *Review & Expositor* 56 (1959) 388–410.
———. "Contribution of Paul Tillich to Pastoral Psychology." *Pastoral Psychology* 19 (1968) 11–16.
———. "Counseling by Seminarians." *Journal of Pastoral Care* 8 (1954) 154–59.
———. "The Diagnostic Use of the Bible: What a Man Sees in the Bible Is a Projection of His Inner Self." *Pastoral Psychology* 1 (1950) 43–46.

---. "Evangelism and Pastoral Psychology." *Pastoral Psychology* 7 (1956) 6–9.

---. "The Gospel and Modern Psychology." *Review & Expositor* 46 (1949) 181–98.

---. "Harry Stack Sullivan, MD: The Interpersonal Theory of Psychiatry." *American Journal of Pastoral Counseling* 1 (1998) 81–84.

---. "The Healthy Minister." *Pastoral Psychology* 9 (1958) 19–28.

---. "The Hindering and Helping Power of Religion." *Pastoral Psychology* 6 (1955) 43.

---. *Holy Spirit and Contemporary Man*. Grand Rapids: Baker, 1974.

---. "Holy Spirit and the Overseer of the Flock." *Review & Expositor* 63 (1966) 187–97.

---. "Holy Spirit as Counselor." *Review & Expositor* 54 (1957) 233–45.

---. *The Holy Spirit in Five Worlds: The Psychedelic, the Nonverbal, the Articulate, the New Morality, the Administrative*. New York: Association, 1968.

---. "In Relation to Theological Education." *Pastoral Psychology* (1970).

---. "Inner World of the Patient." *Pastoral Psychology* 8 (1957) 16–18.

---. *An Introduction to Pastoral Counseling*. Nashville: Broadman, 1959.

---. "Legalism and the Use of the Bible." *Pastoral Psychology* 4 (1953) 29–38.

---. "The Levels of Pastoral Care: The New Testament Concept of a Health-Giving Ministry." *Pastoral Psychology* 2 (1951) 11–16.

---. "A Long Friendship." *Christian Century*, January 19, 1994.

---. "Man of the Month: Edward E Thornton." *Pastoral Psychology* 18 (1967) 4.

---. *Managing Your Stress*. Philadelphia: Fortress, 1985.

---. *The Minister's Own Mental Health*. Great Neck, NY: Channel, 1961.

---. *New Dimensions in Pastoral Care*. Philadelphia: Fortress, 1970.

---. "New Emphases in Psychiatry and Religion: DSM-III." *Union Seminary Quarterly Review* 36 (1981) 141–47.

---. "New Morality: A Psychological and Theological Critique." *Review & Expositor* 64 (1967) 285–96.

---. *On Becoming Children of God*. Philadelphia: Westminster, 1968.

---. "Organizational Development and Pastoral Care." *Review & Expositor* 75 (1978) 349–60.

---. *Pastoral Care and Counseling in Grief and Separation*. Fortress, 1976.

---. *Pastoral Counseling*. Philadelphia: Westminster, 1974.

---. "Pastoral Counseling." *Bulletin of Crozer Theological Seminary* 43 (April 1956) 3–16.

---. *Pastoral Counseling in Social Problems: Extremism, Race, Sex, Divorce*. Philadelphia: Westminster, 1966.

---. "Pastoral Counseling in the Free Church Tradition." *Pastoral Psychology* 12 (1961) 21–34.

---. "Pastoral Psychology: The Next 20 Years in Relation to Theological Education." *Pastoral Psychology* 21 (1970) 49–55.

---. *Pastor's Handbook*. 2 vols. Philadelphia: Westminster, 1980.

---. *The Presence of God in Pastoral Counseling*. Waco: Word, 1986.

---. "Professor as Bishop." *Journal of Pastoral Care* 15 (1961) 65–71.

---. *Protestant Pastoral Counseling*. Philadelphia: Westminster, 1962.

---. *The Psychology of Religion*. Waco: Word, 1973.

---. *The Religious Care of the Psychiatric Patient*. Philadelphia: Westminster, 1978.

---. *The Religious Dimensions of Personality*. New York: Association, 1957.

———. *Religious Factors in Mental Illness*. New York: Association, 1955.
———. "The Religious Understanding of Personality." *Pastoral Psychology* 8 (1957) 46–50.
———. "Response." *Review & Expositor* 94 (1997) 131–34.
———. *The Revelation of God in Human Suffering*. Philadelphia: Westminster, 1959.
———. "The Role of Religion in the Psychoses." *Journal of Pastoral Care* 3 (1949) 21–30.
———. "Rural Pastor as Counselor." *Pastoral Psychology* (1959).
———. "The Significance of the Work of Sigmund Freud for the Christian Faith." ThD diss., Southern Baptist Theological Seminary, 1947.
———. "Some Psychological Implications of the Doctrine of the Kingdom of God." *Covenant Quarterly* 16 (1956) 3–12.
———. *The Struggle to Be Free: My Story and Your Story*. Philadelphia: Westminster, 1983.
———. "The Theological Context of Pastoral Counseling." *Review & Expositor* 94 (1997) 521–30.
———. *What Psychology Says about Religion*. New York: Association, 1958.
———. *When Religion Gets Sick*. Philadelphia: Westminster, 1970.
Oates, Wayne Edward, and Olin T. Binkley. "Olin T. Binkley." *Pastoral Psychology* 10 (1959) 6.
Oates, Wayne Edward, and Thomas W. Chapman. *A Practical Handbook for Ministry: From the Writings of Wayne E. Oates*. Louisville: John Knox, 1992.
Oates, Wayne Edward, and Kirk H. Neely. *Where to Go for Help*. Rev. ed. Philadelphia: Westminster, 1972.
Oates, Wayne Edward, and Charles E. Oates. *People in Pain: Guidelines for Pastoral Care*. Philadelphia: Westminster, 1985.
Oden, Thomas C. *Becoming a Minister*. Classical Pastoral Care 1. New York: Crossroad, 1987.
———. *Contemporary Theology and Psychotherapy*. Philadelphia: Westminster, 1967.
———. *Kerygma and Counseling: Toward a Covenant Ontology for Secular Psychotherapy*. Philadelphia: Westminster, 1966.
———. *Ministry through Word and Sacrament*. Classical Pastoral Care 2. New York: Crossroad, 1988.
———. *Pastoral Counsel*. Classical Pastoral Care 3. Grand Rapids: Baker, 1994.
———. *Pastoral Theology: Essentials of Ministry*. San Francisco: Harper & Row, 1983.
———. *Systematic Theology*. Peabody: Hendrickson, 2006.
Oden, Thomas C., and Don S. Browning. *Care of Souls in the Classic Tradition*. Philadelphia: Fortress, 1984.
Oglesby, William. *New Shape of Pastoral Theology: Essays in Honor of Seward Hiltner*. Nashville: Abingdon, 1969.
Olin T. Binkley Papers (MS 460). Z. Smith Reynolds Library Special Collections and Archives, Wake Forest University, Winston-Salem, North Carolina.
Owen, Jim. *Christian Psychology's War on God's Word: The Victimization of the Believer*. Santa Barbara, CA: EastGate, 1993.
Packer, J. I., et al. *New Dictionary of Theology*. Downers Grove: InterVarsity, 1988.
Peden, W. C. *Christian Pragmatism: An Intellectual Biography of Edward Scribner Ames, 1870–1958*. Newcastle upon Tyne, UK: Cambridge Scholars, 2011.

Pfister, Oskar. *Christianity and Fear: A Study in History and in the Psychology and Hygiene of Religion*. London: Allen & Unwin, 1948.
Pittenger, W. N. *The Christian Church as Social Process*. London: Epworth, 1971.
———. *The Christian Understanding of Human Nature*. Philadelphia: Westminster, 1964.
———. *Process-Thought and Christian Faith*. New York: Macmillan, 1968.
———. *Unbounded Love: God and Man in Process*. New York: Seabury, 1976.
———. *The Word Incarnate: A Study of the Doctrine of the Person of Christ*. New York: Harper, 1959.
Plummer, Keith W. "Canonically Competent to Counsel: An Analysis of the Use of the Bible in Integration, Biblical Counseling, and Christian Psychology with a Canonical-Linguistic Proposal for Reclaiming Counseling as a Theological Discipline." PhD diss., Trinity International University, 2008.
Porter, Ray. *Madness: A Brief History*. Oxford: Oxford University Press, 2002.
Powell, Lyman. *The Emmanuel Movement in a New England Town: A Systematic Account of Experiments and Reflections Designed to Determine the Power Relationship between the Minister and the Doctor in the Light of Modern Needs*. New York: Putman, 1909.
Powlison, David. *The Biblical Counseling Movement: History and Context*. Greensboro, NC: New Growth, 2010.
Pritchard, Gregory, et al. *Approaches to the Understanding of God: Lectures*. Winston-Salem, NC: Wake Forest University Press, 1977.
Pruyser, Paul W. *A Dynamic Psychology of Religion*. New York: Harper & Row, 1968.
Purves, Andrew. *Pastoral Theology in the Classical Tradition*. Louisville: Westminster John Knox, 2001.
Rauschenbusch, Walter, et al. *Christianity and the Social Crisis in the 21st Century*. Edited by Paul Rauschenbusch. New ed. San Francisco: HarperCollins, 2007.
Rawlinson, A. E. J. *The New Testament Doctrine of the Christ*. New York: Longmans, 1926.
Ribble, Margaret A. *The Rights of Infants: Early Psychological Needs and their Satisfaction*. New York: Columbia University Press, 1943.
Rieff, Philip. *Liberal Theology, an Appraisal: Essays in Honor of Eugene William Lyman*. New York: Scribner, 1942.
———. *The Triumph of the Therapeutic: Uses of Faith after Freud*. 40th anniversary ed. Wilmington, DE: ISI, 2006.
Roberts, David. *Psychotherapy and a Christian View of Man*. New York: Scribner, 1950.
Rogers, Carl R. *Client-Centered Therapy: Its Current Practice, Implications, and Theory*. Boston: Houghton Mifflin, 1951.
———. *Counseling and Psychotherapy: Newer Concepts in Practice*. Edited by Leonard Carmichael. Boston: Houghton Mifflin, 1942.
———. "The Nature of Man." *Pastoral Psychology* 11 (1960) 23–26.
———. *On Becoming a Person: A Therapist's View of Psychotherapy*. Boston: Houghton Mifflin, 1961.
———. "A Personal Formation of Client-Centered Therapy." *Marriage and Family Living* 14 (1952) 341–61.
Rogers, Clement F. *An Introduction to the Study of Pastoral Theology*. Oxford: Clarendon, 1912.

Ross, Stephen David. *Perspective in Whitehead's Metaphysics.* Albany: State University of New York Press, 1983.
Rowatt, Wade. "Oates' Theological Model for Psychology and Pastoral Counseling." *Review & Expositor* 101 (2004) 87–95.
Ryckman, Richard M. *Theories of Personality.* 5th ed. Pacific Grove, CA: Brooks & Cole, 1993.
Sabom, W. S. "Heresy and Pastoral Counseling." *Journal of Pastoral Care* 36 (1982) 76–86.
Sampey, John R. *Southern Baptist Theological Seminary: The First Thirty Years, 1859–1889.* Baltimore: Wharton & Barron, 1890.
Scharfenberg, Joachim. "The Babylonian Captivity of Pastoral Theology." *Journal of Pastoral Care* 8 (1954) 133.
Schleiermacher, Friedrich. *The Christian Faith.* Edited by H. R. Mackintosh and James S. Stewart. Edinburgh: T. & T. Clark, 1928.
———. *Christian Faith: A New Translation and Critical Edition.* Translated by Edwina G. Lawler et al. Edited by Catherine L. Kelsey and Terrence N. Tice. Louisville: Westminster John Knox, 2016.
Scruggs, Julius Richard. *Baptist Preachers with Social Consciousness: A Comparative Study of Martin Luther King, Jr. and Harry Emerson Fosdick.* Philadelphia: Dorrance, 1978.
Scott, Donald M. *From Office to Profession: The New England Ministry, 1750–1850.* Philadelphia: University of Pennsylvania Press, 1978.
Shahan, Ewing P. *Whitehead's Theory of Experience.* New York: King's Crown, 1950.
Shands, O. Norman. "Ellis Adams Fuller, Man of God." Founders' Day address, Southern Baptist Theological Seminary, September 16, 1965.
Sherrill, Lewis Joseph. *Guilt and Redemption.* Richmond: John Knox, 1945.
———. *The Struggle of the Soul.* New York: Macmillan, 1951.
Shorter, Edward. *A History of Psychiatry: From the Era of the Asylum to the Age of Prozac.* New York: Wiley, 1997.
Smith, H. S. *Changing Conceptions of Original Sin: A Study in American Theology since 1750.* New York: Scribner, 1955.
Smith, John C. "Wayne E. Oates: Pastoral Theologian." ThM thesis, Princeton Theological Seminary, 1970.
Southard, Samuel. "A Phenomenological Approach." *Christian Century* 90 (1973) 1277–78.
Southern Baptist Theological Seminary. *Southern Baptist Theological Seminary Annual Catalogue.* Louisville: Seminary Press, 1947–1974.
Sperry, Willard Learoyd. *The Ethical Basis of Medical Practice.* New York: Hoeber, 1950.
Spitzer, Robert, ed. *Diagnostic and Statistical Manual of Mental Disorders.* Arlington, VA: American Psychiatric Association, 1980.
St. Amant, C. Penrose. Review of *Christ and Selfhood*, by Wayne Oates. *Review and Expositor: An International Baptist Journal* 59 (1962) 214–15.
Starbuck, Edwin Diller. *The Psychology of Religion: An Empirical Study of the Growth of Religious Consciousness.* New York: Scribner, 1901.
Stokes, Allison. *Ministry After Freud.* New York: Pilgrim, 1985.
Stolz, Karl Ruf. *The Church and Psychotherapy.* Nashville: Abington-Cokesbury, 1943.
———. *The Psychology of Religious Living.* Nashville: Abingdon-Cokesbury, 1937.

Strong, Augustus Hopkins. *Systematic Theology: A Compendium and Commonplace Book Designed for the Use of Theological Students.* Vol. 2. Valley Forge, PA: Judson, 1907.

Sullivan, Harry Stack. *The Interpersonal Theory of Psychiatry.* New York: Norton, 1953.

———. *The Psychiatric Interview.* New York: Norton, 1954.

Sullivan, Harry Stack, and Patrick Mullahy. *Conceptions of Modern Psychiatry.* New York: Norton, 1948.

Thelen, Mary Frances. *Man as Sinner in Contemporary American Realistic Theology.* New York: King's Crown, 1946.

Thiele, William E., Jr. "The Presence of God in Pastoral Counseling." *Theological Educator* 55 (1997) 108–12.

Thornton, Edward E. "The Place of Clinical Pastoral Education in the New Plans of Theological Education." *Journal of Pastoral Care* 20 (1966) 16–23.

Thurneysen, Eduard. *A Theology of Pastoral Care.* 1st ed. Richmond: John Knox, 1962.

Tiebout, Harry. "Conversion as a Psychological Phenomenon." *Pastoral Psychology* 2 (1951) 28–34.

Tillich, Paul. "Communicating the Gospel." *Union Seminary Quarterly Review* 7 (1954) 3–10.

———. *The Courage to Be.* 2nd ed. New Haven: Yale University Press, 2000.

———. "Existentialism, Psychotherapy, and the Nature of Man." *Pastoral Psychology* 11 (1960) 10–18.

———. "Faith and the Integration of the Personality." *Pastoral Psychology* 8 (1957) 11–14.

———. "The Impact of Pastoral Psychology on Theological Thought." In *The Ministry and Mental Health,* edited by Hans Hofmann, 13–22. New York: Association, 1960.

———. "Impact of Pastoral Psychology on Theological Thought." *Pastoral Psychology* 11 (1960) 17–23.

———. *The New Being.* New York: Scribner, 1955.

———. "The Relation of Religion and Health: Historical Considerations and Theoretical Questions." In *The Meaning of Health: Essays in Existentialism, Psychoanalysis, and Religion,* edited by Perry LeFevre, 16–52. Chicago: 1984.

———. *The Shaking of the Foundations.* New York: Scribner, 1948.

———. "Some Hard Questions for Clinical Pastoral Educators." *Journal of Pastoral Care* 22 (1968) 194–202.

———. *Systematic Theology.* Chicago: University of Chicago Press, 1953.

———. "Theology and Counseling." *Journal of Pastoral Care* 10 (1956) 193–200.

Tillich, Paul, and Carl Rogers. "Paul Tillich and Carl Rogers: A Dialogue." *Pastoral Psychology* 19 (1968) 55–64.

Thornton, Edward E. *Being Transformed: An Inner Way of Spiritual Growth.* Philadelphia: Westminster, 1984.

———. *Professional Education for Ministry: A History of Clinical Pastoral Education.* Nashville: Abingdon, 1970.

Tuck, William Powell, ed. *Pastoral Prophet: Sermons and Prayers of Wayne E. Oates.* Macon, GA: Smyth & Helwys, 2017.

Van Leeuwen, Mary Stewart. *The Person in Psychology: A Contemporary Christian Appraisal.* Grand Rapids: InterVarsity, 1985.

Vine, W. E. *Vine's Expository Dictionary of Old and New Testament Words*. Old Tappan, NJ: Revell, 1981.

Vitz, Paul C. *Psychology as Religion: The Cult of Self-Worship*. Grand Rapids: Eerdmans, 1994.

Wayne E. Oates Papers (MS 624). Z. Smith Reynolds Library Special Collections and Archives, Wake Forest University, Winston-Salem, North Carolina.

Weatherhead, Leslie D. *Psychology in Service of the Soul*. London: Epworth, 1929.

Whitaker, Robert. "The Triumph of American Psychiatry: How It Created the Modern Therapeutic State." *European Journal of Psychotherapy & Counselling* 17 (2015) 326–41.

White, Christopher. "A Measured Faith: Edwin Starbuck, William James, and the Scientific Reform of Religious Experience." *Harvard Theological Review* 101 (2008) 431–50.

Whitehead, Alfred North. *Modes of Thought*. New York: Macmillan, 1938.

———. *Process and Reality: An Essay in Cosmology*. New York: Macmillan, 1929.

———. *Religion in the Making*. Cambridge University Press, 1926.

Wild, John Daniel. *The Radical Empiricism of William James*. 1st ed. Garden City: Doubleday, 1969.

Williams, Daniel Day. *The Minister and the Care of Souls*. New York: Harper, 1961.

———. *What Present-Day Theologians Are Thinking*. Rev. ed. New York: Harper, 1959.

Wills, Gregory A. *Southern Baptist Theological Seminary, 1859–2009*. Oxford: Oxford University Press, 2009.

Wilshire, Bruce W. *William James and Phenomenology: A Study of the Principles of Psychology*. Bloomington: Indiana University Press, 1968.

Winfrey, David. "Biblical Therapy: Southern Baptists Reject 'Pastoral Counseling.'" *Christian Century* 124 (2007) 24–27.

Wise, Carroll A. "Client-Centered Counseling and the Pastor." *Journal of Pastoral Care* 7 (1953) 127–36.

———. *Pastoral Counseling: Its Theory and Practice*. New York: Harper, 1951.

———. *Religion in Illness and Health*. New York: Harper, 1942.

Zilboorg, Gregory. *Sigmund Freud: His Exploration of the Mind of Man*. New York, Scribner, 1951.

Zilboorg, Gregory, and George W. Henry. *A History of Medical Psychology*. New York, Norton, 1941.

———. *Mind, Medicine, & Man*. New York: Harcourt & Brace, 1943.

www.ingramcontent.com/pod-product-compliance
Lightning Source LLC
Chambersburg PA
CBHW051110160426
43193CB00010B/1388